War Paths, Peace Paths

Issues in Eastern Woodlands Archaeology
Editors: Thomas E. Emerson and Timothy Pauketat

SERIES DESCRIPTION: Issues in Eastern Woodlands Archaeology emphasizes new research results and innovative theoretical approaches to the archaeology of the pre-Columbian native and early colonial inhabitants of
North America east of the Mississippi River Valley. The editors are especially
seeking contributors who are interested in addressing/questioning such concepts as historical process, agency, traditions, political economy, materiality,
ethnicity, and landscapes through the medium of Eastern Woodlands archaeology. Such contributions may take as their focus a specific theoretical
or regional case study but should cast it in broader comparative or historical
terms.

Scholars interested in contributing to this series are encouraged to contact
Thomas Emerson, ITARP-Anthropology, 23 East Stadium Drive, University
of Illinois, Champaign, IL 61820; teee@uiuc.edu.

BOOKS IN THIS SERIES

Chiefdoms and Other Archaeological Delusions
    by Timothy R. Pauketat
*In Contact: Bodies and Spaces in the Sixteenth- and Seventeenth-Century
    Eastern Woodlands*
    by Diana DiPaolo Loren
*War Paths, Peace Paths: An Archaeology of Cooperation and Conflict in Native
    Eastern North America*
    by David H. Dye

War Paths, Peace Paths

*An Archaeology of Cooperation and
Conflict in Native Eastern
North America*

David H. Dye

ALTAMIRA
PRESS

**A DIVISION OF
ROWMAN & LITTLEFIELD PUBLISHERS, INC.**
Lanham • New York • Toronto • Plymouth, UK

ALTAMIRA PRESS
A division of Rowman & Littlefield Publishers, Inc.
A wholly owned subsidary of The Rowman & Littlefield Publishing Group, Inc.
4501 Forbes Boulevard, Suite 200
Lanham, MD 20706
www.altamirapress.com

Estover Road
Plymouth PL6 7PY
United Kingdom

British Library Cataloguing in Publication Information Available

Library of Congress Cataloguing-in-Publication Data

Dye, David H.
  War paths, peace paths : an archaeology of cooperation and conflict in native eastern
North America / David H. Dye.
     p. cm. — (Issues in Eastern Woodlands archaeology)
  Includes bibliographical references and index.
  ISBN-13: 978-0-7591-0745-8 (cloth : alk. paper)
  ISBN-10: 0-7591-0745-9 (cloth : alk. paper)
  ISBN-13: 978-0-7591-0746-5 (pbk. : alk. paper)
  ISBN-10: 0-7591-0746-7 (pbk. : alk. paper)
  eISBN-13: 978-0-7591-1312-1
  eISBN-10: 0-7591-1312-2
  1. Woodland Indians—Warfare. 2. Woodland Indians—History. 3. Diplomacy—East
(U.S.)—History. 4. East (U.S.)—History. I. Title.

  E78.E2D94 2009
  973.04'973—dc22   2008033902

Printed in the United States of America

♾™ The paper used in this publication meets the minimum requirements of
American National Standard for Information Sciences—Permanence of Paper
for Printed Library Materials, ANSI/NISO Z39.48-1992.

To the memory of the First Nation's honored
diplomats and courageous warriors:

Deganawida (Mohawk)

The Great Sun (Natchez)

Wa-tse-mon-in (Osage)

Powhatan (Powhatan)

Tecumseh (Shawnee)

Contents

List of Figures

Foreword

Today's globalizing world is rife with armed conflict of all sorts and scales. Warlords and war presidents use it, successful diplomats contain it, and ordinary people live in fear of it. We need to understand its causes, consequences, and remedies.

Whatever or whoever causes it, violence—says author David H. Dye—is not a "linear process." Rather, it pervades all aspects of social life and has long-term consequences that can only be understood in historical perspective. The same is true of its antithesis, peace. The job of archaeologists, of course, is to provide that perspective.

David H. Dye does this and more for pre-Columbian eastern North America in the pages that follow. Eastern North America has one of the best-documented archaeological and ethnohistoric records in the world and, thanks to this book, researchers everywhere can begin to understand its complex historical relationship to war and peace. Surprisingly, few others precede him in this effort.

Why no one else has written such a book as this might at first seem to strike one as odd. Surely, the ways in which people fought or made peace mattered as much in the past as they do today. One might think that archaeologists long ago would have not only realized this, but would have devoted considerably more attention to understanding the history of violence and its resolution. Certainly, archaeologists often come upon evidence of inferred warfare—based on evidence of palisade walls, burned villages, and traumatic skeletal injuries. These lines of evidence aren't particularly ambiguous. So why is *War Paths, Peace Paths* the first *book* on the archaeology of indigenous conflict and cooperation in eastern North America?

Part of the answer must have to do with what Lawrence Keeley, in 1996, said was archaeology's tendency to "pacify" the past (see also LeBlanc 2003a). Violence and its resolution were rarely central in explanations of the past, save for evolutionary anthropological arguments about the rise of chiefdoms and states. However, in North America, war and peace have not taken a front seat in explanations.

The reasons for this are not simple, but lie in part in the lingering effects of an antiquated notion that Native Americans were "noble savages" free of the ills of Western civilization, of which organized conflict was one. Thus, finding a several-millennia-old Archaic-period individual who had been scalped—a practice thought by some to have been introduced by Europeans—was national news only decades ago. Likewise, the discovery of a several-centuries-old ditch filled with the skeletons of hundreds of massacred men, women, and children at Crow Creek, South Dakota, was met with disbelief (and threats of violence) in the 1970s (Wiley and Emerson 1993).

Perhaps the pacification of the past is also an unintentional by-product of archaeology's stubborn empiricism. Some insist on finding the smoking gun or signed treaty in the grip of a skeletonized warrior or diplomat before they will entertain any inference concerning the existence of violence or peace making. For that reason, warfare until recently was the exclusive domain of specialists, usually bioarchaeologists, who could reliably identify evidence of traumatic injuries.

As a result, violence has not been effectively integrated into big-picture explanations of the past. The study of warfare is not particularly well developed or nuanced in theoretical terms. In short, the long-term social effects of war and peace have not been thought about too much. Indeed, archaeological models up through the 1990s typically portrayed pre-Columbian North American societies as self-correcting systems comprised of "social interactions" rather than as chaotic fields made up of people with conflicting agendas. Surely, violence—from such a systems perspective—was an aberrant side effect of history and peace was merely the absence of violence, a normal state of affairs that did not need to be theorized.

But what if violence is not aberrant? What if peace making is a cultural process and not the normal state of affairs? Should not "interaction" be parsed into its constituent feuds, raids, ritual adoptions, alliances, fortifications, and warrior cults, among other things (see Hall 1997)? The answer to the last question, after reading Dye's book, is a resounding yes, and allows us to move on to consider the larger rhetorical questions that precede it.

War and peace need to be rethought, theorized anew, and understood historically. Violence restricts movement, socializes the young to act aggressively, alters the demographic profiles of populations, and breeds more violence. Peace allows freedom of movement, exchange, intermarriage, and political expansion. Neither war nor peace is an incidental by-product of history. They are woven into history's fabric. They shape the social landscapes wherein people's futures are experienced. They are experiential processes, with effects that can only be evaluated over the long term.

To evaluate these processes, we need deep-time, data-rich studies. Dye gives us just that, reviewing in the following chapters the sweep of pre-Columbian experience on the continent by tacking between archaeological fact and rich ethnohistoric detail, from the earliest Paleoindian pioneers to those later peoples who met the Europeans. This is Dye's major contribution: he allows us to rethink long-term change by synthesizing the archaeological and textual evidence of indigenous warring and peace making in one of the world's primary culture areas. As such, Dye has written a most important addition to AltaMira's Issues in Eastern Woodlands Archaeology book series.

Timothy R. Pauketat

Preface

War and Peace are not considered antithetical relationships . . . ; rather, they are just two forms of exchange and reciprocity.

(Lizot 1991:70)

Writing *War Paths, Peace Paths* was the culmination of research on the archaeology of warfare in eastern North America while I was a faculty member at the University of Memphis. The first draft of the manuscript was written during a faculty development assignment that released me from teaching, committee work, and other university responsibilities. The freedom from day-to-day commitments and interruptions helped me gather my thoughts and clarify my thinking about the evolution of warfare, and provided the time necessary for writing initial chapter drafts.

In retrospect, my experience as an undergraduate and graduate student helped shape my view of archaeology, the process of investigating the past, and ultimately how I view cooperation and conflict in eastern North America. My interest in institutions that promoted peace and war began in an unexpected and unanticipated way. In fact, I had no interest in warfare during my graduate work. My master's thesis was focused upon the Bilbo site near Savannah, Georgia, and my dissertation addressed Joseph R. Caldwell's concept of primary forest efficiency and the nature of prehistoric subsistence in eastern North America. In the dissertation, I discussed the mechanisms of alliance and violence only in the most general sense. Like Steven LeBlanc (1999:ix), who has written extensively on prehistoric warfare in the American Southwest, I did not set out to study warfare. Throughout my educational experience and my early interest in southeastern archaeology, I saw little connection between warfare and archaeology except in a general way.

In 1981, I began working with Mississippian archaeology and the ethnohistoric accounts written or related by members of the Hernando de Soto expedition who traversed the Lower Mississippi alluvial valley. Memphis is near the area where de Soto crossed the Mississippi River in June 1541, and the expedition accounts provide important insights for archaeologists. Spanish accounts are critical for building models of Mississippian societies that can be tested at nearby archaeological sites, several of which have provided material evidence left by the expedition.

Undertaking research on the de Soto expedition in the mid-1980s brought me into contact with archaeologists, cultural anthropologists, ethnohistorians, and folklorists who were investigating the sixteenth-century Southeast. Much of the pioneering work was led by Charles Hudson of the University of Georgia. In the fall of 1988, Peter Young, the editor of *Archaeology* magazine, convened a number of these scholars at the Southeastern Archaeological Conference meeting in New Orleans. At one point during the evening, he approached me about the possibility of submitting an article on the de Soto expedition for the magazine's forthcoming spring volume. Young was considering an issue devoted to the expedition, and my charge would be writing about the conflict between the native southeasterners and the expedition participants. Although I was somewhat knowledgeable about the de Soto entrada, I was less familiar with the nature of sixteenth-century warfare; but I thought the experience would be worthwhile. During the Christmas holidays I labored through the Spanish accounts, looking for patterns and trends in conflict and violence between the Native people of the Southeast and the Spanish conquistadores. In some respects, I was amazed at how much information was available and how little had been employed by archaeologists for interpreting warfare. The result of my labor was the lead article in the May–June 1989 issue of *Archaeology*.

Afterward, I gave little thought to continuing warfare studies. I was eager to return to Lower Mississippi valley archaeology and ethnohistory, from what I believed was a short interlude in my research interests. But shortly thereafter, I received an invitation from David Hurst Thomas to present a paper in the symposium entitled "Archaeological and Historical Perspectives on the Spanish Borderlands East" at the 1989 Society for American Archaeology meeting in Atlanta. Again, the suggested paper topic was sixteenth-century warfare, with emphasis on the de Soto expedition in the interior Southeast.

I accepted Thomas's invitation and the paper subsequently became a chapter in volume 2 of the *Columbian Consequences* series. This volume, edited by Thomas and published by the Smithsonian Institution Press in 1990, addresses the Spanish borderlands in the Southeast. The *Columbian Consequences* chapter led to a spin-off article on sixteenth-century warfare in the Lower Mississippi valley, which was published in 1994 in *Perspectives on the Southeast*, edited by Patricia B. Kwachka.

I continued giving papers on Mississippian warfare throughout the 1990s. The papers and resulting book chapters concerned various aspects of warfare, such as prestige-goods exchange, European contact, and Mississippian ritual and iconography. The latter topic was particularly interesting because it provided new insights into traditional political and economic interpretations of warfare. In 1995, I began attending a yearly workshop on Mississippian iconography hosted by F. Kent Reilly III at the University of Southwest Texas (then Southwest Texas State University) in San Marcos. I began to look at warfare in terms of ideology and ritual as well as political economy and social evolution. Traditional interpretations of Mississippian iconography linked combat symbolism with warfare. Conversations with the workshop participants over the years convinced me to reconsider the nature of representational or figural art and its reference to quotidian combat. I realized that an important dimension of warfare was in the realm of ritual and myth, and I came to understand iconography as portraying the activities of otherworldly beings rather than humans. Likewise, while warfare certainly was precipitated by ecological and economic matters, it was clear that eastern North American cultures incorporated ideology into warfare to a remarkable degree, and that discussion of warfare could not be addressed through a strict examination of political economy or cultural ecology.

Thomas E. Emerson and Timothy R. Pauketat's invitation to write a volume on the archaeology of warfare as practiced in the Eastern Woodlands of North America initiated another change in my thinking. I came to realize that warfare, as it is expressed in the archaeological record, could not be fully understood without paying close attention to how people cooperated with one another and the extent to which they worked toward peace as well as war.

Archaeology, of course, has great time depth. To appreciate long-term changes and how social institutions promoting peace and war have evolved, one must pay close attention to archaeological evidence. Where archaeology falls short, however, is in the rich detail that ethnography brings to the comparative study of humankind. To investigate cooperation and combat during a time period accessible only via the archaeological record, one must adopt a macroscopic anthropological perspective to delineate patterns and processes of sociocultural change within family groups, tribal societies, and regional polities, in this case those of eastern North America. To examine cooperation and conflict, I draw upon theoretical orientations and information from a number of disciplines and subdisciplines: archaeology, climatology, cultural anthropology, ethnohistory, folklore, iconography, and physical anthropology.

The major theme outlined in *War Paths, Peace Paths*—that cooperation, conflict, and society coevolve—is introduced and explored in chapter 1, then is followed in chapter 2 by an overview of the archaeological approach to social evolution and the study of cooperation and competition. In chapter 3, I discuss how populations from approximately 11,000 to 5000 BC formed alliances and resolved conflicts. Chapter 4 presents the archaeological evidence for the beginnings of intersocietal conflict, especially feuding, and the mechanisms ameliorating conflicts from about 5000 to 1000 BC. The elaboration of feuding between 1000 BC and AD 400 is discussed in chapter 5.

The view that violence increases with social complexity is central to chapter 6, in which I discuss the late Woodland cultures (AD 500 to 1700) of eastern North America. In chapter 7, the relationship between cooperation and conflict in the Northeast is evaluated through a brief examination of the Iroquois Confederacy from AD 1000 to 1700. Chapter 8 is centered upon alliances and conflicts among Upper Mississippian Oneota populations in the Upper Midwest from AD 1000 to 1700. The origins of chiefly alliances and warfare from AD 1000 to 1700 in the Lower Midwest and the Southeast are examined in chapter 9. Chapter 10 is a summary of how cooperation and competition, alliances and conflict, and peace and war coevolved throughout thirteen thousand years of indigenous culture history in eastern North America.

Acknowledgments

Many friends and colleagues helped form the ideas herein through discussions over the years. Special thanks go to my teachers and mentors, Robert I. Gilbert, Jr., Charles H. McNutt, William G. Haag, and Patty Jo Watson, for their influences on my intellectual development. This book has benefited from their wisdom and encouragement.

Kent Reilly and the Texas Iconographic Workshop have had a profound influence on my thinking about iconography, peace, ritual, and warfare. Kent kept the workshop attendees on track by reminding everyone that investigating elite behavior and ritual is critical if we are to understand the nature of culture change through the lens of archaeology. To Kent and the workshop participants I offer my heartfelt gratitude and appreciation for their help.

I owe thanks to my wife, Debbie, and our children, Jennifer, Thomas, and Kakky, for their unfaltering support throughout the entire writing project. They are glad to have the kitchen table back once more.

This book was influenced by ideas and input from a number of people. José Brandão, Adam King, George Lankford, Charles McNutt, Tom Emerson, Dale Henning, Tim Pauketat, Ken Sassaman, Dean Snow, and Patty Jo Watson generously read and commented on one or more chapters. The volume was greatly improved by Patty Jo Watson's meticulous editing of the entire manuscript. I thank these colleagues for their helpful suggestions. Errors and mistakes in facts, interpretation, and reasoning are, of course, mine alone.

Heartfelt thanks and gratitude are extended to those who supplied their photographs: James Duncan, Dale Henning, John Pafford, and John Bigelow

Taylor. The volume was immeasurably improved by the artistic talents of Leigh Ann Dye and Steven Patricia. Permission to use the images of their artifacts and the illustrations from their publications was expeditiously provided by David Hurst Thomas (American Museum of Natural History), Jefferson Chapman (McClung Museum), Jonathan Haas (Field Museum), Strawberry Fields (Tennessee State Museum), Lisa Haney (Missouri Archaeological Society), Mark Norton (Tennessee Division of Archaeology), Robert J. Pearce (Museum of Ontario Archaeology), and Barbara Sirmans (Birmingham Public Library). To each of the individuals and the institutions that provided photographs or images, I offer my thanks and appreciation.

I am grateful for the financial and institutional support received from the University of Memphis. I thank Dean Henry A. Kurtz for a faculty development leave in 2004 and Mervin J. Bartholomew, chair of the Department of Earth Sciences, for his unwavering encouragement and support. Wayne S. Key of the McWherter Library Interlibrary Loan Department did an outstanding job of locating difficult-to-find reference material. His efficiency and dedication in finding articles and books was essential to writing *War Paths, Peace Paths*. In particular, I would like to thank Tom Emerson and Tim Pauketat, who encouraged me to participate in the Issues in Eastern Woodland Archaeology series at AltaMira Press. Their unflagging patience and constructive comments are greatly appreciated.

I am grateful for everyone who supported and helped in the acquisitions, editorial, and production departments at AltaMira Press. I thank Jack Meinhardt, acquisitions editor, for his patience and continuing enthusiasm over the book. Marissa M. Parks, acquisitions editorial assistant, shepherded, guided, and supported the volume through the various stages of acquisition and production. Karen Ackermann, production editor, ably steered the book through the production process, and Jonathan Caws-Elwitt did an excellent job of copyediting. I thank Lori Pierelli for her skills in proofreading the final draft. To each, I am thankful.

CHAPTER ONE

Cooperation and Conflict in Native Eastern North America

The vast majority of societies in which warfare does occur are characterized by the alternation of war and peace.

(Kelly 2000:124)

In December 1607, only seven months after the founding of Jamestown, Captain John Smith was captured by several hundred warriors of the Powhatan Confederacy as he hunted outside the English settlement. Although Smith may have regarded the area in which he hunted as Virginia, the Powhatan warriors almost certainly saw Smith as a trespasser and thief. Soon after his capture, Smith was taken to Werowocomoco, the principal Powhatan town located some twelve miles from Jamestown. To Smith's surprise, he was welcomed by Powhatan and obliged to wash his hands and then dry them with bird feathers prior to being feted.

After a feast of massive proportions, he was promptly stretched out on two large, flat stones, as several of Powhatan's warriors raised their war clubs to bash in his skull. According to Smith's account, Powhatan's twelve-year-old daughter, named Matoaka, rushed to save his life by placing her head between Smith and the threatening war clubs. Matoaka pulled Smith to his feet, dramatically rescuing him from what seemed to be an imminent demise. As quickly as his life had been about to end, Smith was brought back from near death and adopted by Powhatan as a son, thus becoming Matoaka's brother. Smith was then taken to a shrine or temple secluded in the woods west of the village, where Powhatan and his warriors continued the adoption ritual by painting themselves black and perhaps communicating with the ancestors who resided in the west, the Realm of the Dead (Kupperman 2000:114, 174). Powhatan's nickname for his young, precocious, and perhaps dramatic daughter was Pocahontas.

We may never know whether or not Pocahontas actually saved John Smith's life, but Gleach (1997:118–21) convincingly argues that Pocahontas's actions appears to have played a critical role in an ancient adoption ritual. Such ceremonies were both widespread and ancient in eastern North America and were used in one form or another primarily to establish alliances. Pocahontas went on to become a pivotal culture broker between the Jamestown Colony and the Powhatan Confederacy. Smith's near-death experience apparently symbolized his transformation, whereby he became not only a member of the confederacy, but also one of Powhatan's subchiefs and the diplomatic complement of Pocahontas. Now, as English-Powhatan citizens, Pocahontas and Smith were in the unique position of providing balanced and reciprocal hospitality between the English of Jamestown and the Powhatan of Werowocomoco. Through his two children, Powhatan would have access to diplomatic channels and ultimately to the much-desired Western manufactures, especially European axes, knives, and muskets.

In the end, Smith and the Jamestown community failed to understand the implications of the symbolic ritual adoption, in large part because the English colonists did not grasp the reciprocal responsibilities which the adoption and alliance protocol demanded. The unsuccessful brokering between the two polities, despite Pocahontas's efforts, erupted within a few years as the First Anglo-Powhatan War (1609–1613; Grenier 2005:24–25). After a nine-year respite, a massive, coordinated attack took place on March 22, 1622, when Powhatan's brother, Opechancanough, amassed and launched his warriors against the Virginia settlements, bringing about ten years of renewed violence. In this second war, the "First Indian War of 1622–1632," about one-third of the Jamestown population was initially killed in a series of coordinated surprise attacks. The third round of warfare was the "Second Powhatan-English War" (1644–1646), which ended any hopes that the English settlers and Powhatan Confederacy could peacefully coexist. The resulting treaty between the two parties ultimately forced the Powhatans from their homeland.

Trends in Peace and Violence

The pivotal position of adoption, alliance, and diplomacy in Native efforts to secure peace underscores the critical role of ritual in alliance building, cooperation, and violence. In Native eastern North America, as is the case throughout the world, a breakdown in diplomatic efforts often led to unremitting violence. My purpose in writing *War Paths, Peace Paths* is to examine the coevolution of ritual, diplomacy, and sociopolitical organization as it relates to the pursuit of cooperation and conflict in eastern North America, from earliest settlement to about AD 1700, when much of the Native way of life was being drastically changed. In so doing, I attempt to develop a better understanding of the relationships among conflict, the resolution or management of conflict, and our perceptions of the social institutions Native peoples crafted to further cooperation or to wage war.

All human groups have the potential for violence, but they also have the potential for ameliorating violent acts through a variety of domestic, political, religious, and social mechanisms. In some instances, violence may be fomented through misunderstandings between cultures over institutions which served to promote peace, as seen in the example above from early seventeenth-century Tidewater Virginia. Similar scenes would reoccur throughout the Americas, as Natives and colonists continually misunderstood one another, with catastrophic results. When attempts at peace fail, social groups are often forced to resort to violence to resolve their grievances and realign their geopolitical worlds.

I propose that peace and violence in eastern North America over the past thirteen thousand years may be viewed as three broad, interrelated trends. The first and earliest trend, typically found among family-level mobile foragers, is based on personal grudges that are managed through alliances, avoidance, cooperation, negotiation, self-redress homicides, and toleration. Self-redress homicide refers to the action undertaken by relatives who take it upon themselves to seek justice in cases of murder. Violence is typically limited among nomadic, family-level hunter-gatherers because they lack the overarching, cohesive kin organizations that are necessary for coordinating groups larger than the family. Physical aggression is rather rare for family-level foragers because conflict is dampened and peaceful relations are maintained through intercommunity ceremonies, cooperation, exchange, and marriage. When violence does occur it settles disputes, but it is ineffective for controlling people (Knauft 1991:405).

The second trend, characteristic of local groups or tribal societies, is kin-based feuding, in which aggrieved parties seek personal retaliatory justice from any member of the targeted group through blood revenge over grudges (Reyna 1994:40). Vengeance is sought after a killing and is usually limited to one or two homicides at a time by temporary kin militia. Generally, one side takes the offensive, but there is no necessary political objective beyond the maintenance of personal or group honor (Boehm 1987:221). Feuds generally are settled by third-party-assisted dispute settlements and alliances, through complex forms of diplomacy and ritual that bind kin groups together. Anthropologists who study conflict and violence consider feuding to be fundamentally different from warfare (Otterbein 1994), but this is not a universally held position (see Kelly 2000).

The third trend, representative of regional or chiefly societies, consists of warfare and the complex rituals associated with alliances and diplomacy. Chiefly warfare differs from family-level homicides and tribal feuding in that violence now becomes impersonal lethal aggression between communities, and is carried out for political gain. The object of chiefly warfare is the capture, killing, or annihilation of nonspecified members of the enemy political group. The intent of peaceful relations among chiefly societies is the establishment of political alliances among neighboring communities or polities. Complex forms of diplomacy and ritual continue to arise around efforts to form alliances.

A central question in the study of cooperation and conflict in the past is based on the above trends: how do we go about understanding long-term variability in the collective lethal violence of one social group against other groups? And how do we explain the relationship of intersocietal conflict to cooperation and human social evolution? For example, does skeletal trauma represent self-redress homicide, feuding, or warfare? What is indicative of organized violence versus domestic violence or institutionalized, violent social contests and games? Interpersonal cooperation and violence are well documented in the archaeological record, but what are the sources or precipitating factors in the patterning of alliance and conflict institutions? What is the role of ritual and ceremony in efforts to establish and maintain alliances, or to wage war?

Archaeology and the Study of Cooperation and Conflict

Archaeologists have the advantage of well-documented, long-term cultural sequences to aid them in answering these questions. Eastern North America has archaeological evidence of past culture change during more than thirteen thousand years (figure 1.1). Complementing the great temporal depth provided by archaeological research, ethnographic reports and ethnohistoric documents describe in considerable detail the domestic, economic, ideological, political, and social organization for Native peoples of eastern North America. Ethnography and ethnohistory are critical to archaeologists for building models of past human behavior. Archaeologists who work in eastern North America are fortunate to have so many Native groups that were documented

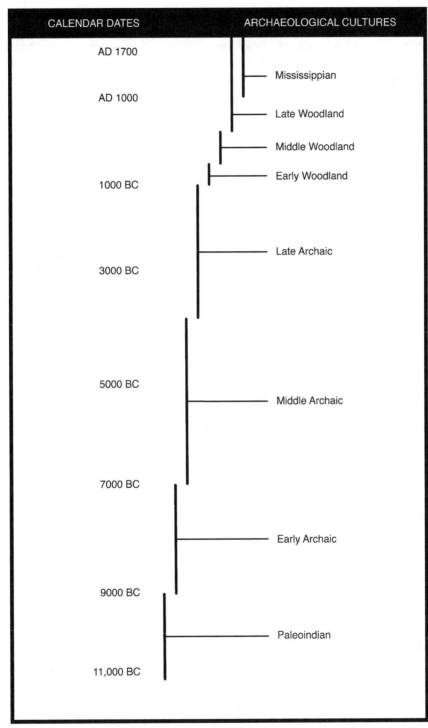

Figure 1.1.   Cultural chronology of eastern North America.

by trained anthropologists. In some instances, the anthropologists themselves were Native speakers. Long-term studies of culture change, based on archaeology, ethnography, and ethnohistory, with attention to peace and war, thus provide opportunities for answering questions that speak to the human capacity for conflict and conflict management; and for examining how patterns of violence and justice-seeking coevolved over time, and how they relate to social and political organization.

Initial European narratives describe efforts made by Native Americans toward peace-achieving mechanisms (including adoption, diplomacy, exchange, and rituals), as well as war-waging, fortification building, military tactics, trophy taking, weaponry, and war rituals. Alliances and tribute relationships for both peace and war are outlined in early documentation. While the archaeological record substantiates many ethnohistoric accounts, documentation of eastern North American endeavors for cooperation and conflict on the part of early hunter-gatherers remains limited. In this book, I discuss those institutions that must have promoted and resolved violent conflict in ancient eastern North America.

In recent years there has been renewed interest in the archaeology of conflict, violence, and warfare among foragers and farmers. A number of these works have stressed general studies of intersocietal cooperation and conflict (Carman and Harding 1999; Carneiro 1990, 1994; Cioffi-Revilla 2000; Dennen 1995; Dentan 2008; Divale 1974; Ferguson 1997; Ferguson and Whitehead 1992; Gat 2006; Guilaine and Zammit 2005; Keeley 1996; Martin and Frayer 1997; Osgood et al. 2001; Otterbein 2004; Raaflaub and Rosenstein 1999; Reyna and Downs 1994; Rice and LeBlanc 2001; Souza 2008). Likewise, the number of studies of warfare in the Americas has risen sharply through the research of archaeologists, cultural and physical anthropologists, and ethnohistorians (Arkush 2008; Arkush and Allen 2006; Brown and Stanton 2003; Chacon and Dye 2007; Chacon and Mendoza 2007; Ferguson 1984; Haas 1990, 1999, 2001; Hassig 1992; Keeley et al. 2007; Kelly 2000; Lambert 1997, 2002, 2007; LeBlanc 1999, 2003a, 2003b, 2006; Milner 1999, 2000; Otterbein 1994; Redmond 1994; Walker 2001; Webster 1999, 2000).

The topic of violence, feuding, and warfare has recently received attention from eastern North American archaeologists and physical anthropologists as well, more so than has the investigation of conflict resolution (Anderson 1994a; Bridges 1996; Bridges et al. 2000; Brown and Dye 2007; Dickson 1981; Dye 1990, 1994, 1995, 2002, 2004, 2006a, 2006b; Dye and King 2007; Emerson 2007; Fontana 2007; Gibson 1974; Hollinger 2005; Jacobi 2007; Keener 1998; Lafferty 1973; Larson 1972; Malone 1991;

Mensforth 2001, 2007; Milner 1995, 1998a, 1999, 2000, 2007; Milner and Smith 1989, 1990; Milner et al. 1991a, 1991b; Owsley and Berryman 1975; Pauketat 1999; Peregrine 1993; Ross-Stallings 2007; Schroeder 2006; Seeman 1988, 2007; Smith 1995, 1997, 2003; Steadman 2008; Steinen 1992; Steinen and Ritson 1996; Strezewski 2006; Trubitt 2003; Williamson 2007).

Archaeological Evidence for Conflict

Understanding the nature of archaeological evidence and the way in which archaeologists utilize information is essential for investigating complex relationships of conflict and cooperation in the past. Evidence for competition and alliances in the archaeological record is highly variable and is often amenable to alternative interpretations. Multiple lines of evidence provide the strongest support for interpretations of past group interaction, whether peaceful or violent.

Archaeology is well suited to identifying the ways in which peace and warfare were conducted and how they related to the social world of foragers and farmers—as well as to the biological and physical world, especially changing climate. Broad patterns and trends may be delineated, as well as the "long-term effects of warfare on population distribution, settlement characteristics, technology, and political centralization" (Milner 2007:183). While proximate or "emic" causes of violence—such as ethnic hatred, sorcery, ferocity, aggression, revenge, retaliation, fear, mistrust, theft, insults, and capture of women and sometimes children—are difficult to detect in the archaeological record, ultimate causes of both peace and violence are generally more accessible. However, as Arkush (2008:563) reminds us, "Most analyses of war's ultimate causes quickly jettison revenge, but it is inescapable for those working at a close scale of analysis, documenting the traumatic abductions, mutilations, and massacres that are the stuff of war." In the end, frequent war is correlated with both a fear of unpredictable natural disasters and a deep-seated fear of outsiders (Ember and Ember 1992).

Archaeological evidence for cooperation and conflict is both direct and indirect. Direct evidence for violence is manifested in skeletal trauma and burned communities. Indirect evidence includes fortifications, settlement patterns, postmarital residence patterns, buffer zones, weaponry, exchange relations, and iconography. Evidence for cooperation is much more difficult to interpret and is always indirect, but may comprise exchange relations, political organization, ritual events, and settlement patterns. Highly crafted exchange items manufactured from exotic materials, such as biface blades; ceramics; pipes; and ritual regalia, including ear spools, headdress elements, pigments, and symbolic weaponry, are found in caches or religious contexts.

Skeletons exhibiting purposeful lethal and nonlethal trauma provide per-haps the clearest and most direct evidence for assessing past intracommunity and intercommunity violence, but most skeletal evidence is limited to the past seven thousand years, thus underestimating the evidence for both coop-eration and conflict in the archaeological record. To evaluate the nature of conflict, osteologists must quantify skeletal evidence for interpersonal vio-lence. Different types of violent and aggressive behavior produce character-istic patterns of skeletal injuries, and only through systematic research of skeletal populations will we understand "the complex interactions between demographic variables, environmental change, and cultural-historical processes that shape our aggressive tendencies" (Walker 1997:175). Such analysis requires a relatively well-preserved and representative skeletal pop-ulation. Among mobile foragers, skeletal populations may be completely lacking, thus severely limiting evidence for assessing the degree of conflict or cooperation for family-level hunter-gatherers.

In eastern North America, osteological remains exhibiting conflict-re-lated wounds date from about 5000 BC through historic times. Skeletal trau-mas include embedded projectile points, cranial blunt-force trauma, and bod-ily mutilation, including scalping and dismemberment (Lambert 2007; Milner 1995, 1999). The removal of body parts is believed to result from trophy-taking behavior and may be evidenced by cut marks on the cranium, vertebrae, and various joints. The patterning of specific types of skeletal trauma, especially scalping and dismemberment, may translate into key sig-natures of intercommunity violence. Missing hands, feet, or heads, especially when accompanied by other evidence of violence, can reflect the taking of body parts as trophies (Chacon and Dye 2007; Hollinger 2005; Milner et al. 1991b; Willey 1990). Likewise, extra body parts associated with burials may signal interment of human trophy remains with the deceased. Parry fractures of the forearm often result from efforts to ward off blows to the head. Cut marks on bone and disarticulated remains can be evidence of mutilation, while cut marks on the cranium generally indicate scalping. Depression frac-tures on the cranial vault provide evidence of blunt-force trauma from war clubs. Skeletal trauma may underrepresent the degree of violence in the past. For example, only about 25–33 percent of the projectiles that come into con-tact with human bodies are likely to strike bone and leave traces of the cause of death (Lambert 1997:93; Milner 2005:150). Thus, the majority of indi-viduals struck by projectile points may go undetected.

Less direct evidence of conflict based on human skeletal remains rests on three categories of information. First, demographic profiles of skeletal popu-lations provide important data on the nature of conflict in the past. Young males may be absent from cemeteries because their deaths took place away from the community, or perhaps they were captured. Likewise, children and females of child-bearing age may be absent from a massacre assemblage because they were captured. Second, carnivore gnaw marks on human skeletal remains may indicate that a victim had been killed away from the settlement, with the body having been recovered after some time had passed. Third, mass burials of individuals of the same sex exhibiting skeletal trauma suggest the ambush of task groups away from the community, as has especially been inferred with respect to groups of women engaged in gathering activities.

Multiple lines of evidence are necessary to differentiate deaths resulting from intergroup combat from other types of traumatic fatalities. Four types of skeletal trauma are typically used to assess the frequency and nature of interpersonal trauma: scalping, decapitation and dismemberment, projectile points embedded in human bone, and blunt-force trauma, particularly in the skull (Steadman 2008:53). Substantiating evidence confirming deaths from intersociety conflict includes "the overall proportion of such deaths in a cemetery sample, the number of fatalities in separate incidents, the nature of perimortem damage to skeletons, and a consideration of the archaeological context" (Milner 1995:237). In some instances, the patterning of multiple skeletal trauma reinforces conflict interpretations. For example, Burial 113, a male between thirty and forty years of age from the Orendorf site, has classic multiple lines of skeletal trauma: a projectile wound of the posterior first thoracic vertebra; blunt trauma to the left mandible and chop wounds on the occipital and left parietal; and extensive cut marks on the skull vault. In other words, the individual was shot, clubbed, and then scalped (Steadman 2008:56). In a recent analysis of the Orendorf skeletal series, Steadman (2008) investigated four components of interpersonal trauma: clear perimortem evidence of interpersonal trauma, inferred perimortem trauma based on archaeological context, antemortem cranial trauma, and postcranial antemortem features.

Individuals exhibiting skeletal evidence of violence may have been injured in ways unrelated to intergroup conflict, including ancestor veneration, domestic abuse, human sacrifice, hunting accidents, internal disputes, intracommunity self-redress homicides, mortuary processing, social contests, accidental falls, ritualized conflict resolution, and sports-related injuries. For example, Mensforth (2001) found in the Green River Archaic of west-central Kentucky that 53 percent of all skeletal trauma was in the form of nonlethal cranial injuries indicative of intragroup, codified, face-to-face fights, such as male social contests. Likewise, Smith (2003) notes in an East Tennessee Mississippian burial population a high frequency of healed and nonlethal, blunt-force cranial trauma, concentrated primarily on the fronts and tops of female skull vaults. She suggests that this pattern "represents gender-specific, codified, face-to-face conflict resolution" (314) rather than intergroup feuding or warfare. Ante-mortem trauma of the facial bones may be indicative of ritual violence or trauma directed toward females (Lambert 1997; Walker 1997). Human ritual sacrifice may have been widespread, serving numerous purposes. Contexts for such sacrifices may have included retainer burials, the provision of spirit-trail companions, and rituals that mimicked combat (Hall 1997).

Cut marks and disarticulated remains may result from human remains being processed in conjunction with mortuary ritual. Olsen and Shipman (1994:385–6) note the difficulty of discerning dismemberment and disarticulation resulting from conflict-related mutilation, on the one hand, from trophy-taking behavior stemming from disarticulation as part of secondary burial process, on the other. But Hollinger (2005:36, 124) states that "artifacts made of human bone recovered from archaeological contexts may have been the result of trophy taking since veneration of ancestors through modification of human remains is almost completely absent from the ethnohistoric record of the Midcontinent." Context is critical to determinations of mortuary processing versus dismemberment resulting from trophy-taking behavior. Modified human remains resulting from secondary burial practices are more likely to be found in cemetery contexts. Human trophies, on the other hand, typically are interred as grave goods or are discarded in nonfunerary refuse pits or midden contexts (Knight 2004).

Direct evidence for warfare may also be seen in large-scale, intentionally burned settlements (Fontana 2007:52). Houses and sometimes entire communities may be accidentally consumed by fire, or houses may be burned by their owners after abandonment; but it is unlikely that houses would have been intentionally fired, unless considerations related to dilapidation, pest or rodent infestations, or religion outweighed the economic advantage of recycling structure materials or retrieving them for use as fuel (Hollinger 2005:40). Discrimination between accidental conflagration and intentional burning may be possible by examining the contents of building floors. Evidence for intergroup conflict such as raiding may be seen in the patterning of specific structures targeted and destroyed at a site, especially above-ground storage facilities, ancestor temples or charnel houses, chiefly residences, and palisades.

For example, late in the twelfth century, Aztalan, a heavily fortified Mississippian site in eastern Wisconsin, shows clear indications of being torched by Oneota raiders. Large sections of the palisade, some of the houses, and a charnel structure were all burned. In addition, butchered human remains further indicate that the community was destroyed, not by an accidental conflagration, but by an intentionally set fire in the context of violent conflict (Hollinger 2005:141). Desecration of charnel houses or ancestral shrines was a high priority in attacks on mound centers in the Southeast and Midwest between about AD 1200 and 1700. Firing temples or ancestor shrines generally took place in conjunction with burning palisades and houses (Dye and King 2007).

The more common and diverse forms of archaeological evidence for violence are circumstantial or indirect and may include fortifications, settlement patterns, weapons, exchange patterns, and iconography. The presence of fortifications, intentionally constructed to repel an offensive attack, is one of the most obvious and unambiguous archaeological indicators of severe intercommunity conflict (Fontana 2007; Jones 2004; Keeley et al. 2007; Lafferty 1973; Milner 2000; Schroeder 2006; Trubitt 2003). Baffle gates, bastioned palisades, and V-sectioned ditches are unequivocal characteristics of defensive fortifications (Keeley et al. 2007). Fortification features have been identified among many, if not most, of the precontact societies in eastern North America (Milner 2000). Fortifications are among the most visible archaeological indicators of intersocietal conflict, or at least the potential for conflict, and typically occur in contexts of elevated levels of warfare.

By investigating the physical features of a fortification system, archaeologists can uncover information regarding the frequency, scale, and type of warfare taking place. Defensive walls and ditches are sensitive archaeological markers for threats of sustained and forceful external violence. The expenditure of labor, resources, and time in excavating postholes or trenches, securing timbers, fastening posts, and plastering wooden palisade walls underscores the belief that threats were sufficiently real, serious, and frequent enough to warrant this type of construction (Fontana 2007:65–6). Vencl (1999:67) notes that "fortifications are above all the materialized expression of the human fear of being attacked, and losing life, freedom or property." The construction of fortifications reflects the weapons systems of the time. For example, the enemies of the Iroquois League abruptly incorporated flanked designs into their village defenses by the 1660s, upon the introduction of the concerted use of iron axes, muskets, counterpalisades, and shields by the Iroquois (Keener 1998:96).

When threatened with attack, the most obvious options available to eastern North American populations would have been to scatter into the surrounding countryside, abandoning their possessions; or to remain in the village or town, protecting themselves, their resources, and their possessions by building a defensive fortification system (Milner 1998a:75). For example, the

Mississippian inhabitants of the Moundville site in east-central Alabama built a 5-kilometer palisade wall with some 125 bastions in about AD 1200, at a time when the town's ruling elite were creating a major regional center. The surrounding countryside was being politically consolidated, and the rulers were actively protecting themselves, their population, and their resources from outside threats. The likelihood of attack was sufficiently serious that much of the domestic activity at Moundville took place within the palisade walls (Dye 2006a).

In ancient eastern North America, a basic dichotomy existed in fortification construction between the chiefly societies of the Lower Midwest and Southeast and the tribal-scale societies of the Upper Midwest and Northeast. Mississippian chiefdoms generally, though not invariably, had towns fortified through elaborate defenses including ditches, embankments, and palisades. In the northern Eastern Woodlands, on the other hand, the walls were often flimsy, being constructed expediently to meet the needs of the moment (Milner 1999, 2007). Exceptions existed, however. The Caddoans of the Southeast did not fortify their settlements, while the historic-period Huron and members of the Iroquois League built robust defenses. The strength of the defenses is a general indication of the strength of the attacking forces.

Settlement patterning provides another distinctive archaeological marker of conflict. Communities may be clustered together for defense, thus separating themselves from their antagonists by buffer zones of considerable distances (Hally 1993). The nature of relationships among local groups, villages, and towns may be evidenced by the extent of surrounding buffer zones, and by the degree and directionality of exchange. Sites located on defensible land forms such as bluff-tops, islands, meander bends, peninsulas, or ridges may reflect defensive concerns. In the Mississippi alluvial valley, for example, Mississippian sites are often located within meander bends, where inhabitants employed large cutoff lakes as water barriers that restricted access to the palisaded towns. On smaller river systems, short palisades might be constructed across meander-bend necks to take advantage of the landscape for defensive purposes. Use of the physiographical setting may change as the intensity and nature of warfare evolves. Populations may disperse in response to endemic conflict, or may nucleate in the face of increased hostilities.

Changes in housing configuration have been used as a key to increases in intersocietal conflict. House size may be indicative of postmarital residence rules (Ember 1973), which in turn may be associated with increased conflict (Divale 1984). Hollinger (1995) describes a shift in postmarital residence patterns among Oneota groups in the Upper Midwest, noting that a link between "increasing emphasis on cultivated foods would have encouraged an increase in the frequency of matrilocal residence decisions. An increase in matrilocal residence would have facilitated shifts in emphasis from internally focused hostilities toward external parties" (163). He sees changes taking place from patrilocal (AD 900–1400) to matrilocal (1400–1650) and back to patrilocal (1650-1700) postmarital residence patterns in Oneota settlements. Similar changes have been noted for Fort Ancient (Henderson et al. 1992) and Iroquoian (Hart 2001) residence patterns.

Buffer zones are large, uninhabited areas between neighboring communities that are maintained through fear of raiding parties. Buffer zones may define cultural, linguistic, and political boundaries based on natural features such as ridge systems, rivers, or other natural physiographic divisions (De-Pratter 1983:33). Death was a real possibility beyond the community's safe zone. Many individuals seem to have been taken by surprise and killed outside the safe zone, to judge from the number of skeletons that were buried some time after death (as evidenced by weathering and carnivore damage to the remains). Enemy raiders often lay in ambush for unsuspecting victims. Hunters venturing into buffer zones were as much raiding parties as they were hunting parties, with the hunter potentially becoming the hunted.

The further one trekked into the buffer zone, the greater the risk of running into an enemy hunting or raiding group. The size of the buffer zone was dependent upon population densities of the groups in question: the higher the population density, the narrower the buffer zone because "they become more costly economically to create and because the security belt they provide was less necessary" (Keeley 1996:112). As a result of infrequent visitation, buffer zones may have been attractive locales for people hunting, gathering, and procuring vital resources such as high-quality lithics, despite the inherent danger.

Weapons provide one of the critical pieces of archaeological information in assessing the degree and nature of conflict in the past. Weapons used in warfare are often difficult to distinguish from implements used in butchering, hunting, and woodworking, although specialized weapons become evident as violence becomes increasingly institutionalized and ritualized over time. Two general types of weapons are noted in eastern North America: utilitarian and sociotechnic, or symbolic (Taylor 2001). Utilitarian weapons were used for cutting, defense, piercing, and striking. Symbolic weapons were important prestige goods used as markers of sociopolitical status and employed as ritual paraphernalia.

Striking weapons (Brasser 1961; Van Horne 1993) include a variety of war clubs. Brasser (1961) identifies six main types of war clubs in postcontact eastern North America: slingshot, hammer, pickax, sword, gun-shaped, and ballhead. Van Horne (1993:62–73) lists six types for the Southeast: stick with inset projection, globe-headed, swordform, swordform with globe-head, spatulate, and staff. War clubs were the preferred shock weapon for close-quarter combat. Warrior prestige was gained by obtaining war honors through personal, one-on-one combat, and war clubs afforded warriors the best opportunity to engage in hand-to-hand fighting with the enemy. In the Southeast, warriors used lances, quarterstaffs, and slings as striking weapons, in addition to war clubs (Jones 2004:123).

Cutting tools, especially knives, were employed by warriors for a variety of utilitarian purposes, but the primary uses may have been dismemberment and scalping, rather than hand-to-hand combat. Knives used for "butchering" humans have largely gone unnoticed in the archaeological literature, as they generally are interpreted as hunting accoutrements. But chipped-stone bifaces, such as Ramey knives, may have functioned as dismemberment or scalping implements. Burials of elite adult males are often accompanied by bifacially knapped blades.

Piercing weapons include two types: the spear and the arrow. Both weapons were used for hunting game as well as human enemies. Three stages in the evolution of piercing weaponry can be identified in eastern North America. First, spears were used singly: thrusting spears seem to have been the earliest piercing weapon, brought into eastern North America by Paleoindians. Thrusting spears appear to have been replaced around 8500 BC by spears with lighter dart points that were propelled by atlatls. The spearthrower added an extra joint to the arm, which increased the efficiency of the thrusting motion. Finally, the bow and arrow, introduced into eastern North America around AD 600, was more accurate and lighter than the spear. Warriors and hunters used the self-bow. A replica of a Virginia self-bow was found to have a "weight of 46 pounds at 28 inches of draw and a cast of 173 yards." It was "soft and pleasant to shoot, and could do effective work either as a hunting or a war implement" (Hamilton 1982:32). Bone or deer antler points lashed on cane arrows, used in conjunction with the self-bow, were particularly effective against wooden armor in the Southeast (Jones 2004:142–3).

Archaeological evidence of defensive weapons, including body armor and shields, is attested through iconographic images and early historic accounts (Taylor 2001). Body armor throughout eastern North America was similar in basic design, the primary concern being to protect the arms, back, chest, head, and thighs. Covering for the body was made from wooden slats or rods tightly bound together with cords. Armor was not used as much in the Lower Southeast as it was in the Upper Southeast, Midwest, and Northeast. Circular shields with carrying handles or straps, large enough to cover the head and body, were manufactured from thick, tough rawhide or bark strips. In the Southeast, shields were made from wickerwork of woven split cane and in a variety of sizes and shapes. A wooden hoop ran around the shield's circumference to provide stability and strength. Wooden helmets were used, as were turbans made from bark or cloth (Emerson 2007); both were worn throughout much of eastern North America by warriors, to protect against club strikes to the head (Jones 2004:11–12).

Symbolic, or sociotechnic, weaponry was an exchange item in eastern North America as early as Paleoindian times. The use of hypertrophic, or exaggerated, weaponry is documented from Dalton (Sloan) points found in cemeteries and caches dating between 8500 and 7900 BC (Walthall and Koldehoff 1998). Throughout prehistory, hypertrophic weaponry was manufactured in the form of symbolic versions of knives, projectile points, clubs, and the component parts of spears (atlatl weights, or bannerstones). Spear and arrow points, atlatl weights, and clubs all attest to the central role of weaponry in the belief systems of eastern North America.

Three sociotechnic artifact types that typify symbolic weaponry—clubs, knives, and projectile points—have been identified from the Spiro site in eastern Oklahoma. Sociotechnic weapons were modeled upon utilitarian weapons, but differ from them in "(1) the use of relatively soft or brittle materials absent in forms showing heavy or prolonged use wear, (2) the incorporation of superfluous attributes that compromise any presumed effectiveness in performing work, and (3) the exaggeration or diminution of artifact size beyond the limits of mechanical utility" (Brown 1996:469). Sociotechnic clubs found at Spiro were crafted in three major forms: the ax, the falchion (or long, thin-edged biface form), and the mace.

Exchange among local groups provides another area of indirect archaeological evidence for intersocietal conflict. Relationships among contemporaneous neighboring groups may be inferred from exchange items resulting from intergroup interactions. Societies that are close enough to one another that interactions would be expected to take place should provide evidence of hostilities. When known local or interregional exchange items are lacking, then hostilities may be inferred.

Prehistoric art may include images associated with combat, feuding, or warfare. The clearest examples illustrate victims, warriors, and weapons, which are depicted in stone, copper, ceramic, and shell. Middle Woodland examples crafted from mica and showing human forms with severed feet, hands, and heads may illustrate trophy taking. After AD 1200, a veritable explosion of iconographic imagery portrays evidence of violence and combat throughout much of eastern North America. Where suitable smooth surfaces exist, combat-related motifs may be found as petroglyphs or pictographs on the walls of caves and bluff shelters and the surfaces of boulders or bedrock outcrops. Such motifs may include arrows, atlatls, bows, celts, clubs, and maces. Anthropomorphic images, in conjunction with combat weapons, are found as early as the tenth century AD at Picture Cave in eastern Missouri (Diaz-Granados 2004).

Figurines that depict the accoutrements of twelfth-century warriors, carved from Missouri flint clay, have been discovered at the Cahokia site (Emerson and Hughes 2000; Emerson et al. 2003). Mississippian "Birdmen" with feather headdresses incorporating human heads are modeled in copper, marine shell, and wood (Brown and Dye 2007). Images of the Birdman brandishing a mace in his right hand and holding a trophy head in his left hand are recorded on copper repoussé plates and marine-shell gorgets. Pipes show bound captives, and warriors using shields. War-related symbols, including falcons and raptor-like "Thunderer" motifs, are commonly found throughout the Upper Midwest (Hollinger 2005). Throughout the midcontinent, raptors symbolized Upper World spirit beings, such as the Thunderers, who were associated with war (Benn 1989; Hall 1997) and are illustrated on ceramics and human bone (Hollinger 2005).

Archaeological Evidence for Peace

Archaeological signatures for the presence of peaceful or cooperative relationships among communities are less well developed than are the criteria for violence and warfare. Three lines of evidence may provide data for peaceful relations or alliances among regional groups: exchange patterns, ritual paraphernalia, and settlement patterns. Negative evidence, such as lack of skeletal trauma in human remains, burned settlements, and fortifications, also provides important information for intersocietal peace, or at least establishes the level at which cooperative relations existed among various groups. Haas (2001:332) notes that "as the presence of clusters of markers of conflict and defensive posturing is a measure of the presence of war, the absence or disappearance of such markers in the historical sequence of a society can be taken conversely as a measure of the reign of peace." Peaceful relations among neighboring groups may also be inferred from examination of evidence for patterns of exchange. The establishment and maintenance of vigorous exchange patterns may indicate powerful positive relations among exchange partners.

Throughout eastern North America, alliance building and peace-promoting endeavors were highly developed through diplomacy and ritual. The presence of ritual paraphernalia and accompanying regalia are key markers for assessing the degree and nature of interaction among groups. Ceremonial paraphernalia associated with rituals that sought to establish and maintain peaceful relations may include ceramics, ceremonial accoutrements, gorgets, pipes, shell cups, and symbolic weaponry. For example, Long-Nosed God maskettes crafted from copper or marine shell are believed to have been important in the creation of alliances in the twelfth and thirteenth centuries in the Midwest (Duncan and Diaz-Granados 2000). Likewise, "friendly intertribal relations were mediated . . . by exchanges of shell beads" in much of the Eastern Woodlands (Hall 1997:57–58).

Settlement patterns provide an important indication of peaceful relations. When settlements are located in unprotected or nondefensive positions, the level of conflict may be low, or conflict may be absent. Settlement patterns change over time as social and economic changes take place, but settlements are also sensitive indicators of political relations among regional populations.

Evaluating the degree of conflict and cooperation among contemporary populations throughout eastern North America requires the use of direct and indirect evidence. While assessments of violence have attracted the attention of archaeologists over the past several decades, cooperative relations among neighboring groups have not been investigated so frequently. Although warfare has been discussed more often than mechanisms promoting peaceful relations, our understanding of the nature, range, and variability of violent conflict is still inadequate. In this book, I propose that for nearly half the time that Native Americans lived in eastern North America—approximately six thousand years—peaceful relations characterized these family-level hunter-gatherers, and that violent conflict among social groups emerged only with increasingly complex forms of social and political organization.

In chapter 2, I present an overview of the evolution of Eastern Woodland cultures and summarize some of the basic tools that archaeologists use in the investigation of cooperation and conflict. With evidence derived from archaeological research, the relationship between conflict and cooperation may be studied in order to provide an assessment of Native American life over the past thirteen thousand years.

CHAPTER TWO

Archaeology and the Study of Violence and Cooperation

*If resort to violence is part of the human tool kit, so too is resort to coopera-
tion, generosity, and trust.*

(Johnson and Earle 2000:16)

I draw from several fields of study to model the coevolution of cooperation and
conflict, but I believe that archaeology is the primary vehicle for understanding the relationship between peace and violence in the Eastern Woodlands
prior to European contact. A major question posed by the scientific investigation of homicides, feuding, and warfare—beyond the simple question of why
intersocietal conflict takes place—is that of how aggression and violence are
expressed or suppressed under varying domestic, economic, political, and social
circumstances. How do people resolve episodes of violence and maintain
peaceful coexistence? Are we violent because we are genetically wired for aggression, or is conflict a product of our increasing dependence on and development of culture? How do warfare and peace articulate with and relate to the
rest of society? Are times of peace unusual, or is the practice of peaceful intersocietal relations as much a part of our nature as our capacity for violence? Finally, do aggression, violence, homicide, feuding, and warfare, on the one
hand, and institutions of diplomacy, alliance, cooperation, and peace, on the
other, take forms appropriate to the domestic, economic, political, and social
systems in which they find expression? Although the study of human conflict
and cooperation in the past may seem trivial compared to current pulses of
seemingly endemic world violence, understanding the nature of intersocietal

efforts at promoting peace and waging war is of great importance if we are to understand why our species has such a propensity for violent behavior and yet can also be so successful in establishing and maintaining peaceful relations.

In this book, I look at the archaeological evidence for the relationship between peace and war, both being based on various forms and degrees of alliance and cooperation, over some thirteen thousand years in eastern North America. Archaeologists have made great strides in learning about the nature of human society in North America and how it changed over time (Fagan 2005; Milner 2004; Pauketat and Loren 2005). The study of culture change is at the heart of anthropological archaeology, and eastern North America is well suited to the study of how human society was transformed from early family-level foragers to regional, multivillage polities. Institutions of peace and war play a significant role in culture change. Analysis of their interconnected relationships is critical for understanding the nature of intergroup conflict and cooperation in eastern North American.

My thesis in the present work is that two basic and critical aspects of human existence, cooperation and conflict, are intertwined in complex ways, and that peaceful cooperation and violent conflict have evolved in tandem over several thousand years. As human societies have developed, so too have the institutions of cooperation and violence. Throughout the long cultural sequence in eastern North America, diplomacy has been used to achieve desired states of political and social balance through threats of warfare and maintenance of alliances. In many instances in the past, societies may be "at war" with one neighbor while enjoying cooperative arrangements with another. Thus, peace and war are not linear processes. Intersocietal relationships are bound together in complex ways, changing over time, creating and recreating matrices of domestic, economic, political, religious, and social relationships among neighboring groups, which slowly change in an ebb and flow of antagonistic relations coupled with warm and trusting alliances. These partnerships gradually change over time, as relationships are altered: the bitter enemy becomes the ally, and the trusted host schemes over the treacherous feast. Thus, cooperation and conflict might be regarded as "intersocietal engagement," in that they are but two aspects of a single political and social process.

Numerous theories have been proposed for the archaeological study of violent conflict. Individual theories are neither right nor wrong, but they vary in their ability to aid archaeologists in understanding the changing nature of conflict in the past, and how cooperation and violence are expressed in various levels of economic, political, and social integration in social systems. In this book, I employ a social-evolution approach. Social evolution refers to the development of increasingly complex levels of sociopolitical integration, and to how social change is interpreted through the archaeological record. It pays particular attention to population growth because of its consequences for how people meet their basic needs and solve the problems caused by their needs and wants. Growth in population creates problems that must be addressed and solved by technology, the social organization of production, and political regulation, as well as by ritual, ideology, and cosmology. The necessity of solving these problems results in sociocultural evolution (Johnson and Earle 2000:2). A social-evolutionary perspective is useful because it allows archaeologists to gauge changes in levels of social integration against the varying dimensions of peace and conflict.

Johnson and Earle (2000:15) identify three levels of economic, political, and social integration in their social-evolutionary perspective: family-level group, local group, and regional polity. Their social-evolutionary perspective forms the basis for much of my discussion. I use these levels of sociopolitical integration to organize and contextualize complex and dynamic economic, political, and social relationships among people in the Eastern Woodlands prior to European contact.

Ethnographic descriptions, in many respects, provide models fundamentally different from those based upon archaeological evidence, especially for social groups who once lived in eastern North America. The use of a social-evolutionary perspective is a heuristic device, not a theoretical position into which archaeological data and interpretations should be forced in a unilineal sequence. For example, McElrath et al. (2000:8) note that

> Although it may be argued that broad-scale cultural changes are reflective of regional developments and that specific localities are simply the parochial expressions of these phenomena, shoehorning a historically complex sequence of specific ethnic occupations of the American Bottom into an evolutionary scheme denies the historicity of social change and the individualized forces involved in cultural development. Such an approach ignores the historical processes of social development that would explain, for example, why Mississippian culture emerged in the American Bottom and not in the lower Illinois Valley, why Middle Archaic Helton phase peoples were sedentary in the lower Illinois Valley but apparently not in the American Bottom, and so on.

The archaeological record for eastern North America is a complex sequence of occupations by ethnically distinct, historically divergent, and politically diverse populations whose trajectories of political, religious, settlement, social, and subsistence systems are nonunilineal and multifaceted. Eastern North American societies were historically linked and interdependent upon one another. Social change is seen from the perspective of environment, culture, and human agency. Evolutionary sequences need not be unilineal or gradualist, but can and should incorporate historically contingent processes. "No single local or regional chronological sequence can be expected to validate a 'model' of social evolution" (McElrath et al. 2000:10).

How do we assess a group's interaction in a regional context? What is the social mechanism for establishing relationships among groups who may be competing for resources, yet who may be engaged in mutually beneficial and cooperative alliances and rituals? In eastern North America, ever larger circles of domestic, political, ritual, and social activities must be considered in terms of peaceful and hostile relations for both individual societies and their long-range interactions with regionally cooperative and competitive groups. Social groups interact within multilayered networks. An emphasis on "cause-and-effect relationships" obscures the variation that lies at the heart of our knowledge concerning eastern North American societies. The "study of cultural evolution does not end with a reconstruction of the 'genealogies' of cultures. But without such a reconstruction, it will never begin" (Tschauner 1994:90).

To develop a comprehensive understanding of social life and culture change, one must study a large, geographically continuous area such as eastern North America with attention to its subunits, such as the Gulf Coast, Mid-Atlantic, Midsouth, Midwest, Mississippi Valley, Northeast, Southeast, Trans-Mississippi West, and so forth (see figure 2.1.). Eastern North America was a social world of shifting centers and peripheries. The cultural landscape was marked by population centers that were at different and uneven cultural stages of development. The significance of historical events and variation, especially the nature of cooperation and conflict, will become clearer as we examine the broad historical development of cultures within geographically delineated regions. There are multiple pathways to the emergence of social hierarchies and the ways in which people identify their relationships with each other, and the ways in which they define themselves in terms of cooperation and conflict.

Although there has been a general trend from less centralized to more centralized social groups in eastern North America, the specific historical events and relationships that characterize populations are complex, oscillating, and nonunilineal. Culture change over the broad expanse of time cannot be adequately explained solely by reference to simple cause-and-effect relationships, or to gradual changes in social, economic, political, and ideological systems. Finally, my postulated evolutionary sequences are not intended to be rigid evolutionary schemes, but rather hypothesized contexts within which cooperation and conflict may be discussed.

Figure 2.1. Map of eastern North America.

Eastern North America: Social Evolution and Conflict

Eastern North America is characterized by deciduous forests in the eastern portion and tall-grass prairies in the western area (figure 2.2). Few if any of the ethnographic groups upon whom Johnson and Earle (2000) based their social-evolutionary model occupy comparably rich and diverse environmental settings. Thus, Johnson and Earle's model of the evolution of human societies, while useful for broad generalizations concerning social evolution, may be significantly limited in its application to eastern North American societies.

Figure 2.2. Satellite image of eastern North America. (*Natural Colour Mosaic of North America*, www.intute.ac.uk/sciences/worldguide/html/image_1559; courtesy of NASA).

The earliest people to enter eastern North America were low-density, family-level foragers. In such societies, egalitarian family-level, or "hearth," foragers are self-sufficient, the family group acting as the primary subsistence unit. Such groups usually number about five to eight persons, interacting with larger, extended-family camps or hamlets periodically, as opportunities arise and needs dictate. Demographic patterns may be characterized as fission-fusion. Leadership is ad hoc, and even skillful and renowned individuals do not have power over others. Descent is typically bilateral, which means that kinship ties to the mother's and father's relatives are equally emphasized, and postmarital residence patterns are flexible.

Depending on the extent of their self-sufficiency, family-level groups may form camps of one or two families, or hamlets composed of several families. Daily problems of unpredictability regarding food or other basic needs are ameliorated by reciprocity among kin and friends. Access to resources is maintained through an extensive network of kin and friendship ties, based on positive relationships among members of the local camp. Social networks are materialized through the exchange of valuables, such as fine-grained chert or other essential raw materials. Positive social relationships are critical to survival, and aggression is actively discouraged. The central principle for family-level foragers is to minimize risks through their economy and social organization.

Family camps are minimal human social communities, composed of closely related kin. Among low-density foragers, these groups number fewer than one person per ten square miles, and often fish, gather, or hunt within a home range that is not strictly defended against outsiders. Exclusive claims are not made over territory, but families may "own" key resources that may be protected from trespassers. Resources are secured via a simple division of labor by sex. When resources are highly localized, risk-management needs are increased, or specific subsistence activities call for groups larger than the family, then camps of twenty-five to fifty persons may form, but they just as quickly dissolve back into single-family camps. When tasks require labor to be organized or mobilized, leadership positions arise on an ad-hoc basis and are both ephemeral and context-specific: that is, leaders do not remain leaders for long. Likewise, rituals are conducted according to the immediate needs of individuals or the family.

In terms of eastern North American archaeology, the family-camp organization corresponds well with what archaeologists know about the time period from earliest settlement to about 5000 BC. While the first North Americans may have been family-level camp or hearth groups, the rich resources of the Eastern Woodlands may have allowed these initial foragers to maintain higher population densities, such as family hamlets, early in the settlement history.

The family hamlet has a higher density of people than family camps, generally one person per ten square miles to two persons per square mile. Initial efforts at horticulture may augment wild foods, upon which the family continues to rely heavily, but storage is more prevalent. The hamlet forms and reforms as specific resource availability is utilized by family groups, who change locations to maximize efforts at fishing, gardening, gathering, and hunting. The hamlet is not a well-defined political entity because leadership is still ad hoc and based on context. Ceremonialism is not highly developed.

The family-hamlet pattern may correspond to social groups in eastern North America from about 9000 to 5000 BC, but it may also characterize an earlier period. Neither the family-level camp nor the hamlet typically engages in feuding or warfare. Territoriality and exclusive access to resources are virtually nonexistent. Although home bases are large with respect to population densities, defense of territory is not practical. Therefore, confrontations among family groups are rare, with the exception of impulsive homicides, which may occur when personal hostilities erupt over mates or previous homicides, for example.

Warfare and intergroup aggression are virtually nonexistent among mobile, family-level foragers, whether organized as camps or hamlets; but raids due to feuding may take place as population densities rise. Trespass is often resented where families have usufruct rights to specific resources, which they may defend in the face of theft. Fighting may occur between individuals who hold personal grievances or grudges against one another over homicides, mates, resources, or sexual jealousy. Such fights are usually nonlethal, although deaths can occur. Organized intersocietal conflict may have been infrequent to nonexistent prior to the development of more complex integrated forms of society. That is, before about ten thousand years ago, when human social groups became increasingly sedentary and segmented, feuding and warfare may have been rare to nonexistent, but murder and homicide would have been present. Peace would be maintained through occasional feasting and gift exchange. Outward signs of violence would be discouraged. Responses to conflict would include nonphysical means such as avoidance, discussion, restraint, and toleration.

In small, family-level hunting-and-gathering societies, aggression among members is personal. Resolution of a violent act usually results in a homicide, the killing of a killer. Violent persons and bullies are typically executed by an "agent" of the community. Such acts generally do not lead to a cycle of revenge killing in which blood feuding continues unabated. Much of the skeletal trauma seen in the early prehistory of eastern North America may be the result of these conflict-resolving homicides, rather than the more socially or politically organized raids and ambushes that are signatures of feuding and warfare. Ascertaining the differences in the archaeological record among self-redress homicides, feuding, and warfare based on skeletal trauma is difficult.

Local groups in the eastern North American archaeological record appear around 5000 BC, as family-level foragers become increasingly sedentary, population densities climb, and more complex social institutions emerge. Unlike family-level groups, local groups are composed of many families and are often five to ten times the size of family-level groups. The centripetal pull that brings multiple families together is usually some common interest, such as food storage, defense, or resource abundance. Social segmentation or subdivision takes place along kinship lines, which serves to form corporate groups. The local group cooperates in raids, rituals, and large-scale construction projects. Local groups tend to be either acephalous, village-sized units or intergroup collectivities, which are larger groups integrated by regional networks of exchange and headed by charismatic leaders whose power is achieved on the basis of personal abilities.

The acephalous local group has a population density greater than that of the family-level hearth. It usually forms a village or community of hamlets composed of some one hundred to two hundred people, often subdivided into segmented social units such as clans or lineages. These hamlet-sized kin segments number about twenty-five to thirty-five persons. The subsistence economy often focuses on domesticated species, although wild resources may dominate in some societies. The local group is integrated both politically and ritually and led by a headman. The group typically fragments into its constituent smaller kin groupings, seasonally or otherwise periodically, as a result of internal disputes. Ceremonialism is important for publicly identifying and defining local groups and their complex regional interrelationships. Resources are held exclusively by kin groups, and territorial defense is common. The initial concentration of wealth occurs in local groups, and force becomes an implement for its acquisition and transfer.

In local groups with segmented social systems, such as clans or lineages, feuding comes to the forefront, being organized by charismatic leaders and regulated by the collective members of the social group. Feuding is endemic, and intercommunity relationships of various sorts are critically important for community security, but such relationships are contracted on an individual, family-by-family basis. Cooperation is attained through various forms of exchange and feasting, which serve to foster and cement alliances. In eastern North America, the beginnings of local camps and their segmented social systems seem to appear around 5000 BC, but episodes of complexity are also present earlier.

The intergroup collectivity is managed by a charismatic leader. Such groups are more integrated than acephalous local units and are often found in higher population densities. Feuding between territorial groups is usually endemic and intense. The local community of perhaps three hundred to five hundred people is territorially based, and the territory is vigorously defended against outsiders. The community typically contains multiple clan or lineage segments dispersed throughout the group's well-defined territory.

The local group's representatives in the regional intergroup collectivity, the charismatic leaders, are essential for managing risks, organizing kin militias, and negotiating and contracting intergroup alliances through feasting and exchange. Leaders also maintain internal group cohesion by adjudicating disputes. Finally, leaders represent the group in initiating, conducting, and coordinating major rituals that formalize the local group's intercommunity relationships. A charismatic leader's power, however, is dependent on personal initiative, and may wax and wane over time based on an individual's ability to compete with rival leaders. From about 1000 BC to AD 400, leaders and their managed intergroup collectivities may be seen most clearly when wealth and prestige goods are exchanged over long distances and are prominent in the archaeological record.

Territoriality and feuding are common among local groups. As population and competition increase, territories are diligently defended and carefully demarcated against neighbors. Local groups often occupy a world of aggressive male behavior, which is typically rewarded by the community. Local groups are linked into intergroup collectivities by the exchange of valuables and by strongly integrated networks of marriage and alliance.

With the development of lineages, clans, or other forms of social segmentation, human conflict becomes more effective and deadly, as violence is more structured and organized. In fact, tribal warriors are noted for their fierceness (Chagnon 1997; Redmond 1994). Tribal or local-group feuding originates in the development of an organization supporting the maintenance of kin militia units. These social groups act with a sense of shared responsibility, and react as kin in forming raiding parties. Kin militias are small, temporary, and informal organizations ranging in size from five to thirty individuals, who serve under leaders who build alliances through feasting and exchange. Command hierarchy in kin militias is rudimentary, and leaders generally mold acquiescence to their opinions by cajoling or pleading rather than by issuing commands (Reyna 1994:42).

Individual, personal grudge resolution, an important motivation for tribal raiding parties, could be amplified over time, precipitating the formation of social factions and short-lived intra- and intertribal alliances. Reyna (1994:42) argues that "kin militia that acted upon grudges often were not fixed community, village, or descent group units. Rather, they seem to have been evanescent congeries of kin and allies thrown together for one or two operations."

Reyna (1994:42) identifies three patterns of tribal fighting:

> First, a kin militia would raid a people against whom it had a grudge, kill a few, and then run for home. Second, kin militias would raid a people against whom they harbored grudges a number of times over a brief period such as a year, satisfy these grudges, and then never raid again. Third, kin militias might raid a people against whom they harbored grudges a number of times over a number of decades finally culminating in a battle.

Kin militias, although capable of organized violence, lack the capacity to sustain raids for more than a few weeks, so the victors leave their neighbors' territories after a raid. With only elementary powers to disperse their enemies (Carneiro 1994), tribal societies have limited power over their opponents. Among segmentary lineage systems characterized by long-term use of restricted resources and intruded on by invasive tribal societies, competition may arise to drive competitors from the area. This "predatory expansion" principle results in temporary consolidation of fragmented tribal polities for "concerted external action" (Sahlins 1961).

In the case of classic blood feud, raids upon encampments often result in mass burials. Surprise attacks, in which an unsuspecting enemy is ambushed, characterize feuding. Typically, dawn raids are carried out against neighboring settlements. The archaeological evidence for raids is also seen in individuals with multiple wounds, as raiders are able to kill from a distance with spears and/or bows and arrows. Wounds resulting from clubs are more typical once access to the camp or village is gained.

The archaeological expression of collective responsibility for vengeance might be indicated when the practice of pin-cushioning, or delivering multiple wounds to a single victim—which is suggestive of vengeance killing—becomes routine. The size of the raiding party is usually equal to the number of arrows or spears delivered in the coup de grace volley. Group liability may be expressed by the killing of children who are members of the malefactors' social group. Wounded individuals are able to withdraw to the rear for safety in the case of battles between two lines of combatants, resulting in either healed skeletal elements or single interments given proper burial.

With the incipient growth of social hierarchies based on the growth of aristocratic lineages in chieftaincies (Carneiro 1998; Redmond 1994, 1998), and their elaboration in chiefdoms (Earle 1997), organized violence is once again transformed. Some local groups become regional polities, as chieftains begin to inherit political offices that later become institutionalized chiefly positions. In regional polities, the ruling elite or chief establishes order by means of the ideological/political organization. Regional peace is imposed and maintained within the polity. While peace reigns internally, the chief wages violent and systematic warfare externally against some neighboring polities, while welding alliances with others.

Local communities that incorporate under the control of an effective chief eventually fragment, often at the time of the chief's death, into constituent communities. Intense competition takes place among elites within regional polities for political offices that control revenue-producing resources. The subsistence economy from which surplus could be derived in eastern North America was based upon productive natural resources and tropical cultigens such as corn, beans, and squash. The subsistence economy was carefully managed to maximize surplus production, which was translated into an effective power base. Political survival derives in part from the exchange of prestige goods, which provides elites with opportunities for investment and control. Surplus production also helps finance operations in ideological, economic, military, and political spheres. Clearly defined offices of leadership emerge at the local and regional levels as the regional integration of the polity proceeds. Institutionalized offices are occupied by members of the hereditary elite, who use their ritual responsibilities to legitimize their leadership positions.

Chiefly warfare was waged by means of a corporate organization that included a chief's retainers, who formed a council, and the militias they called up from neighboring, allied polities (Reyna 1994:43-44). Militia units might include warriors from the low hundreds to several thousand (Carneiro 1990). While raids were carried out by small, private war parties, large, national militias could be deployed in general massed attacks. Small groups acted as either partisan war parties, or as groups of raiders who formed part of a "national" war effort. War councils held small grievances in check and forged alliances with friendly polities. Councils of war controlled large national wars. While small raiding parties could wear down an enemy over time, the ultimate goal of a national war was "the total destruction of the enemy or their capitulation on issues in dispute" (Eid 1985:134).

By comparison with kin militias, chiefly militias were capable of superior and improved tactics (Turney-High 1991:25–26) because of improvements in command structure. These military improvements enabled chiefs as commanders to issue orders through their retinues, which gave chiefs the authority and power to punish disobedient warriors. Religious cults further strengthened chiefly authority by identifying "the interests of the war god with those of the chief" (Reyna 1994:44).

The Origin of War
Is War Making Integral to Our Ancestry?

Recent comparative studies of hunter-gatherers by anthropologists Douglas P. Fry and Raymond S. Kelly (Fry 2006, 2007; Kelly 2000) suggest that there is great time depth for humans in their attempts to avoid conflict. According to Fry (2006:1), "Violence tends to grab the headlines, but violence constitutes only a minute part of social life. To focus too much attention on the aggression is to totally miss the 'big picture.'" Fry's concern is with the nature of violence among simple nomadic foragers and how the interpretation of human aggression informs us about our past. He does not deny that increased levels of violence characterize social behavior among complex hunter-gatherers and farmers, but he argues that violence was not part and parcel of our heritage, nor do humans have an instinctual basis for aggression, violence, and warfare. Of course, Fry is not the first scholar to suggest that war making is not integral to our hominid ancestry, but he presents a detailed discussion of the human potential for peace and how simple hunter-gatherers use a variety of social strategies and behaviors to dampen external and internal conflicts. As is the case with Fry, Kelly also employs a comparative ethnographic analysis of simple foragers to isolate distinctive features of peaceful hunter-gatherers. He notes that the frequency of warfare is low among unsegmented mobile foragers and high among mobile and seminomadic segmental hunter-gatherers.

War councils, formal forums for overseeing military operations, also brought improvement in the command structure. Held to discuss tactics and strategies, war councils depended on wise council from priests, intelligence from spies, and military advice from experienced warriors. Command structure also depended on the existence of a real military hierarchy. Chiefs commanded their retinues, who in turn oversaw the graded ranks of warriors. The military hierarchies of chiefdoms possessed rules about chains of command that allowed a chief to maneuver "formations within his militia in different ways so as to create surprise, to concentrate force at critical points, to utilize terrain, etc." (Reyna 1994:45). Chiefs had the capability to commit their militias in restricted campaigns, with clear political objectives, that could result in great slaughter.

Chiefly warfare was chronic in regularity and frequency because warfare was now an instrument of chiefly public or governmental policy. Political objectives might include chiefly grudge resolution that arose out of elite conduct of public affairs. Force could be used to appropriate social labor and material goods as tribute. With chiefly militias, "violence could be used to create, maintain, and transform social relations" (Reyna 1994:46), providing chiefs with constitutive powers over social relations. Chiefdoms had the organizational means to aggregate or accumulate polities to their corporate structure by violence.

Peace and War in Eastern North America

In many ways, eastern North America is a unique world, different from the rest of the Western Hemisphere in terms of climate, environment, and history. With massive and extensive forests that produced a variety of wild plant foods and abundant game, eastern North American coastlines, prairies, and woodlands gave rise to a series of complex Native American foraging and farming cultures. Institutions of cooperation and conflict were enmeshed in the domestic, ideological, political, and social fabric of these evolving societies long before European contact, having been a critical part of Native American society for several thousand years.

Until recently, great forests covered the eastern third of North America, from the giant conifers in the Great Lakes region to the stately live-oak and magnolia forests of the Gulf and lower Atlantic Coasts. From the rich tidal marshes of the Atlantic Ocean to the tall-grass prairies of the Midwest and Eastern Plains, eastern North American cultures thrived, first as hunters and gatherers, and later as settled farmers who lived in villages and towns. Game animals and wild plants were unevenly distributed, and changes in forest composition reflected differences in climate, elevation, and latitude. From the muddy back swamps and fertile natural levees of the Lower Mississippi Valley, to the mixed hardwood and boreal forests of the Northeastern Woodlands, to the tall-grass prairies of the Midwest, aquatic resources, forest animals, and plant foods varied according to the land's natural ecology and climatic oscillations.

The different ecological zones gave rise to differing cultural adaptations by their inhabitants, the amounts and reliability of food resources shaping their lifestyles. Differences in the local availability of acorns, fish, and whitetail deer were of critical importance in terms of survival, and so alliances were forged among neighboring groups of hunters and gatherers—and later among groups of villager farmers, who not only depended on garden and field produce for their survival, but who were also affected when weather patterns changed. When local plant resources failed and game animals migrated to adjacent territories where food was more abundant, then local groups faced difficult decisions. Periodic hunger and starvation were grim reminders of the fragile existence humans maintained, not only with the plant and animal world, but also with their neighbors and the deities who controlled their lives and everyday events.

To maintain the delicate relationships ensuring survival, native peoples of eastern North America created numerous ways to offset adverse conditions through alliances, marriage arrangements, population movements, prayers, raiding, residence patterns, rituals, and theft of resources. From earliest times, alliances based on diplomacy became an ecological safety net, an insurance policy providing mutual benefit for those who could maintain strong and secure bonds with their neighbors in times of need. Exotic tokens of wealth and prestige were exchanged among community leaders. Men and women chose marriage partners from neighboring territories to build strong exchange and kin relationships, which provided the basis for long-lasting alliances. Rituals and prayers were offered to the deities and ancestors who interceded on behalf of the supplicants. Movement away from areas of conflict was desirable when vacant zones were available. However, in the case of environmental circumscription or territorial packing, theft of neighboring resources was a viable alternative to starvation. Raiding neighboring settlements where local resources and stored food supplies were abundant often provoked retaliatory attacks, however.

Supernatural aid was sought to entice animals that had migrated into neighboring territories. Rituals and solicitations directed toward deities in the hope that they would influence game movements and increase the numbers of forest animals were widespread throughout the Eastern Woodlands at the time of European contact. When rituals and prayers were not enough, people called upon hard-earned alliances crafted through diplomacy, and kin networks established through intercommunity marriages, to urge their neighbors to join them in raids against those who were temporarily blessed with abundance. Prayers served to invoke from deities the power to successfully attack one's enemies, to find game, and to return home safely with food or scalps.

In most cases, alliances and marriage arrangements worked to everyone's benefit. But, when necessary, game animals in neighboring areas could be taken surreptitiously at territorial boundaries. Instances of thievery may have gone undetected in many cases. However, confrontations would have erupted between neighboring groups as they tried to protect their resources. And perhaps, on rare occasions, blood was spilled. When a killing did occur over access rights to resources, revenge was necessary to settle the score of human lives. Rituals would have been activated for the concerned parties to work through the protocol of compensation or begin a long and deadly round of blood feuding. While raiding was probably deeply rooted throughout much of eastern North American prehistory, the flash point that resulted in violence and bloodshed may have been reached only on rare occasions. It was the threat of violence that was endemic, rather than violence itself.

Eastern North America provides archaeologists with an ideal region in which to consider the conditions under which warfare evolved. Devoid of people prior to settlement by Upper Paleolithic foragers, the archaeological record is understood sufficiently well that basic questions about the dynamics of violence and social-group conflict over some thirteen millennia can be at least tentatively answered. What changes took place in conflict over time, from earliest settlement to the time of European contact? What was the nature of conflict among simple mobile hunters and gatherers, and how did intersocietal conflict change as people began to cultivate locally available plants? How did people go about creating ways to avoid conflict, and how successful were they in establishing and maintaining cooperative relations? What prompted outbreaks of hostilities, and how were they resolved when they occurred? To what extent did European contact in the sixteenth century escalate violence? I address such questions in this book.

Warfare in the Eastern Woodlands underwent a series of transformations, from a lack of warfare initially to chiefly warfare at European contact in the sixteenth century. As foraging societies began to develop social segmentation, raiding and predatory expansion became more prevalent. In time, chiefly warfare, based on raiding, incorporated formal institutions and inherited offices as part of elite aggrandizement. Before warfare took on the aggregative powers of chiefdoms, however, it grew out of human decisions to engage in violence or to develop social mechanisms to dampen or quell conflicts through rituals which promoted cooperation and peace. The earliest foragers who entered eastern North America undoubtedly already possessed a cultural ethos that reduced competition and promoted restraint in order for them to survive.

CHAPTER THREE

Family-Level Foragers and the Resolution of Homicides

Anyone studying the first Americans sets sail in hazardous academic seas, beset on every side by passionate emotions and contradictory scientific information.

(Fagan 1987:7)

When the first people entered the Americas, did they bring violence and warfare with them? The earliest hunters and gatherers, who were never numerous, left only stone tools and the areas where they gathered wild plants and butchered game, quarried stone tools, and camped. Such skimpy evidence provides few clues as to their way of life, their relationships with each other, or the nature of their interactions with adjacent groups. Over the years, archaeologists have pieced together the broad outline of the remarkable story of these Ice Age foragers who settled eastern North America. From these studies, an assessment of conflict and cooperation can be made for the earliest inhabitants of eastern North America.

As an undergraduate, I was fortunate to study archaeology in one of the richest prehistoric regions in eastern North America, the Lower Tennessee River valley. One day, while conducting a surface survey at Kentucky Lake Reservoir in west-central Tennessee, one of the Tennessee Valley Authority's impoundments of the Tennessee River, I walked across a high terrace overlooking the river and adjacent floodplain. Thousands of broken chert artifacts, evidence of a prehistoric archaeological site, were scattered across the plowed field.

Paleoindian Foragers and Pleistocene Extinctions

Upper Paleolithic foragers may have settled eastern North America toward the end of the Allerød warming trend from 12,000 to 11,300 BC, just after a major continent-wide wave of Pleistocene extinctions. Although many megafauna became extinct, mammoths and mastodons seem to have survived for another eight hundred years or so. The massive extinction of Pleistocene megafauna may have been caused by some combination of human predation, reduced food supplies, disrupted birth schedules, and changes in ecosystem and climatic conditions.

The sudden and rapid onset of the Younger Dryas cold interval around 10,900 BC was a time of markedly colder conditions. A sudden temperature decline brought about changes in the distribution of floral and faunal communities, widespread drought, and possibly a moderate lowering of sea level. The emergence, diversification, and expansion of distinctive subregional forager traditions at the time of the cold interval served as a trigger, bringing about the final wave of extinctions that saw mammoths and mastodons die out. Hunting over great distances to exploit widely dispersed large mammals changed to a hunting pattern that emphasized more localized movements directed toward a wide range of smaller animals.

The number of large mammals that became extinct in North America at the end of the late Pleistocene is staggering: bears, camels, giant sloths, horses, mammoths, mastodons, saber-toothed tigers, and several forms of bison. Before this extinction, the diversity of large terrestrial mammals in North America was similar to that of modern Africa.

After selecting some stone tools and chipping debris samples, I walked over to a ridge overlooking the river. A well-made biface fragment caught my eye. I could tell from the chipping pattern and shape, as it lay partially buried in the ground, that it was not typical of ones I had seen in museum collections. This one was different. In fact, I could see it was a fluted Paleoindian spear point. The distinctive flute was obvious even from a distance of ten feet. Fluted points have been documented by archaeologists as being associated with extinct Ice Age mammoths on the High Plains. And so, at that moment, I knew that an Ice Age hunter had made this spear point.

I had located a prehistoric site that belonged in the set of sites that archaeologists view as the initial Paleoindian pioneer staging territories in eastern North America (Anderson 1990). Some of the earliest inhabitants of the Western Hemisphere had settled here some thirteen thousand years ago. The Lower Tennessee valley would subsequently fill with people, as population increased over the centuries. The large Paleoindian territories would shrink into increasingly smaller hunting domains for later people, creating tensions and stress for small, mobile foraging bands. The Tennessee Valley provides evidence for some of the earliest conflict in North America. Intersocietal tensions began with the Paleoindian people who first settled along the major rivers of eastern North America, hunting, gathering, fishing, and making stone tools, such as the spear point I had found that day on the Tennessee River terrace.

Organized intersocietal conflict is typically lacking in unsegmented societies, social groups that have not developed lineages, clans, or sodalities (Kelly 2000). Paleoindian bands appear to have been integrated as small, mobile, independent families, loosely connected by kin networks, but with no higher order of social integration (such as lineages or clans), suggesting that Paleoindians did not engage in prolonged feuding or warfare.

Recent research has reevaluated the origin of warfare, leading anthropologists to believe that intersocietal conflict is rare to nonexistent among nonsegmented foraging societies in resource-scarce areas. In such environments, people apparently must cooperate to survive; that is, they do not have the luxury of fighting among themselves, although organized homicides and spontaneous conflicts over resources do occasionally occur (Knauft 1991; Reyna 1994). Among nonsegmental, simple family-level foragers, raiding, warfare, and the defense of territory are virtually nonexistent.

What was the nature of intersocietal conflict among pioneer hunter-gatherers who crossed through the Arctic gateway into the Western Hemisphere? How did social conflict become transformed as foragers adapted to changing environmental and social conditions? When did feuding or warfare begin in eastern North America? How did self-redress homicide, capital punishment, and spontaneous conflicts over access to resources evolve into blood feuding? In this chapter, I examine the nature of conflict among the earliest inhabitants of North America and attempt to answer some of these questions, despite the paucity of evidence.

The entry of Early Paleoindian foragers into the Americas marks one of the great events in the history of human population movements. For the first time since the initial dispersal of *Homo erectus*, or closely related hominids from Africa between 1.5 and 2 million years ago, hunters and gatherers journeyed into a hemisphere devoid of humans. The sixteen-million-square-mile Western Hemisphere was populated by Pleistocene megafauna that were unfamiliar with the invading human hunters, who possessed great intelligence and had highly developed skills and weaponry with which to exploit the virgin landscape.

Initial forager population densities were presumably thin, perhaps as a result of a "pioneer phase of colonization." The resulting archaeological sites would be few, small, widely dispersed, and generally invisible—or at least rarely observed—in the archaeological record. The succeeding "residential phase of colonization" would leave a more readily detectable archaeological signature on the landscape, resulting in an increased threshold of visibility, such as the widespread Clovis horizon (Adovasio and Pedler 2005:49).

The advantage conferred by Clovis fluted bifaces may have been more social and political than technological. The distinctive fluted bifaces may have served as integral components for social/political bonding in widespread exchange networks (Meltzer 1993). Caching exotic, symbolic, and hypertrophic weaponry, manufactured through highly skilled crafting, was an early manifestation of what became a long-lasting tradition in eastern North America of ameliorating conflicts through the exchange of valuables.

Some Paleoindian family groups may have entered eastern North America prior to or during the Older Dryas, an abrupt and short-lived cold snap between 12,000 and 11,700 BC that witnessed an increase in winter precipitation and shorter growing seasons in the Northeastern Woodlands (Fairbanks et al. 1992). If Paleoindian populations came out of the northwest, they could have expanded eastward during a warming trend after the Older Dryas—perhaps just below the glacial margin, along the Northern Plains tundra. Migrating eastward and southeastward, they may have followed well-established game trails along river terraces, or navigated the major rivers of the Northern and Central Plains, such as the Arkansas, Missouri, or Platte, in small boats or canoes (Englebrecht and Seyfert 1994). These rivers would have led Paleoindian foragers to the resource-rich Mississippi River valley and its tributaries. From here, the great Eastern Woodland rivers, the Cumberland, Ohio, and Tennessee, would have attracted foragers to rich hunting-and-gathering grounds along the broad alluvial valley floors, adjacent terraces, and nearby uplands, where they could have readily developed a broad-spectrum subsistence strategy (figure 3.1). The proximity of large populations of game, and the local availability of the high-quality, highly desirable cherts that were necessary for stone-tool manufacture, would have provided strong incentives for colonizing and settling resource-rich sections of these rivers.

The importance of high-quality cherts for establishing alliances and participating in exchange networks is seen in the presence of nonlocal cherts in Clovis assemblages, which "could signal alliances between groups with long-term, routinized distributions across the landscape, that is, people of places" (Sassaman 2005:83). The presence of nonlocal, lithic raw materials in archaeological assemblages is an indicator of interactions between communi-

Figure 3.1. **Paleoindian hunters and gatherers, Tennessee, ca. 10,000 BC (courtesy of Frank H. McClung Museum, University of Tennessee, Knoxville; painting by Greg Harlin).**

ties. Long-distance exchange of exotic cherts among later societies has roots extending back to the Paleoindian stage.

Clovis populations may have been too sparse and transient to establish boundaries among themselves (Meltzer 1988), but the exchange of exotic cherts among these populations may signal the early establishment of such boundaries. If so, long-distance exchange of symbolic and hypertrophic weaponry would have been helpful in establishing marriage ties and resolv-ing conflicts across social boundaries. Intergroup alliances may have resulted from open-ended and flexible social relationships, facilitated by the seasonal aggregation of neighboring groups. Alliance formation may also have grown from the several millennia of settlement in those areas of eastern North America that were rich in subsistence and raw-material resources.

There was considerable variation among Paleoindian foragers, with widely varying degrees of mobility and subsistence strategies (Adovasio and Pedler 2005:51). In some areas, Clovis foragers made "redundant, even permanent use of preferred locales" (Sassaman 2005:83). Large hunting territories soon became the cores of staging areas (Anderson 1996a). Initial population con-centration in eastern North America is believed to have taken place during the second cold period, the Intra-Allerød, an abrupt, short-lived cold event around 11,400 BC (Ellis et al. 2004; Stuiver et al. 1995). After the Intra-Allerød, the Late Pleistocene forests and grasslands resumed the long-term warming trend as climate ameliorated again, giving rise to a more homoge-nous forest cover (Graham et al. 1996; Jackson et al. 2000). In the Deep South, warm temperate forests prevailed, while boreal forests predominated in the Upper Midwest. Between these two forest types, cool temperate forests with a mixture of conifers and northern hardwoods grew in the Midwest and Midsouth (Delcourt and Delcourt 1987).

Studies of modern hunter-gatherers indicate that lethal conflicts among Clovis foragers upon entering eastern North America may have been re-stricted to self-redress homicides or capital punishment. Kelly (2000) argues that Upper Paleolithic foragers in general had low levels of conflict, although conditions favoring sporadic competition were likely to be present as re-source availability fluctuated at any given location from year to year. Among Clovis families, spontaneous conflicts may have taken place over access to limited goods such as high-quality flint sources; but feuding and war were probably lacking because social segmentation does not appear to have been present. Instead, violence would have been limited to spontaneous homi-cides resulting from individual aggressions that would have flared up over personal issues such as conflict over homicides and mates.

In the environment of the North American tundra and boreal forests, co-operation among local groups would have been maximized and competition would have been minimized, in an effort to survive harsh conditions and lim-ited resources. Unsegmented societies represent a cultural organization well suited to those who colonize previously uninhabited territories or environ-mental zones, especially where critical goods are scarce (Kelly 2000:127). Warfare is therefore assumed to be initially absent among Early Paleoindians, because violence is assumed to be rare among unsegmented foraging societies in tundra or boreal forests. In more productive environments, such as deciduous forests where plants and animals are abundant, efforts to restrict access to critical items may have had early beginnings.

According to Kelly (2000:135), the initial societies that

> passed through the Arctic gateway to the New World were thus those that achieved a degree of regional integration through some combination of intermarriage, visiting, gift exchange, joint feasting, and festive intercommunity gathering entailing singing and dancing. Such practices fostered a state of positive peace that provided a basis for sharing and cooperation. In other words, it was not merely the absence of war but the presence of a positive peace that facilitated Upper Paleolithic migration.

Early Paleoindians lacked formal structural organization beyond the level of the family group. Such unsegmented or nonhierarchical societies are typically organized along two basic principles. First, bilateral kin relations allow regional integration through intermarriage. Mates are often chosen during occasional social gatherings and rituals, when family groups rendezvous at joint-use camps. Second, unsegmented foragers have a nonhierarchical, egalitarian social organization. The lack of hierarchies helps reduce or curtail conflict. Pioneer foraging societies, including those that came through the Arctic gateway to the Western Hemisphere, almost certainly shared several social principles: the family-level and local group organization, bilateral kinship relations, and unsegmented or nonhierarchical social organization (Whallon 1989). Prior to entering eastern North America, ancestral Paleoindians probably practiced self-redress or capital punishment, the killing of a killer. Capital punishment entails organized, planned, and premeditated attacks by family members against murderers who are explicitly targeted for their prior lethal violence.

After initial settlement, eastern North America continued to be sparsely populated by small groups of foragers who roamed over thousands of square miles within the territories of resource-rich staging areas. These flexible, egalitarian bands, consisting of only a few families each, regularly moved in search of food and resources, especially the high-quality cherts that were essential for crafting stone tools, and which were used to tip thrusting spears and as butchering knives. While highly mobile Clovis hunters probably sought out any remaining large Pleistocene mammals, such as mastodon, they would have had a broad-based diet, targeting a wide range of plants and animals. Hunting bison, deer, elk, and small mammals, they also gathered seasonally available fruits, nuts, seeds, and vegetable foods and caught fish in lakes and streams (Anderson and Sassaman 1996).

In open continental environments, unsegmented foragers tend to move away from conflict. An encounter between two groups of hunters seeking to exploit the same area is likely to create buffer zones between their respective bands. When there is no opportunity to withdraw, they first maintain a display of strength, in which the weaker party may leave. If not, then open confrontation may take place. Conflict over resources in the early stages of Paleoindian colonization may have been reduced by family groups moving away from conflict or developing alliances based on exchange of scarce or exotic goods, such as high-quality, fine-grained cherts.

The Clovis to Middle Paleoindian transition, around 8800 BC, witnessed a fundamental reorganization of culture and technology across much of eastern North America (Anderson 1996b). Most of the unglaciated Eastern Woodland terrain was thinly populated. Geographically restricted and stylistically distinctive spear points appeared, indicating that Paleoindian groups throughout eastern North America were beginning to establish regional population concentrations, cultural diversification, and territorial distinctiveness. Large hunting territories, centered upon limited sources of high-quality cherts, seem to have filled and expanded rapidly. Colonizing groups appeared on the Gulf Coast a few hundred years after the initial staging areas were settled, establishing new foraging territories. By 8800 BC, Paleoindians had also moved into the northeastern Canadian Woodlands. Neither of these areas were prime, resource-rich environments for Clovis foragers, suggesting that the more desirable Paleoindian territories in the Midsouth and Midwest had been occupied and filled (Anderson 1996b). Population packing in the initial staging areas, and the resulting tension among bands following population increase, may have prompted some foraging bands to move into these "marginal" areas.

When spontaneous conflict over access to resources occurs between neighboring foraging groups, they tend to move apart, reducing or removing the underlying cause of conflict. When possible, foragers will move into unpopulated areas, even if these are less desirable, to avoid or reduce conflict (Fry 2006, 2007; Johnson 1982). Had this been the case with the Clovis establishment of new territories adjacent to the original staging areas, then some degree of tension resulting from population increase would have been evident, signaling progressive intensification of conflict. Unless population numbers are held in check, group size among foragers will increase significantly upon entering unpopulated, rich-resource areas, giving rise to elevated competition with neighboring groups.

Resource scarcity is considered a precipitating condition for lethal conflict. The incidence and severity of spontaneous conflicts over access to resources are correlated with the degree to which access to those resources is restricted as population increases bring about greater impact on them. Frequency of conflict does not covary with population density, but frequency and severity of spontaneous conflicts do covary with resource availability (Kelly 2000). Thus, the more resources are restricted, the more likely it is that conflict will take place. Higher resource restriction or environmental circumscription (Carneiro 1988) amplifies the incidence and severity of conflicts. Thieving trespassers who precipitate spontaneous conflicts over access to resources are targeted explicitly for lethal violence. In such cases, raids are not organized, planned, or premeditated, but they do entail organization, as group members are recruited for the specific purpose of carrying out an armed ambush.

The principal objective of trespass is to secure subsistence or lithic resources. If contested, members of the trespassing group either leave or prepare to fight. Recourse to armed conflict is only a means to a resource-acquisition end. Each of the contending forces is made up of individuals who routinely hunt or gather as units. The implements they carry for resource procurement—including clubs, digging sticks, knives, paddles, slings, spears, and stones—can also be employed effectively as weapons against people. The sites of conflict are usually territorial edges where thieving neighbors prey on resources.

Fights among foragers may be initiated by neighbors attempting to exploit the resources of another local group, and may expand as relatives and friends on both sides become involved. Injuries and fatalities sometimes occur as a result of intergroup altercations. "What is typically manifested as a brawl or melee over contested resources was thus manifested externally by the outright killing of trespassers" (Kelly 2000:137). Bands claim exclusive rights to hunting territories, and hunting without permission by trespassers potentially leads to conflict if resident hunters encounter the intruders or discover recent evidence of their trespass.

Territorial violation is seen as a criminal act of theft, which may precipitate an unanticipated clash between two groups of hunters or gatherers. Spontaneous conflicts over access to resources are usually localized because of seasonal overlaps within ecological niches. In some instances, rival claimants fight for control of contested resources, with the stronger party taking possession and the weaker party withdrawing.

By approximately 8500 BC, some foragers may have created relatively complex societies. The continuing stylistic drift of hafted bifaces, due to increasing territoriality coupled with relatively rapid adaptation to the diverse and changing Early Holocene environments, resulted in the emergence of several distinctive regional styles—such as Dalton, which flourished in the Midsouth and southern Midwest. These regional projectile-point styles would have differentiated one local group from another, serving to restrict access to critical resources among neighboring groups.

The Dalton archaeological record "unequivocally speaks of boundaries and alliances" (Sassaman 2005:83). Some Dalton locales have produced unusually large and exotic, high-quality lanceolate blades that were cached (Walthall and Koldehoff 1998). These symbolic, hypertrophic blades measure up to thirty-eight centimeters in length and exhibit remarkable workmanship in exotic cherts (figure 3.2). The preferred raw material, high-quality Crescent Quarry Burlington chert found just southwest of St. Louis, was chosen for its superior flint-knapping ability. The symbolic blades have been found in more than thirty locations along a seven-hundred-kilometer stretch of the Lower Mississippi Valley, from the American Bottom to northeast Arkansas, and along the Illinois, Mississippi, and Missouri rivers (Morse 1997).

The Dalton exchange network, marked by the distribution of Dalton hypertrophic, chipped-stone blades, was geographically extensive along the Lower Mississippi Valley. It is not surprising that this exchange network was established along the braided-stream portion of the Lower Mississippi Valley. The braided-stream regime of eastern Arkansas was one of the richest resource zones for Paleoindians in eastern North America, and the Mississippi River would have offered excellent opportunities for interaction and exchange throughout the region (Anderson 2002; Morse 1997).

The Dalton people created formal cemeteries, burying their dead with unusually large and elaborate bifaces (Morse 1997). The manufacture and exchange of symbolic weaponry helped to create and maintain alliances and to reinforce status differentiation among individual families. Oversized Dalton bifaces have been referred to as "primitive valuables" (Walthall and Koldehoff 1998:266), and their production and exchange among hunter-gatherers is often viewed as integrating groups into regional alliance networks that facilitated information exchange, marriage arrangements, peace maintenance, and resource management. Manipulation of valuables may structure social interactions through ritual acts in the context of group aggregations. The power of such valuables resides in their ability to reproduce social alliances among neighboring forager groups (Johnson and Brookes 1989). Possession and use of any such item amounts to a statement that asserts identity (Sassaman 2005:85).

The transition from the Late Paleoindian period to the Early Archaic period is characterized by the use of new hafted-biface styles. The Early Archaic period is an arbitrary juncture in the history of forgers in eastern

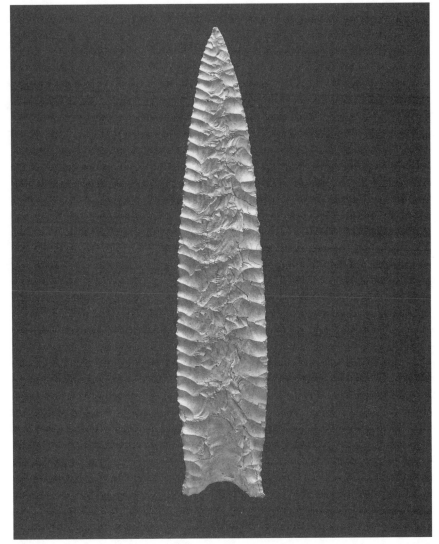

Figure 3.2.   Dalton symbolic weaponry, Pettis County, Missouri (courtesy of John Pafford).

North America, marked primarily by changes in hafted bifaces (Smith 1986). Otherwise, the Late Paleoindian period changes almost imperceptibly into the Eastern Archaic stage (Adovasio and Pedler 2005:51). The transition is set at around 8000 BC, with the return to a general warming and drying trend in the years following the cold episode of the post–Younger

Dryas climate interval (Ellis et al. 2004). These climate changes would have had a major impact on local cultures, as Eastern Woodland hunters and gatherers gradually adjusted to changing environmental regimes. Modern floras began to appear, including plants that would be domesticated in later times, and they were intensively collected. The warming climate resulted in replacement of Terminal Pleistocene conifer-hardwood communities in eastern North America by the resource-rich, mixed-hardwood forests of oak and hickory that moved northward from their refuge in the lower Southeast (Delcourt and Delcourt 1987).

In the Early Holocene, during a warming trend between the Younger Dryas and post–Younger Dryas climate intervals, the Laurentide ice sheet continued to melt and retreat northward into central Canada, creating large glacial lakes that formed in depressions carved by the retreating ice lobes. The treeless tundra extended south of the receding edge of the glacial margin and north of the band of open boreal forests, which were bounded by glacial lakes to the northwest, glacial ice to the north, and tundra to the northeast.

To the south of the boreal forests, the complex mosaic of mixed conifer–northern hardwoods forest, temperate deciduous forest, and prairie developed in synchrony with glacial melting. The narrow band of mixed conifer–northern hardwoods forest broadened and shifted northward. The deciduous forest developed as a coherent forest type at the southern limit of the mixed conifer–northern hardwoods forest region, occupying a large area of the Midwest and Midsouth from the Atlantic Coast to western Arkansas, and from central Alabama to central Indiana. It expanded northward in reaction to both warmer climates and rapidly retreating glaciers, replacing the northeastern boreal pine forests and creating a rich forest habitat for deer, turkey, and small mammals. The southeastern evergreen forest spread northward from central South Carolina to southern Arkansas, while extending south to the Gulf Coast and into Florida, replacing the sand-dune scrub. To the west, the southeastern evergreen forest was replaced by prairie in eastern Texas and Oklahoma and northeastern Kansas (Delcourt and Delcourt 1987:97–98). Much of eastern North America now consisted of resource-rich deciduous forest and mixed conifer–northern hardwoods forest.

As a result of the increase in forest biomass, people were present in relatively large numbers across eastern North America, having become fully adapted to the Holocene environment. Increased population densities are evidenced by large numbers of Early Archaic sites and numerous artifacts widely distributed over eastern North America (Anderson 1996b:160–63). As human populations continued to increase, group ranges became progressively smaller due to demographic packing. For example, a Clovis territory that was originally located along one or more river systems might have been reduced to a single drainage by Late Paleoindian times. Finally, such a territory might have shrunk to a portion of that drainage during the Early Archaic period. Early Archaic foragers continued the Paleoindian pattern of seasonal movements of local groups composed of some twenty-five to fifty people related by kinship or marriage ties. Annual fall aggregation events would have been held to enable alliance formation and maintenance, information and resource exchange, marriage opportunities, and social visits, (Daniel 1998).

Gradual abandonment of the Paleoindian tool kit may have been directly related to the emergence and increasing importance of a more general foraging strategy over eastern North America, in response to postglacial warming and the rapid expansion of deciduous forests. A shift to residential mobility and expedient tool production, from the earlier Paleoindian technology with its emphasis on curation, seems to have taken place. Technological organization, diet, and mobility strategies among modern foragers are linked closely with local effective temperature (Binford 1980:13–16).

With changes in forest and faunal composition, a gradual shift took place toward a more generalized Early Archaic hunter-gatherer economy characterized by relatively large territories and mobile foraging. While overall lifestyle apparently changed little from the earlier Paleoindian culture, there was a major difference in the settlement-subsistence system. Seasonal population movements, incorporating base camps in fertile river valleys with upland camps nearby, began during Early Archaic times. Late summer/fall/early winter base camps were now inhabited regularly. Located within major river drainages, early, cool-season base camps were chosen to take advantage of the availability of local food resources and materials for tool manufacture, with special attention to local chert quarries. In early spring, hunters and gatherers moved from floodplain base camps into small, regularly spaced foraging camps. During the summer months, they hunted and gathered in the adjacent uplands. The adaptation and the lifestyle they forged characterized and shaped much of the ensuing Archaic period (Anderson et al. 1996:8; Caldwell 1958).

Changes from side-notched to corner-notched projectile points between 7500 and 6900 BC may have reflected a shift in weapon use, from thrusting spears to atlatls or spear-throwers that propelled lighter spears (Chapman 1995:38). Bannerstones, a uniquely Eastern Archaic trait, emerged around 6500 BC in the Lower Midwest, Midsouth, and lower Atlantic Slope (Sassaman and Randall 2007). Their use as burial accompaniments in mortuary ceremonialism signals a continuation of the early emphasis on symbolic weaponry as marking individuals with some degree of importance or elevated status.

Early Archaic egalitarian hunting-and-gathering bands were loosely tied together, periodically coalescing into macrobands. Interaction networks are demonstrated by the wide distribution of exotic lithic resources and the exchange of symbolic weapons, used for alliance formation. The key to successful exploitation of river valleys may have lain in the practice of alliance formation and aggressive territorial defense. Reciprocal obligations based on broad exchange networks were vital for establishing and maintaining stable and long-term security. Alliances made life more secure in environments characterized by patchy food resources and overcrowding. Strong border maintenance would serve as a deterrent to resource theft. Conflict among foraging bands would have increased as a result of stress over unpredictable resources (Sassaman 1996).

As populations increased over the centuries due to foraging bands fissioning into new constituent groups, annual hunting-and-gathering ranges decreased. Over time, the net effects would have been increased tensions and strained social relations among neighboring bands over access to resources (Anderson 1996a, 1996b). These tensions may have erupted locally into intergroup attacks, although alliances may have helped dampen or ameliorate hostilities.

The hypothesized transition from capital punishment (self-redress homicides) to spontaneous conflicts over access to resources may represent the early phases of a feuding style of conflict. The majority of armed conflicts among unsegmented hunters and gatherers are spontaneous. Anticipation of conflicts over resources often leads to a policy of surprise attacks on unsuspecting hunting parties who trespass on adjoining territories. When conditions for an immediate attack of trespassers are unfavorable, offended hunters may follow the trespassers to their encampment, waiting for an ambush opportunity. The central motif is the punishment of thieving trespassers, with attacks directly consequent upon such theft. Violence here differs from earlier times in that the locale shifts from the scene of the crime to the perpetrator's encampment, and any member of the enemy community may be attacked.

In the case of the killing of an individual from an enemy group, responsibility for vengeance generally devolves upon the close relations of the slain person. There is subsequently a coordinated and preplanned effort to fulfill vengeance obligations, the target of which may be the malefactor. However, if the trespasser cannot be killed, then someone else, often a relative, will be substituted, leading to pitched battles between families. Social substitution is conditional and may or may not be applied. Thus, kin-group responsibility for revenge is recognized, while full kin-group liability is not, as the malefactor is the preferred target rather than a member of that individual's kin group. Responsibility of the kin group for a death, and their pursuit of justice, are the last steps prior to the emergence of classic blood feud (Kelly 2000).

A shoot-on-sight policy whenever the avengers of a killing have the advantage of surprise may preclude any other type of interactions, such as exchange, intermarriage, and visiting. Kelly (2000) considers the shoot-on-sight policy a comprehensive "state of war" punctuated by episodic hostile encounters. In such engagements, casualties are inflicted, and when a party of trespassing hunters is surprised, the wounds are usually fatal. As men hunt, they also engage in patrolling their resource territory.

One of the few sets of human remains dating to the time period between 8000 and 4000 BC is the Windover site (ca. 6000 to 5000 BC) in east-central Florida, where 168 individuals were recovered from a peat matrix (Dickel et al. 1988; Doran 2002). While self-redress may have been commonplace during the seventh to fourth millennia, the Windover evidence suggests that feuding was beginning to emerge in eastern North America. Skeletal trauma at Windover includes healed ulnar fractures, cranial depression fractures, and trauma resulting from spear points.

One burial (number 154), an adult male in his late forties interred with abundant grave goods, had two well-healed fractures, a right-orbital-floor blowout fracture and a shaft fracture of the left ulna, perhaps a parry fracture. The blowout fracture resulted from traumatic impact to the eye orbit, perhaps by a bone or deer antler point, causing a compression fracture. "Bluntly pointed, hollowed base antler and bone points are one of the most abundant artifacts found at Windover, and we know they were used for interpersonal violence because one was found deeply embedded in the auricular rim of a male pelvis" (Dickel et al. 1988:169). Cranial depression fractures were recorded for three adults and two subadults. Ulnar fractures were noted for over ten percent of all adults, but were not associated with subadults. Two individuals, a male and a female, exhibited bilateral midshaft "parry" fractures (Dickel et al. 1988). The assemblage of skeletal trauma at Windover suggests that many individuals were victims of a series of raids stemming from feuds with neighbors, rather than of self-redress revenge homicides over murders or sexual jealously.

In summary, violent conflict among Paleoindian and Early Archaic populations may have been limited to the pursuit of capital punishment resulting from adjudicating murders and trespass. Foragers, who inhabit environments characterized by low resource density, diversity, and predictability, typically have low levels of conflict over resources. Capital punishment of killers or trespassers demonstrates several principles. First, armed conflict is collective and has specific objectives. Second, sanctioned by the group through moral justification, participation is esteemed in such violent acts. In these societies, spontaneous conflicts over access to resources; feuding; and warfare would be insignificant or absent, with lethal violence being restricted to isolated incidents widely spaced in time. Generally, when the family and kin of a homicide victim seek revenge, they attack the perpetrator, resulting in the murder of the murderer. In this way, individuals prone to lethal violence are removed from the local group (Whallon 1989), and violence is contained by preventing continuing retaliatory acts as in feuding.

An ethos of cooperation for foragers in resource-poor environments serves to limit conflicts among unsegmented societies. Emphasis is placed on the reestablishment of sharing and goodwill after violence occurs (Knauft 1994). The near absence of violent conflict among local groups of unsegmented foragers is primarily the result of cooperation among family-level groups who inhabit resource-scarce environments. In areas of abundant resources, raiding is often more frequent or prevalent. Typically, households in such environments avoid competition by scattering. As population increased in eastern North America, territorial range and mobility decreased, resulting in elevated levels of conflict. During the Middle Archaic period, the nature of conflict and of attempts to resolve violence would undergo a major transformation. While feuding may have been rare in the past, it would now move to center stage.

CHAPTER FOUR

❧

Complex Hunter-Gatherers and the Origin of Feuding

Peace is as demanding a state as war, requiring for its maintenance effort, eco-nomic sacrifice, and even occasional violence.

(Keeley 1996:156)

The period from about 5000 to 1000 BC witnessed the transition from non-segmental foragers to segmental societies and the transformation of patterns of cooperation and conflict. These tribal-like local groups initially arose in the resource-rich river valleys of the Southeast and lower Midwest. Although segmental local groups are difficult to recognize archaeologically (Braun and Plog 1982), key characteristics of such groups in the Eastern Woodland ar-chaeological record include communal rituals, complex monumental earthen construction, symbolic weaponry crafted from exotic materials, long-distance exchange, and the beginning of a feuding style of conflict (Anderson 2002; Sassaman 2005).

Sea-level stabilization around 5000 BC has been postulated as contributing a significant impetus to the rapid rise of cultural complexity. Hunter-gatherers in eastern North America turned to higher-quality and more pre-dictable foods, such as fish, in lower-river floodplains. In alluvial valleys, the relative abundance of organisms available to humans increased significantly. For example, in the Lower Mississippi alluvial valley, 5,000-year-old faunal assemblages are 50–90 percent fish (Day et al. 2007:170).

A common fishing, gathering, and hunting economic pattern character-ized most eastern North American local groups, although there was a great deal of diversity in scale, complexity, and elaboration. In general, small groups of foragers were dispersed over the landscape (figure 4.1). What differentiated these populations from earlier hunters and gatherers was their increased seasonal occupation of base camps, the elaboration of communal activities, and "heightened differences in wealth or surplus" (Caldwell 1958:21). The authority of tribal leaders was impermanent, being centralized and pronounced only during communal events, such as monumental construction projects and feuding. Public offices and organizational structures may have been virtually nonexistent except at communal gatherings (Anderson 2002). During times of raiding, the structural pose of peacetime, with its egalitarian decision-making bodies, may have changed to a different po-

Figure 4.1. Archaic hunters and gatherers, Tennessee, ca. 5000 BC (courtesy of Frank H. McClung Museum, University of Tennessee, Knoxville; painting by Greg Harlin).

litical stance or organization after the conclusion of the precipitating event or activity. A "war" leader, for example, could head a hierarchically ranked "war" organization; but after the conclusion of the raid, the organizational structure would be dismantled, as warriors and "war" leaders returned to their nonraiding "civilian" functions (Gearing 1958).

The emergence of segmental social groups is thought to be a key characteristic of tribal or local-group feuding sparked by diplomatic and alliance potential, resource availability, population density, conflict intensity, and possibilities for interaction. There appears to be a greater chance for conflict among local groups when resources are extensive but finite and, to some extent, unpredictable (Anderson 2004). The transition from spontaneous conflicts over access to resources to retaliatory, revenge-based violence lies in "restricted resource availability relative to population in environments rich in subsistence resources" (Kelly 2000:143).

Physiographic structure—coastlines, rivers, and mountain ranges and passes—shapes the potential for social interaction and affects the likelihood for the emergence of complex societies (Clark and Blake 1994). Not surprisingly, evidence for the first complex societies in eastern North America appears in especially productive, resource-rich areas: the Lower Mississippi Valley, the Atlantic and Gulf coasts, and the major river systems of the midcontinent. These factors, coupled with regional population growth, contributed to the emergence of cultural complexity, as seen in the growth and elaboration of monumental construction, intercommunity raiding, and long-distance exchange networks.

Conflict prior to 5000 BC among eastern North American foragers may have been characterized by spontaneous fighting for access to resources, the continuation of an earlier Archaic mobile-forager pattern. However, by 5000 BC conflicts may have intensified, with the development of revenge-based blood feuding in resource rich areas. Feuding is one outgrowth of increasingly intensified bouts of spontaneous lethal conflict over resources among segmental groups.

The distinction between unsegmented and segmental organizational types differentiates mobile forgers with low levels of conflict from increasingly sedentary hunter-gatherers with intermediate to high levels of raiding. Revenge is the most prevalent cause of intersocietal conflict, including feuding among segmental societies (Kelly 2000:76). Vengeance leads to a cycle of reciprocating attacks employing social substitutability in retaliation for past homicides, which, in turn, have generally stemmed from conflicts over resources. An atmosphere of raiding, based on unending quests for revenge, develops in rich environments in which comparatively high population densities are sustained over extended periods, and local groups are unable or unwilling to move away from each other when conflicts over resources arise. Thus, feuding has its origins in segmental hunting-and-gathering societies that begin to emphasize social substitutability and increased group cohesion and integration based on defending claims to fixed territories in resource-rich environments (Kelly 2000).

The elaboration of peacemaking practices and alliance formation is critical for dampening conflicts. The establishment of peace often entails rituals and compensatory gift giving between previously feuding local groups on the verge of hostilities. Peacemaking practices often include compensation for past homicides. The concept of death compensation may arise in lieu of retaliatory vengeance if peacemaking and alliance institutions are in place. The exchange of goods, as part of the compensation package, may include both staple and wealth items. The concept of "covering the dead," widespread throughout the early historic Midwest, was an institution of compensation involving goods exchanged in place of retaliatory vengeance (White 1991). The circulation of Middle Archaic tokens of exchange, such as bannerstones; hypertrophic biface blades; large, grooved stone axes; engraved bone pins; marine shells; and pieces of copper, almost certainly includes items used for death compensation resulting from revenge killings (figure 4.2).

Once the transition is effected from capital punishment and spontaneous conflict over access to resources to vengeance-based raiding, resource availability is further reduced by restriction and tightening of fixed territorial boundaries and the development of buffer zones. Foragers avoid border areas when such zones become too dangerous to exploit, which serves to establish a no-man's-land between local foraging groups. The unutilized zone may confine communities to relatively sharply defined territorial areas centered on highly desirable and localized resources.

Revenge-based raiding by segmental social groups is often motivated by collective kin-group responsibility, payback vengeance, social-group liability, and territorial defense. Raiding behavior results in a distinctive patterning of violence, which provides an archaeological signature for the emergence of classic blood feuding. Territorial defense is evident in ambushes or confrontations that take place away from habitations, perhaps in defense of boundaries or during encroachment into another group's area. Protection and defense of resources results in higher incidences of single-adult-male burials. Payback vengeance is marked in the archaeological record by overkill and raids on encampments. Overkill is seen in pin-cushioning, where extreme or excessive violence is inflicted upon the victim, reflecting deep emotional involvement. Raids upon encampments, habitations, or set-

Figure 4.2.   Middle Archaic symbolic weaponry, Jersey County, Illinois (courtesy of John Pafford).

tlements, evident in the age/sex distribution of multiple burials, generally result in multiple deaths at the same time, necessitating mass graves. In general, more women and children are killed than men. Mass burials of predominantly women and children are considered one form of evidence for segmental-social-group feuding.

Pin-cushioning is an act of collective responsibility for revenge, taking the form of overkill, where numerous spears or arrows are used to reinforce an act of revenge rather than simply to accomplish an act of killing. Spears are often left in place so there will be no question as to the raiders' identity. In accordance with the principle of social substitution, children are killed in acts of revenge because they are members of the social group responsible for past deaths.

In the evolution of collective violence, social substitution is a key criterion for the origin of feuding. Social violence evolves from a state of conflict lacking social substitution, characteristic of nonsegmented foragers such as Clovis groups, to an intermediate form where a "malefactor if possible" form of retaliation is evident (represented by Late Paleoindian/Early to Middle Archaic populations). Finally, social substitution results in widespread vengeance-based blood feuding that encompasses territorial defense, collective responsibility, payback vengeance, and group liability, a syndrome perhaps characterizing late Middle Archaic groups.

Kelly (2000:60) proposes six incremental stages in the progressive transformation of conflict, beginning with homicide and spontaneous conflicts over access to resources of nonsegmented social groups and ending in the classic blood feuds of segmental social groups. The six stages are:

> (1) no counteraction, (2) the legitimation of capital punishment through public opinion in the absence of specification of a party or entity responsible for its achievement, (3) the stipulation of relational, kin-based vengeance obligations that generate a de facto vengeance group, and (4) kin group responsibility for carrying out vengeance against the malefactor (alone) vested in the extended family and/or kindred of the homicide victim. The transition to kin group member liability—in which the malefactor is the preferential but not the only recognized target of vengeance (stage 5), or in which any member of the killer's group is susceptible to vengeance (stage 6)—constitutes a watershed in that these stages are restricted to societies with segmental forms of organization.

With the evolution of segmental social organization, we see the development of descent groups, food storage, increased population density, and feuding. Lineages, clans, or sodalities develop from descent groups. Social segments allow integrated forms of social organization for feuding and alliances, and for the stockpiling of food. When food is stored, it inevitably becomes a key military objective for raiding parties (Kelly 2000:68–71). Food storage and segmental social organization go hand in hand. Institutionalization of large-scale or "communal" food storage, then, is an initial trigger in the coevolution of intersocietal violence and society.

In segmental foraging societies, marriage, a transaction between social groups, creates group-to-group relations. Linkages produced by exogamous unions may be vehicles for military and peace alliances in which local groups band together to raid neighboring groups, or join forces to defend themselves against attacks from their neighbors (Kelly 2000:64). Marriage as a transaction between social groups, and/or the presence of descent groups, go hand in hand with the development of kin-group liability for vengeance.

By about 7000 BC, scattered foraging populations in eastern North America were responding to continued changing environmental regimes. With the general warming and drying trend of the Hypsithermal (Ellis et al. 2004:359), foraging populations became increasingly reliant on hunting deer, turkey, and small mammals; fishing in local lakes and rivers; and gathering seasonal plant foods, especially acorns and hickory nuts (Smith 1986). Smaller-sized territories may have resulted as population increased in resource-rich river valleys where animal and plant foods were concentrated. At the same time, carrying capacities declined in less favored areas, resulting in increased alliance formation and escalated conflicts over resources.

A slight increase in the mean annual temperature and a decrease in rainfall may have reduced the overall carrying capacity of the land, as the Hypsithermal climatic episode brought about drier conditions with warmer summers and colder winters. Throughout much of the Northern Hemisphere, seasonal extremes may have stressed local foraging populations (Anderson 2001:158). The generalized hunter-gatherer economy began to shift toward increasingly restricted mobility and a narrower range of foods.

In response to the climatic warming episode and resulting changes in the availability of local resources, the Middle Archaic period witnessed a host of cultural adjustments. For example, a dramatic increase in the use of abundant riverine aquatic species such as shoal-adapted mollusks and shallow-water fish may have brought about the gradual adoption of sedentary lifeways in many parts of eastern North America after 7000 BC.

Climate during the Middle Archaic was characterized by alternating periods of warm and cool conditions. An abrupt cooling trend known as the "8,200-Year-Old Cold Event," which occurred between 6400 and 6000 BC, was the most widespread and strongest Holocene cooling episode (Alley et al. 1997). Cool conditions prevailed again at 5800, 5100, 4600, and 3500 BC, with intervening warm periods. The last cooling trend is known as the Holocene Neoglacial (Ellis et al. 2004). These and other climatic events had variable effects throughout eastern North America, but almost certainly brought about some degree of stress and adjustment among foraging populations. As early as 5800 BC, incipient horticulture or gardening was taking place on a local scale by foragers, who first cultivated squash and gourd (Fritz 1990).

Around 2,800 years ago, the last fragments of the Laurentide ice sheet melted in northern Canada. The boreal forest moved northward into the rapidly retreating tundra whose southern boundary was in central Canada. The mixed conifer–northern hardwoods forests occupied the Great Lakes region and expanded in width. The deciduous forest region likewise moved north-ward to southern Minnesota, central Wisconsin, Michigan, and southern New England; but retreated on the east, south, and west in response to changes in the distribution of prairies and the southeastern evergreen forest. To the west, the closed deciduous forest became a more open savanna near the prairie-forest border.

Prairies extended from Houston to Winnipeg across the continental inte-rior, and eastward as a prairie peninsula to central Illinois (King 1981). The southeastern evergreen forest expanded northward into the Ozarks of Mis-souri and northeastward on the Atlantic Coastal Plain as far north as New Jersey. A rise in sea level resulted in the development of extensive coastal swamps and marshes along the Atlantic and Gulf Coastal Plains (Delcourt and Delcourt 1987:98).

Across the Lower Southeast, pine forests began to expand again, replacing extensive upland and river-valley oak forests. Cypress stands developed in backswamps and along oxbow lakes (Watts et al. 1996). In the Lower Mid-west and the Midsouth, the Middle Archaic climate appears to have been hotter and drier than at present, leading to a reduction in upland vegetation, increased surface erosion, and aggrading river floodplains (Schuldenrein 1996). The warming and drying trends may have rendered riverine areas more favorable and upland areas less desirable to foraging populations. For groups restricted to upland environments, the decline in resource structure may have generated conflicts over subsistence resources.

Increasing population levels may have further restricted group mobility in many parts of eastern North America. Some areas, including large portions of the Atlantic and Gulf Coastal Plains, appear to have been lightly popu-lated because of the expansion of pine forests and the corresponding decrease in the incidence of the more productive oak forests (Sassaman 1995). Ex-pansion of pine forests at the expense of oaks, increased seasonal temperature extremes, and evidence of widespread aridity may have led to a consolidation of people in areas where hardwood forests continued to thrive, such as the river valleys of the Midsouth and Lower Midwest and resource-rich areas along the coastal margins (Smith 1986).

Why did complex societies first emerge in eastern North America around 5000 BC, and not before? The answer to this intriguing question may lie in widespread aridity and the resulting expansion of pine forests. Population pressure may have been a significant variable of cultural elaboration as group circumscription in comparatively resource-rich zones placed pressure on, and generated competition for, resources. As populations grew and mobility de-creased, competition and interaction among foragers appears to have increased, forcing people into increasingly restricted territorial ranges. Critical population-density and spacing thresholds were thus reached at a time when climatic uncertainty was increased (Anderson 2001).

A greater frequency of El Niño events, and an increased intensity to these events, appears to have coincided with the end of the Middle Archaic (Robdell et al. 1999), producing highly variable climatic conditions in eastern North America, which resulted in unpredictable and patchy resource distribution. These changes may have prompted greater cooperative efforts, such as elaborate mound building, long-distance exchange networks, complex ritual behavior, formal alliances, and extensive raiding among the region's populations.

Regional political conditions, as well as increasing population levels, played a major role in shaping the exploitation of aquatic resources. The variety, range, and dietary significance of targeted plants and animals did not change substantially from the Early Archaic, with two exceptions. As early as 5800 BC, riverine resources, especially mollusks and fish, began to be collected in significant numbers. Second, some native plants began to be cultivated. Emergence of cultural complexity and increasing sedentism has been linked to an elevation in the aquatic resource base, which in turn resulted in sharp escalation in the kinds and amounts of riverine aquatic species available to Middle Archaic hunters and gatherers (Smith 1986:22). Well-documented key features of the Middle Archaic foraging adaptation include multiseasonal base camps, semipermanent habitations, multiregional exchange networks, monumental construction of earthen mounds, increases in sedentism, specialized plant gathering, territorial boundary marking, and alliances. There is also increased evidence for feuding (Anderson 2002).

Tribal organization clearly emerged in the latter part of the Middle Archaic period, although it is possible that tribal societies were present at earlier times (Anderson 2004). The emergence of local groups may have been ephemeral, without a great deal of stability, longevity, or complexity; but during the Middle Archaic, local groups began to develop lineages, clans, or sodalities. Evidence for long-distance prestige-goods exchange, feuding, and monumental construction indicates that family-level society had been transcended. Mound centers in eastern Louisiana and southern Florida are examples, although given the labor represented in their construction; these societies appear to be culminations, rather than beginnings, of tribal organization. The first clear evidence for widespread tribal social organization includes long-distance exchange networks, increased social interaction, subsistence intensification, monumental construction, ceremonial behavior, a new emphasis on individual status, lapidary crafting, territorial marking by cemeteries, buffer zones, alliances, and intergroup conflict.

The Poverty Point Site and Complex Hunter-Gatherers

Between approximately 1650 and 700 BC, Lower Mississippi Valley hunter-gatherers constructed an impressive monument of earth in northeastern Louisiana. The Poverty Point site inhabitants built a complex array of mounds and ridges overlooking the Mississippi River floodplain. The central site area consists of six rows of concentric ridges, which form five aisles. The ridges, at one time standing 4 to 6 feet high and 140 to 200 feet apart, form a partial octagon measuring three-quarters of a mile at the outermost margin and enclosing a 37-acre plaza. A 70-foot-tall bird-shaped mound dominates the 400-acre site. Archaeologists believe the ridges served as building foundations, while the plaza functioned as the site of dances, games, rituals, and other public activities.

High-quality chert and other stones, crafted into projectile points and other tools, have been found at Poverty Point. The raw materials were exchanged by hunting-and-gathering groups from as far away as the Ouachita and Ozark mountains and the Ohio and Tennessee river valleys. The extensive exchange network attests to the complex hunting-and-gathering society that built the Poverty Point earthworks.

Poverty Point remains a mystery, but certainly one of the major purposes of the massive and widespread exchange system and the central gathering place was the amelioration of conflict and maintenance of cooperation among loosely affiliated hunter-gatherers. Poverty Point may be a temporal flowering of an adjustment to hunting-and-gathering conflict reduction. With the rise of tribal groups throughout eastern North America, exchange systems flourished; and one component of the exchange of exotic materials is the crafting of alliances and death compensation.

Rising population densities reached the upper limits of the carrying capacity of annual foraging ranges, as indicated by the almost exclusive use of local raw materials (Blanton and Sassaman 1989). Middle Archaic populations in the rich-resource zones of the Midsouth and Midwest were clearly engaged in long-distance exchange, intercommunity conflict, alliance formation, mound construction, and formal-cemetery creation.

Sedentism and Middle Archaic cemeteries appeared as early as 4000 BC in some resource-rich areas. With the emergence of fixed territories, perhaps during a warmer and drier period that tended to restrict denser human populations to river valleys, there may have been competition for resources, resulting in sporadic tribal feuding and territorial marking by mounds and cemeteries. The relatively sudden establishment of cemeteries and burial mounds near resource-rich river valleys may mark a dramatic change in Archaic lifestyle (Charles and Buikstra 1983). Middle Archaic folk lived in base camps and even year-round settlements that flourished because of the diverse and relatively abundant nearby food resources. The prominent Middle Archaic bluff-top cemeteries were monumental structures that served as indicators of hereditary rights to important local resources and were energetically defended. If a group wished to claim rights of ownership and inheritance to resources, one logical way to do so would be through maintenance of corporate cemeteries.

With the emergence of tribal organization in eastern North America, violent conflict among hunter-gatherer groups is manifest (Bridges et al. 2000; Smith 1997). Increased exploitation of riverine resources, especially shoal environments, brought about population growth in resource-rich zones. Economies specializing in intensive harvesting of narrow-spectrum subsistence items often exhibit increased conflict resulting from efforts to restrict access to critical resources in favored localities through territorial control. Intergroup conflict may have emerged because of increased territorial boundary marking and enforcement (Price and Brown 1985:12), as well as population growth brought about by innovations in subsistence technology, such as storage. The combination of environment and demography may have set the stage for the early appearance of preagricultural, hunter-gatherer conflict (Haas 1999:22–23).

Milner (2004:47) notes:

> Tensions would have been likely to erupt into outright violence when people were unwilling or unable to relinquish claims to favorable places; that is, when they could not easily resolve their differences by simply walking away. Conflicts probably broadened and intensified when neighboring groups fell on hard times, making it more difficult for people to move or expand their territories in search of desperately needed food.

Initial evidence of feuding in eastern North America appears in approximately 5000 BC in the Midsouth and Midwest (Bridges et al. 2000:36; Mensforth 2007; Smith 1997; Walthall 1980:64). One of the clearest examples of intersocietal conflict is the Mulberry Creek site (Shields 2003), a large shell midden located at the confluence of Mulberry Creek and the Tennessee River in northwest Alabama (Webb and DeJarnette 1942). Well-preserved human remains that were revealed here provide unmistakable evidence of feuding (Jacobi 2007).

A mass burial of three males was discovered by Work Progress Administration excavators in a large circular grave. Each male had met a violent death, and they were all buried, unceremoniously and one on top of the other, in a semiflexed posture, which was unusual for the site. The rib cage of the upper-most individual, a twenty-five- to thirty-year-old male (Burial 83), had been penetrated by three dart points. Another adult male, twenty-two to twenty-six years old (Burial 84), exhibited seven dart points: four in the thoracic cavity, one in the mouth cavity, one that had come from behind and had lodged in a vertebral centrum, and another that had struck frontally and was embedded between two neural processes. The hands and forearms of this burial were miss-ing, indicating perimortem dismemberment, a practice associated with trophy taking and feuding. The third individual, Burial 85, was an eighteen- to twenty-year-old male with a dart point embedded in his spinal column.

The Mulberry Creek mass grave represents early and clear evidence of vi-olent death, perimortem mutilation, and feuding in the Eastern Woodlands. The victims conform closely to archaeological expectations of social substi-tution and a raiding type of conflict which is expressed as pin-cushioning, trophy taking, and mass graves. The Mulberry Creek site victims foreshadow a pattern of mortality and trophy taking that increasingly incorporated dis-memberment as an important component of intergroup conflict. Trophy tak-ing is such a significant element in the development of social complexity that Anderson (2002) considers it a signature characteristic for the emer-gence of tribal organization.

According to Shields (2003:175),

> archaeological and osteological data indicate that the Mulberry Creek site was first used for shellfishing, tool manufacture, and as a spot to bury the dead dur-ing the latter portion of the Middle Archaic Period (ca. 7,000–5,000 B.P.). It is during this segment of the site's occupation that the rights to engage in these activities were most fiercely contested between small groups of mobile hunter-gatherers.

Worsening intergroup relations coincided with greater exchange in exotic items, suggesting that diplomatic efforts, alliance formation, and perhaps compensation payments (incorporating gift giving) were becoming necessary and widespread. Mutually understood, shared symbols are found on carved bone pins (Jeffries 1996). Distinctive symbolic weaponry, although appearing as early as 6500 BC, continued in importance in the form of hypertrophic or exaggerated biface blades and atlatl weights in the form of bannerstones (fig-ure 4.3). The large sizes; elaborate shapes; high degrees of polish; and espe-cially good craftsmanship, from exotic materials, of the bifaces and atlatl weights transcended the technical requirements or tolerances of ordinary hunting, perhaps signaling encoded cultural information (Sassaman

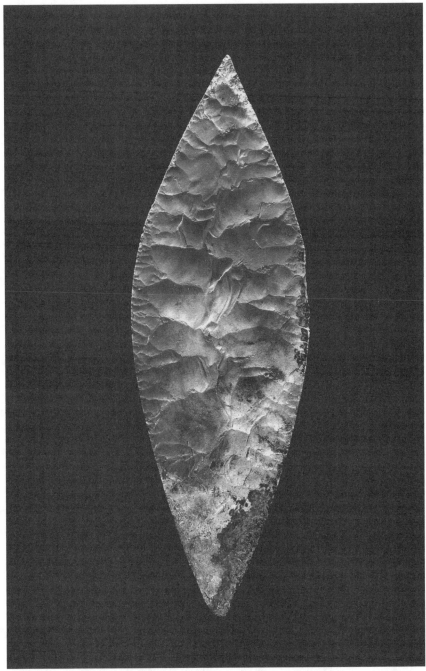

Figure 4.3.   Late Archaic symbolic weaponry, Stewart County, Tennessee (courtesy of John Pafford).

2005:85). Elaborate, hypertrophic forms of bannerstones were designed to make emphatic statements about cultural identity, especially in the context of interprovincial alliances. Unlike Middle Archaic populations, who routinely interred bannerstones with the dead—giving them a specialized role in mortuary ceremonialism—Late Archaic groups used bannerstones as an active medium of social interaction among the living, in the social arena of contested landscapes, ethnic diversity, and shifting alliances. Sassaman and Randall (2007:208) note that "the sense of alterity embodied in bannerstones at this point was likely contested and perhaps polysemic, but nonetheless emphatic."

Feuding at this time is reflected in buffer zones, violent deaths (broken bones, embedded projectile points, and scalping marks), mass burials, and trophy-taking behavior. The increase in archaeological evidence for feuding suggests that food or other resources may have been contested by local groups, resulting in retaliation for trespass and theft. Success in feuding was a means of acquiring status; but the tokens of exchange, often associated with females and children in addition to males, suggest that alliances were based on kin connections and that death compensation was assigned to immediate kin.

Trends initiated in the Middle Archaic period continued to grow in scale and complexity over the course of the Late Archaic period. A variety of well-documented regional cultures is evident: Shell Mound Archaic cultures of the Midsouth and Lower Midwest (Lewis and Kneberg 1959; Webb and De-Jarnette 1942), Benton culture of the Midsouth (Johnson and Brookes 1989), Stallings Island culture of Georgia and South Carolina (Sassaman 1993), Helton and Titterington cultures of Illinois and Missouri (Fortier and Emerson 1984), Nebo Hill culture of the Lower Missouri River valley (Reid 1983), Mount Taylor culture of Florida (Piatek 1994), Old Copper culture of the Great Lakes Region (Stoltman 1986), Poverty Point culture of Louisiana (Gibson and Carr 2004), and Green River Shell Mound Archaic of Kentucky (Marquardt and Watson 2005), to name a few. These societies participated to varying degrees in long-distance exchange networks. Some individuals had higher status than others, as is reflected in relatively elaborate assemblages of grave goods.

By the Late Archaic period, essentially modern climates, sea levels, and vegetation had appeared. Mollusk use in the interior continued, and use of coastal resources became widespread. Increases in regional population levels are evidenced by sites now spread throughout all of eastern North America (Anderson 1996b; Smith 1986). Amelioration in climate appears to have contributed to these developments, with temperature, precipitation, and lake levels reaching conditions similar to those at present (Webb et al. 1993:454–57). Intensive collection of a wide range of wild plants assumed greater importance in the ecologically rich areas of the Midsouth and Lower Midwest.

By 1200 BC, local plants, including goosefoot, knotweed, little barley, sumpweed, sunflower, and local squashes or gourds, were being domesticated by eastern North American populations, who had been collecting them as wild plants for millennia. The nutritional value of such plants is extremely high: some oily seeds, like marshelder and sunflower, proved to be excellent sources of fat, while starchy seeds such as chenopodium (goosefoot), knotweed, and maygrass were used for their carbohydrates. Limited cultivation increased the available food supply and, consequently, human population levels, tying people to specific tracts of land where their gardens were located. Cultivation resulted in a further reduction of group mobility (Gremillion 1996). Harvest yields comparable to those for maize can be obtained from some of these plants (Fritz 1990). Evidence for domestication is rare in areas of low population density such as the Atlantic and Gulf Coastal Plains, Florida, the Lower Mississippi Valley, and the Northeast, suggesting that these populations maintained a generalized foraging pattern. Not surprisingly, evidence for feuding is lacking in these areas.

Late Archaic societies inhabited a biological, climatic, political, and social landscape different from that of their Middle Archaic ancestors. Regional population levels increased markedly, helping drive major changes in sociopolitical organization. Thus, significant fluctuations in alliances, feuding, horticulture, population growth, and subsistence intensification are evident in different parts of the region.

While Late Archaic foragers had a generally egalitarian form of social organization, some individuals had achieved higher status than others, perhaps based on their roles as ad hoc leaders in alliances, construction of public monuments, exchange, mortuary ceremonialism, raids, and ritual. Leaders participated in long-distance exchange networks spanning much of the region. As Middle Holocene and Initial Late Holocene population levels grew, competition and interaction between groups appears to have increased also, as indicated by growth in collective behavior (Anderson 1996a). For example, massive earthen-mound construction at a number of locations in the Lower Mississippi Valley, dating between around 4300 and 3700 BC, required the cooperation of large numbers of people (Saunders et al. 1997).

The Poverty Point site, dating from between 1600 and 1100 BC, and contemporaneous mound centers in the Lower Mississippi Valley comprised an

Figure 4.4.   Poverty Point site, West Carroll Parish, Louisiana (© 2004 S. N. Patricia, RA).

extensive interaction and exchange network that made use of raw and crafted materials from across much of the Lower Southeast and up the Mississippi River into the Midwest (figure 4.4). The Poverty Point tradition was the pinnacle in a lengthy and widespread tradition of mound building in eastern North America (Gibson and Carr 2004). Driven by competition for status between individuals and groups, the need to create ties among large numbers of people may have increased during climatic deterioration or uncertainty, and it may also have increased as a result of the necessity to create allies in the event of increased feuding over trespass and food sources (Hamilton 1999). Mound complexes reflect the cooperative involvement of peoples from across a large area, and mark the emergence of increasingly elaborate forms of tribal organization (Anderson 2002).

Under conditions of increasing population density in the Late Archaic, and in the absence of a dramatic change in subsistence, cultural ecological stability without population reduction may have been possible only where resource procurement zones could be utilized beyond those of the immediate corporate group territory (Brose 1979:7). Exchange would have brought about the circulation of artifacts, raw materials, and food, and the parceling out of hunting and collecting rights.

Food shortages may have stressed Late Archaic hunter-gatherers, as population increased and well-defined, restricted territories became smaller, bringing about foraging for less-preferred food plants and increased energy expenditure in food collecting and processing. As alternative resource areas became inaccessible, raiding one's neighbors, while relying on kin and exchange partnerships for alliances and aid, became a viable option. The demise of bannerstones as an exchange item around 1200 BC signals a change in the components of the interregional alliance protocol, if not the function and nature of the exchange system itself.

Raiding, resulting in violent death and alliance formation, continued in the Midsouth and Midwest during the Late Archaic period. A pattern of feuding characterized by trophy-taking behaviors, human bone modification, mass burials, pin-cushioning, broken and fractured bones, and embedded projectile points was in place by the Late Archaic (Bridges et al. 2000; Jacobi 2007; Mensforth 2007). For example, the Cherry site in the Lower Tennessee valley features a mass grave that may contain the victims of a small massacre. Mortality from violence was about 10 percent at the Cherry site, much higher than at other Archaic communities in the region. Sites located along the main Tennessee River channel exhibit less perimortem violent trauma than do sites such as Cherry that straddle ecological zones, suggesting that intergroup conflict may have erupted, in part, as a result of competition over resource-rich areas (Smith 1997:256–59).

In general, there was a low but sustained level of mortality from violence during the Late Archaic, with some examples probably resulting from interpersonal disagreements and social-group contests. Periods of more organized intergroup raiding by somewhat formal kin groups apparently took place, resulting in the deaths of multiple individuals (Bridges et al. 2000; Mensforth 2007).

The use of modified human bones as grave accompaniments began in the Late Archaic period (Jacobi and Hill 2001), with graves containing modified human remains such as skull cups and gorgets, carved fibulae and radius awls/pins, and modified and cut tibia and femur shafts (Smith 1997:257–58). Trophy-taking behavior at such an early archaeological horizon among intensive hunter-gatherer-gardeners may have been one avenue of prestige enhancement, indicating the "catalytic" role of feuding in the development of incipient social complexity (Smith 1997:257). Success in feuding may have been one means for acquiring status among Late Archaic populations (Anderson 2002).

The Middle and Late Archaic periods provide convincing evidence of the key characteristics of local-group or tribal societies in eastern North

America: a raiding style of feuding based on social substitutability, and an increased emphasis on alliances and on conflict-resolving or conflict-dampening mechanisms. Patterns of long-distance exchange, monumental earth construction, and skilled crafting of exotic symbolic weaponry continued into the next millennium, when cooperation and conflict were transformed into new social and cultural achievements.

CHAPTER FIVE

The Rise of Agriculture and the Elaboration of Feuding

The elaboration of Middle Woodland human bone trophies may . . . reflect a shift to a more complex, competitive, and stratified tribal social system in which interregional trade and warfare alliances played a central role for the first time in American prehistory.

(Nawrocki 1997:24)

Many of the Late Archaic cultural trends, such as widespread exchange and monumental construction, along with increased emphasis on horticulture and a lineage-based political economy, continued in the period from 1000 BC to AD 400. The Late Archaic time span provides important evidence for the interplay of peace maintenance and conflict escalation in eastern North America. While feuding, once entrenched in an area characterized by segmental organization, would have been difficult to minimize, it may have been possible to dampen hostilities through alliances and death compensation based on exchange relationships. The appearance of tribal societies as early as the Middle Archaic (Anderson 2002) suggests that local-group or tribal violence during the Woodland stage had been embedded in Eastern Woodland prehistory for several thousand years. The Early Woodland period is an especially important time in the organization of cooperation and conflict because it may represent a shift in emphasis between a Late Archaic style of feuding or raiding and a much-changed Middle Woodland pattern of conflict.

Intersocietal conflict is not well documented among Early Woodland hunter-gatherer-gardeners. Our understanding of tribal raiding and trophy-taking behavior in the Late Archaic is based on well-documented occurrences of violence, so it is surprising to find such a paucity of archaeological evidence in the succeeding first millennium BC. Feuding almost certainly did not disappear among these foraging and gardening societies. Evidence in the Midwest suggests that intersocietal conflicts and alliances continued, but in altered form.

The lack of evidence for feuding in the archaeological record may result from several factors. One is the relatively short time span between Late Archaic and Middle Woodland. Only eight hundred years or so transpired between the end of the Late Archaic period and the rise of Middle Woodland Hopewellian societies. Second, there is a general lack of Early Woodland burials in comparison to the large numbers of Late Archaic burials. The latter are especially abundant in shell middens along major rivers of the Lower Midwest and Southeast, where evidence of Late Archaic intersocietal conflict is abundantly clear in the well-preserved human skeletal remains. In fact, much of the Late Archaic evidence for raiding comes from shell middens, which provide excellent environments for osteological preservation. By Early Woodland times, changes in settlement patterns included relocation of hunting-and-gathering camps away from shoal areas. Thus, large numbers of well-preserved human remains that might yield evidence of skeletal trauma and trophy-taking behavior are not available. Third, feuding may have been absent or greatly reduced as a result of strong alliances and peacemaking mechanisms based on exchange of gifts and spouses. Formal trading partnerships and creation of real and fictive kin ties through ritual events would have facilitated peaceful social interaction.

In many respects, earlier Archaic trends were intensified during the Early Woodland period; but, overall, there were abrupt societal changes. Early Woodland societies were less complex than those of the preceding Late Archaic populations. Across eastern North America, population densities were lower, the range of settlements and the range of settlement types were more restricted, and long-distance exchange was diminished. Climatic change may have been a catalyst for widespread cultural transformations between 1000 and 400 BC. Kidder (2006:196) implicates climate change as a causal agent for the Late Archaic to Early Woodland transition: "Global climate changes greatly increased flood frequencies and magnitudes in the Mississippi River watershed and were one cause of cultural and behavioral changes that mark the end of the Late Archaic in parts of eastern North America."

Early Woodland people throughout eastern North America continued a hunting-and-gathering lifestyle that had been forged in the Archaic stage but gradually added cultivation of indigenous plants, manufacture and use of pottery, and construction of earthen monuments. Widespread use of Woodland pottery, a key marker for the period, is associated with more efficient processing of cultivated native plants. Strong continuity is also seen in ritual programs between Late Archaic and Early Woodland populations (Clay 1998:15).

The continuation of raiding is assumed to be widespread despite the paucity of confirming data. Perhaps central to Early Woodland adaptations in much of eastern North America was the successful negotiation of alliances among leaders of small, mobile foraging groups. The ability of Early Woodland populations to lessen hostilities and maintain cooperation in the face of potential intergroup conflict may have been critical for survival. Their solution to unpredictable resources, varying climatic and environmental conditions, and potentially aggressive neighbors may have been found in strong alliances, predictable economic patterns, and ritual observances.

Life for the average Early Woodland person was still similar to the earlier Late Archaic lifestyle in many areas of eastern North America. Most populations, in general, still focused on hunting deer and small mammals, fishing in local streams and rivers, gathering wild plants, and supplementing the diet with native cultigens. People appear to have been living in small, more-or-less egalitarian social groups, with a community size of a few dozen people, perhaps represented by several families. In many areas, these hunting-gathering-gardening local groups were still dispersed across the landscape, despite the increasing use of native cultigens (Clay 1998:14). Social links were maintained through exogamy (marrying out). In some areas, minimal investment was placed in camp facilities, with few permanent shelters being constructed; while in other areas, communities were occupied year round, with well-defined structures and dense occupational middens (Anderson and Mainfort 2002).

Many Early Woodland communities were composed of relatively autonomous mobile foraging populations who lived in small, dispersed seasonal camps within geographically and socially circumscribed territories. While a relatively egalitarian form of social organization may have been widespread, some degree of social segmentation—either unranked or minimally ranked lineages, clans, and sodalities—seems to be evident.

Shortly after 1000 BC, Woodland pottery became widely adopted, being used primarily in cooking (Sassaman 1993). The widespread appearance of pottery is associated with an increased exploitation of wild plants and domesticated seed crops. Seeds, along with other plant foods, could be cooked and made palatable through extended simmering or boiling (Fiedel 2001).

The relatively fragile pottery technology may have brought about some degree of decreased group mobility. The ubiquitous grit-tempered, cord-marked Woodland pottery became thinner through time, as a shift took place from heating the pot's contents through stone boiling to a cooking process in which the pot was placed directly over a fire. The widespread adoption of pottery facilitates the recognition by archaeologists of discrete archaeological cultures, perhaps indicating the territorial units of tribal groups (Anderson and Mainfort 2002:5).

Simple horticulture continued to be an element of the overall hunting-and-gathering adaptation. By around 1000 BC, many native and foreign plants were being widely cultivated, including goosefoot, gourds, Jerusalem artichoke, knotweed, little barley, maygrass, squash, sumpweed, and sunflower (Cowan and Watson 1992). These highly productive and nutritious cultigens included both oily and starchy seed complexes. Many of these cultigens were first produced in quantity during the Early Woodland period (Gremillion 2004), although the degree of use varied regionally.

Earthen burial mounds existed in many areas of eastern North America during the Early Woodland period (figure 5.1). Mortuary facilities, including charnel structures and burial mounds, were often located away from domestic settlements, suggesting that mound complexes brought people together from a number of communities, a pattern dating from well back in the Archaic stage

Figure 5.1. Grave Creek Mound, Marshall County, West Virginia (courtesy of Michael Keller).

(Anderson 2002). On the other hand, earthwork construction was abandoned in many areas of the Southeast, and in some cases occupation ceased at formerly dominant centers such as the regionally important Poverty Point site.

Long-distance exchange declined markedly in many areas of eastern North America when compared with the preceding Late Archaic period; but in other areas, such as the Ohio Valley, special locales were involved in Early Woodland interregional exchange (Clay 1998:12). Toward the end of the Early Woodland period, there was a more intensive exchange of scarce and exotic materials. The exchange system and associated rituals helped maintain contacts among far-flung individuals and groups. Competition and conflict among Early Woodland groups is evident, for example, in the Peter enclosure in northwestern Ohio. The enclosure was first stockaded, then provided with a ditch and an interior bank (Clay 1998). Activities at the site revolved around the acquisition and manufacture of exotic artifacts, such as barite and galena.

Near the end of the Archaic, a cold, wet interval associated with a severe global temperature downturn followed the warm/dry Sub-Boreal stadial. This "1159 BC Event" caused social unrest throughout many parts of the world (Kuniholm 1990). Two to three centuries later, another cold event occurred (Van Geel et al. 1999). These episodic periods of climatic change may have been stressful for eastern North American hunter-gatherer-gardeners (Gunn 1997). Anderson (2001) and Kidder (2006) associate these climatic changes with the collapse of Late Archaic exchange networks and the abandonment of earthen construction across much of eastern North America. Two short-term cold events during the first centuries of the Early Woodland period may have made it difficult for many local populations (Fiedel 2001). As a result, feuding may have increased if Early Woodland populations were stressed.

In some areas, local groups appear to have congregated periodically and then dispersed within well-defined territories. Projectile points, bannerstones, and ceramic styles display increasing local variation, suggesting they served as stylistic boundary markers for tribal groups (Brose 1994). Increased population growth in the northern parts of eastern North America may have led to greater definition and circumscription of local territories. A web of reciprocal obligations and gift giving would have served to move a variety of exotic goods from one area to another as part of formal exchange networks that underwrote alliances, which were critical for intergroup cooperative relations and conflict settlement.

One prominent element in the Early Woodland period was widely shared materialized ideology in the form of atlatl grips or handles crafted as "birdstones," which were widely exchanged throughout the Midwest (figure 5.2).

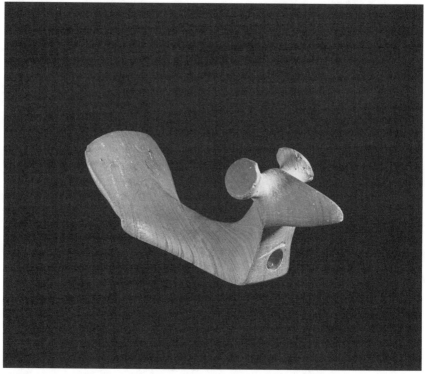

Figure 5.2. **Birdstone, Floyd County, Georgia (courtesy of American Museum of Natural History; © 2004 John Bigelow Taylor).**

Hall (2006:474) argues that birdstones "represented a composite earth and sky deity who possibly also figured as a spirit patron in group initiation rituals" such as puberty rites for age-graded societies. The relationship of a guardian spirit and vision-quest candidate in an age-graded sodality was likened to that between an adopting father and an adoptee. The uniformity of "birdstone" distributional patterns is indicative of a spirit patron shared within a tribal sodality such as a warrior society. Members of the younger group would be adopted by a guardian spirit, a patron in the vision quest. Birdstones were part of a reptilian-related cosmology that may have included spirit adoption as part of mourning and world-renewal rituals. As the basis for intercommunity alliances, spirit patrons and spirit adoption were transformed in later Hopewell interactions.

The Early Woodland landscape was occupied by a mosaic of highly localized complexes. As population densities rose, group territories became better defined and increasingly circumscribed and protected. Ethnic boundaries continued to be marked by cemeteries and artifact styles. The greater structuring of the social landscape may have dampened conflict among tribes. Increasing emphasis on exchange and mortuary ritual further served to lessen the potential for conflict, as they promoted alliances, diplomacy, and social interaction. With the growing sense of corporate identity, lineages and clans carefully balanced the need to monitor critical resources within their territories with the need to maintain rights of access to resources in neighboring areas. Alliances, exchange, mortuary ritual, and other social processes were used to negotiate access to food and resources in neighboring territories. Raiding would have been a last resort, when alliances, kin ties, and negotiations faltered in times of elevated stress.

The Ohio valley Adena complex (ca. 400 BC–AD 250), with its distinctive mortuary-ritual, was shared by many local cultures. Ritual sites, composed of accretional burial mounds, mortuary camps, ceremonial circles, and large earthwork enclosures, are part of a larger, distinctive ritual landscape that reflects cooperation and alliance among small, mobile social groups (Clay 1998). Early Adena burial centers were marked by an egalitarian burial program, utilitarian grave goods, and smaller earthen burial mounds, while later Adena ritual landscapes and burials were more elaborate.

The use of human trophies was part of the mortuary program by Late Adena times. For example, trophy taking is evident in the use of human trophy skulls at the Late Adena Cresap Mound in West Virginia (Dragoo 1963). Glacial Kame individuals from the Drew Cemetery in southwestern Ohio, some of whom were mortally wounded and decapitated, signal a raiding style of violence at the Adena-Hopewell transition (Budinoff 1976). Small, relatively autonomous, and dispersed Adena social groups, characterized as egalitarian hunting-gathering-gardening, may have had distinctive forms of tribal violence, expressed in raiding and trophy-taking behavior.

Economic and political conflicts may have been worked out through mortuary ritual in the sacred landscape. Ritual events, including the burial program, represented the arena for negotiations among small-scale polities, who may have had potentially conflicting economic and territorial interests. These intergroup negotiations would have had the potential to dampen tribal intercommunity violence and ameliorate blood feuding. However, the presence of trophies in the region indicates that negotiations and alliances may not have always been successful.

Across much of the Eastern Woodlands between roughly 200 BC and AD 400, many diverse communities interacted with one another, in a widespread and extensive exchange system based on shared religious rituals and associated iconography (Anderson and Mainfort 2002). Hunters and gatherers continued to supplement their diet with native cultigens, in much the same economic pattern as their Early Woodland ancestors. Likewise, community organization did not change fundamentally, being based on dispersed populations. Climate improved during the Roman Optimum (200 BC to AD 400), a time of warm temperatures. Raiding, consistent with tribal intercommunity conflict, is evident in the form of trophy iconography, human skeletal trophies, and weapons, both utilitarian and symbolic.

Middle Woodland Hopewell was a remarkable cultural florescence of tribal societies that engaged in elaborate burial customs, complex exchange networks, and massive earth construction. Ohio Hopewell probably gave rise to or shaped in some way various regional ceremonial and trading nodes throughout much of the Eastern Woodlands, either through direct contact or indirect exchange (Brose and Greber 1979; Charles and Buikstra 2006).

Middle Woodland social organization consisted of a number of widespread, interacting, and more or less egalitarian tribal lineages or clans, whose members claimed descent from common or mythic ancestors. Some of these clans or lineages appear to have been wealthier and more powerful than others, exercising considerable control over long-distance exchange, public rituals, and monumental earth construction (Anderson and Mainfort 2002:10). Middle Woodland tribes congregated around mounds and earthworks, focal points for rituals, and then dispersed to small seasonal settlements (Cowan 2006; Yerkes 2006; figure 5.3). Feasts at the earthworks would have served to integrate dispersed kin-based segments of the tribes (Knight 2001).

Ohio Hopewell people cultivated chenopod, knotweed, maygrass, sumpweed, and sunflowers that supplemented the mainstays of the diet, namely, fish, game, and wild plant foods. The mobile Hopewell made regular trips to mounds and earthworks throughout the year for adoption, alliances, exchange, feasting, mortuary rituals, and social interaction. Following these visits, small kin groups dispersed to different locations during different seasons to fish, gather nuts and wild plants, harvest native cultigens, and hunt.

Climate during the Middle Woodland may have warmed from the previous Early Woodland cold climate. The mild Roman Warming, or Sub-Atlantic climatic amelioration, may have facilitated the development of Hopewell culture in eastern North America (Griffin 1961:712–13). Rapid fluctuations in climate were not so common or extreme during the Middle Woodland period as in the preceding Early Woodland, and this may have placed less stress on subsistence systems. More moderate conditions may have allowed the regular production of surpluses, helping fuel Middle

Figure 5.3. Middle Woodland village gardeners, Tennessee, ca. AD 300 (courtesy of Frank H. McClung Museum, University of Tennessee, Knoxville; painting by Greg Harlin).

Woodland ceremony, exchange, and monumental construction (Anderson 2001:165).

Hopewell societies were semisedentary tribes that traveled to locations where food was abundant during different seasons of the year, which resulted in dispersed settlements within a defined territorial area. To avoid isolation and maintain necessary alliances, Middle Woodland tribal groups required some means of social integration across large sections of the Eastern Woodlands. Constructing earthworks and participating in mortuary feasts and rituals appear to have been ways in which neighboring tribal communities negotiated exchange networks, strengthened alliances, and maintained some degree of social connectedness or cohesiveness (Cowan 2006; Yerkes 2006). The ritual landscape of burial mounds, mortuary camps, and ceremonial earthworks, especially in the Midsouth and Lower Midwest, are expressions of negotiations among neighboring tribal groups to maintain critical social linkages.

Increase in mound construction during the Middle Woodland is associated with mortuary feasting and burial of the dead, which brought people together from a number of neighboring communities. The massive ceremonial mounds and geometric earthworks in the Ohio valley evolved from the burial mound complexes of the Adena peoples (Clay 1998). Major and minor ceremonial mound and burial complexes, found in the Southeast, Midsouth, and Midwest, witnessed periods of florescence, stability, and then decline (Anderson and Mainfort 2002:13; figure 5.4). These trends appear to be correlated with tribal organizational changes and shifts in regional patterns of exchange. The success of individual leaders or lineages in one area may have brought about changes in neighboring localities (Hantman and Gold 2002).

Small earthen burial mounds and associated mortuary facilities were constructed in many areas of the Eastern Woodlands. These facilities are not the central places of group territories, but rather sacred landscapes located between neighboring groups. Mound groups served to integrate regional populations and link them to short-term, specialized mortuary facilities. In most instances, monumental earthworks and other ritual facilities were located in boundary areas along drainage divides, or along small tributaries near the margins of local tribal territories. Allied groups would have used these sites for collective rituals, including complex mortuary processing, preparation of the dead, graveside feasting, and construction of accretional burial mounds (Anderson 2002; Knight 2001). Additionally, they may have been the sites of alliance formation, diplomatic entreaties, exchanges of symbolic tokens, and rituals associated with death compensation.

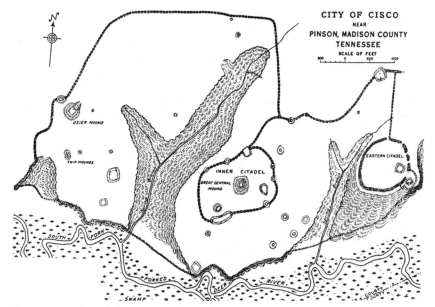

Figure 5.4.   Plan of Pinson Mounds, Madison County, Tennessee (from Myer 1922, revised by Mark Norton).

Platform mounds were constructed and used as public architecture for mortuary ritual in some areas and for feasting activities in other locations (figure 5.5). These ceremonial facilities were the probable arenas of competition and ceremony among unranked lineage heads (Anderson and Mainfort 2002). Most people appear to have been buried in communal charnel houses, low conical mounds, or graves associated with houses. A small number of individuals were accompanied by nonlocal, exotic grave goods and were given elaborate burial in log-lined tombs under conical mounds. Classic Middle Woodland Hopewellian artifacts include copper panpipes, copper celts, and copper earspools; prismatic blades; galena; cut copper and mica; ground stone celts; platform pipes; and symbolic weaponry, such as hypertrophic bifaces (Seeman 1979; figure 5.6).

In the Midwest and Midsouth, there is a marked increase in burial-mound construction and complex mortuary processing programs, particularly in southern Ohio and Illinois (Brown 1979). The Southeast and Northeast have relatively fewer mounds in comparison to the Lower Midwest, and artifacts occur sparingly in these mounds (Seeman 1979). Between 100 BC and AD 200, some especially distinctive copper artifacts were in circulation: panpipes, bicymbal earspools, beads, celts, and reel-shaped gorgets. Ground stone celts are

Figure 5.5. Saul's Mound, Pinson Mounds, Madison County, Tennessee (© 2004 David H. Dye).

found throughout the Eastern Woodlands as mortuary accompaniments, but copper celts are restricted to the Midwest (Faulkner 1996). Copper celts may have symbolically represented warrior prestige. Greenstone ax heads or celts were interred as burial accompaniments, conferring some degree of elevated status on preeminent individuals (Walthall 1980:119). Presumably, many celts were socketed in wooden handles for use as warclubs, as well as for employment in land clearance and woodworking.

The Middle Woodland economy was based in part on chenopod, sumpweed, and sunflower, cultigens grown in parts of the Midwest and Midsouth (Fritz 1993). Evidence for some significant degree of horticultural dependence includes land clearing on upland and floodplain sites, the manufacture and use of hoes, construction and use of storage facilities, and the manufacture of specialized ceramic vessels for cooking and storing native cultigens (Gremillion 2004). Maize and tobacco were introduced into the Eastern Woodlands during the Middle Woodland period. While maize was eventually adapted for intensive use in some places (by AD 1000), tobacco and other native plants were utilized over a large area by Middle Woodland peoples, as evidenced by the widespread occurrence of Middle Woodland pipes (Smith 1992). Animal-effigy pipes may have portrayed spirit helpers from which warriors sought supernatural aid as part of the ritual of smoking.

With improving climate and increased dependence on native cultigens, population probably expanded, and territories decreased. Increased conflict and increased dependence upon and elaboration of exchange systems and alliances resulted. This prompted the circulation of artifacts, raw materials, and food, as well as the parceling out of hunting and collecting rights. Cooperative mortuary ritual reflects the tendency for dispersed social groups to expand exchange opportunities, in order to buffer themselves against subsistence shortages and dampen potential hostilities. Alliances, economic reciprocity, and amelioration of revenge-based raiding would be beneficial in an environment with built-in uncertainties. Alliances could

Figure 5.6.   Three obsidian bifaces, AD 400, Hopewell site, Ross County, Ohio (courtesy of Field Museum; © 2004 John Bigelow Taylor).

be maintained, cemented, and expressed in the establishment of marriage partners and the promotion of exchange among exogamous groups (Clay 1998:14).

While there is no evidence for hereditary leadership positions, spectacular burials and associated grave assemblages are assumed to commemorate highly successful individuals, who gained prestige by gift giving and by enlisting community aid in the pursuit of social and ritual agendas. Community leaders were involved in coordinating, supporting, encouraging, and overseeing collective rituals, monumental construction, alliance building, and exchange networks. Competition among individuals would have generated an accumulation of wealth and prestige. Thus, long-distance interaction and exchange would have enhanced individual status, created alliances, smoothed vengeance desires, and prevented subsistence uncertainty by cementing economic ties among neighboring local groups.

As part of the overall transformation of intersocietal conflict from Late Archaic to Middle Woodland, raiding may have been increasingly channeled into the ritual requirements of alliances and exchange. While trophy taking was a minor element of the Late Archaic mortuary pattern, the use of human trophies became a major component of the Middle Woodland mortuary program.

Hopewell communities "lived lightly on the land" (Greber 2006:104), and settlement patterning, subsistence orientation, and social interaction are difficult to document. Likewise, direct physical evidence for tribal raiding is virtually nonexistent; but circumstantial evidence points to a style of raiding that also took place "lightly on the land." Evidence of Middle Woodland feuding comes from several sources. One important piece of information is the association of human trophies with mound burials. The individuals buried in mounds are a highly select portion of the population. While few burials indicate evidence of violent death, a large proportion of them are accompanied by modified human remains identified as trophies (Seeman 2007). Burials include corpses without heads, and are sometimes accompanied by isolated skulls and other body parts. Extensively modified bones are also present, including human mandibles and maxillae ornaments, and fingerbone pendants. Human bone modification is well documented in Middle Woodland Hopewell contexts; examples include human remains fashioned into flutes, rattles, skullcap gorgets, sucking tubes, and whistles (Bullington 1988:229; Seeman 1988, 2007).

Tribal leaders can be both renowned shamans and great warriors. During times of intercommunity violence, shamans plan, organize, and command raids; recruit warriors; and plan alliances for attacks on common enemies.

They act as hosts in "war"-related rituals and can assume varying degrees of authority over other warriors as leaders of raiding parties. Organized violence bestows considerable personal power on shamans, who can coordinate and command aggressive acts. They gain wealth through looting the communities they raid, and the resulting wealth items can then be parceled out as rewards to allies, which builds networks of intra- and intercommunity alliances. From women taken in raids they increase their progeny and domestic productivity, and from the wives gained through allies they enlarge their kinship and diplomatic networks.

Among local or tribal societies, intercommunity conflict can be interspersed with periods of relative peace. For example, a community might engage in a full spectrum of relationships with other communities. Hostilities may be carried out against enemy communities upon whom revenge raids are targeted. The same communities may conduct sporadic exchanges, but they are still liable to revenge raids. Finally, allied communities may regularly engage in feasting and exchange, culminating in reciprocal exchange of women.

Autonomous tribal communities oscillate between raiding and exchange with other communities: exchanges are peacefully resolved "wars," and "wars" are the outcome of unsuccessful transactions (Lévi-Strauss 1943:136). Peaceful relations are sought and maintained through intercommunity exchange. The diplomatic nodes and intercommunity alliances that result from these exchanges can then be important for mobilizing allied raiding parties in times of conflict, and for seeking refuge. Feasting and exchange are the tribal institutions upon which political and military alliances are established with other communities. Conflict and cooperation are continuously present in the building of intercommunity alliances, which embody the sociopolitical dynamics of tribal communities (Redmond 1998:82). The oscillation between violence and peace in intercommunity tribal relations swings from one reciprocal form of exchange to another. Exchange of crafted goods, women, and information in times of relative peace may be quickly replaced by raids and counterraids in which goods and women continue to circulate throughout the region. Neutral relations do not exist among local groups. Either they are engaged in peaceful relations and exchange a variety of resources, or else they are enemies and raid one another (Lizot 1991:69).

Competition within and among tribal or local groups is not well understood or documented, but ethnographic information about tribal societies suggests that considerable conflict can take place among neighboring groups. Ethnographically documented tribes frequently exhibit extensive and clearly demarcated territories, often extending over thousands of square miles and involving large numbers of people, who engage in persistent raiding (Anderson 2001; Redmond 1994).

Current archaeological evidence of Middle Woodland intercommunity violence suggests a pattern of small-scale raiding among neighboring kin groups, with the goals of protecting a group's own assets and appropriating neighboring resources. Trophy-taking behavior underscores the symbolic role of intergroup conflict. Middle Woodland intergroup violence appears to have low archaeological visibility but nevertheless may have been widespread and symbolically entrenched. Tribal societies integrate people over large areas, yet—except in temporary circumstances such as raiding or collective ceremonial activity—they lack the authority structures and institutional organization by which constituent populations are kept under the direct control of one group or segment. These characteristics of tribal societies seem to facilitate or curb intersocietal conflict.

The Late Archaic pattern of trophy taking that emphasized scalping, dismemberment, and pin-cushioning is represented in the Middle Woodland period, but with a profound transformation. During Middle Woodland times, human bone became a widespread medium for the first time in eastern North America (Seeman 2007). It was an important raw material for the production of a variety of standardized forms, including transformative and mythic themes on flutes, sucking tubes, rattles, whistles, and gorgets. Human skulls and mandibular parts are found across the span of Hopewell interaction. Human bone was modified by being cut, ground, drilled, polished, and painted, and it was frequently used in the context of burial accompaniments. Trophy skulls (with single drilled holes) and highly modified mandibles and maxillae (extensively cut, ground, and polished) were buried with a narrow segment of the population, mainly young adult males (Buikstra 1979; Johnston 2002; Nawrocki 1997; Seeman 1988, 2007).

Violence was probably part of life for Havana Hopewell populations (Charles et al. 1988). A number of investigations into Havana Hopewell cemeteries indicate the presence of trauma such as parry fractures on ulnae and depression fractures on skulls (Conner and Link 1991:31–35; Frankenberg et al. 1988). During the Middle Woodland period, a small core unit may have had the capability of affecting the economic and social structure of groups in peripheral areas through violent means (Jeske 2006:305). If so, then raids based on feuding may have been part of Havana Hopewell social relations.

Modified human bone—rattles, flutes, gorgets, and tubes—were interred as grave accompaniments (Seeman 1988, 2007). In fact, most decorated bone artifacts in Ohio Hopewell contexts were crafted from human bone (Willoughby and Hooton 1922:9). Trophy skulls and evidence for scalping have been reported for several Hopewell sites (Shetrone 1926). For example, at the Turner site in Ohio, sixteen male skulls were found in association with two adults. Thirteen skulls had superficial scratches indicative of scalping (Willoughby and Hooton 1922). Seeman (1988:572) suggests that intentionally, but minimally, modified human skull trophies present in Ohio Hopewell sites were predominantly curated young adults, and that they primarily occurred as burial accompaniments. Human trophy skulls "probably are tangible signs to potential friends and allies of success in warfare" (Seeman 1988:573). Reexamination of skeletal material is needed to ascertain the presence of violent trauma. "Assessment of the nature and extent of violence in Middle Woodland societies is critical for understanding the dynamics of long-distance contact, alliance, and avoidance behaviors. Even small-scale, guerrilla-style raiding may have a strong impact upon the internal organization of a peripheral polity" (Jeske 2006:308).

In Hopewell contexts, human jaws are modified in much the same way as those of predatory animals, linking human trophy taking with the more ancient practice of taking and displaying animal trophies. Modified ornaments made from the jaws of predatory animals, especially wolves, were suspended as bodily adornment and placed in mortuary context. The mingling of over one hundred worked jaws of predators with those of humans in the Tremper site cache in southern Ohio (Mills 1916:285; Shetrone and Greenman 1931:507) strengthens Seeman's (2007) interpretation.

Cut human and animal jaws appear to have been modified to be worn and seen. Found only in burial contexts, cut human jaws were worn around the neck and on the chest or torso, and perhaps sewn onto garments. Others were suspended from the wrists (Meinkoth 1995:54; Seeman 2007). The latter instance is reminiscent of Plains warriors who on ritual occasions adorned their wrists with scalps and human hands (Bowers 1965:317).

Hopewell headgear symbols incorporate predatory animals and human trophies, including predators or scavengers devouring human heads (Perino 1968:121; Shetrone and Greenman 1931:416; Willoughby and Hooton 1922:159), raptors with human crania headgear (Moorehead 1922:166), and anthromorphic figures equipped with detached human heads (Dragoo and Wray 1964:fig. 7). The trophy theme supports the idea that animal predators feeding on human heads relates metaphorically to success of warrior shamans in raiding (Seeman 2007). Hopewell iconography has a shamanic caste and includes the themes of human and animal connections, world renewal, ancestor veneration, and human trophies (Brown 1997:468, 473; Seeman 2007). The trophy iconographic theme includes detached human heads and hands, in addition to headless and footless torsos.

Shamans

Warriors and Diplomats

Shamanism may have been one avenue for Middle Woodland alliance building and raiding. The great variety of Hopewellian effigy platform pipes may be the product of a transition from Early Woodland warrior age-grade rites to more individualized warrior ceremonies in Middle Woodland times, including pursuing solitary vision quests and seeking personal spirit guardians prior to entry into warrior societies. The abundance of reptilian icons at the beginning of the Early Woodland period and their presence but relative scarcity in Hopewellian imagery may signal a trend away from egalitarian access to supernaturals by warriors and a trend toward an ancestral supreme being and the emergence of elite warrior lineages or privileged religious associations. The patron of an elite lineage can be perceived as an apical ancestor exclusive to that warrior society and legitimizing its leadership. The transition would have been expedited if the original Early Woodland shared-spirit patron was transformed in Middle Woodland times into the patron of shamanic-based warrior societies.

Shaman warriors may have been associated with raiding activities and altered states of consciousness; tobacco-pipe smoking; and bird, bear, and human transformational imagery. Shaman warriors were individuals whose otherworldly sources of power would have given them the authority to gather kin-based militias and deploy and direct them against neighboring groups. In addition, shamans served as diplomats whose shamanistic performances not only aided in consolidating kin-militia forces and leading them in raids against enemies, but also helped secure alliances. Alliance building and militia formation may have taken place in the context of feasting, gift exchange, and mortuary ceremonialism at the great ceremonial centers.

Interpretations of Middle Woodland exchange typically center on political, economic, religious, and social principles, but intercommunity conflict is rarely included in explanations of ceremonial centers or exchange systems. Intersocietal conflict necessitates territorial alliances and regional mechanisms to help mediate intergroup disputes. Raiding and, possibly, limited warfare were perhaps infrequent, but these were still ominous threats. Raiding may have been regulated by a ritual cycle that was acted out at the impressive Hopewell earthworks, where social exchanges and ritual displays took place. Because most eastern groups during the Middle Woodland remained relatively mobile, intercommunity violence had not reached the point at which social groups were forced together for defense, as happened in later centuries.

Near the end of the Middle Woodland period a panregional trend toward larger settlements was taking place. Increased settlement aggregation may have resulted from its high resource potential, and from defensive response to increased competition. During the fifth and sixth centuries in the Midsouth and Midwest, nucleated villages began to form in some areas. Changes taking place in eastern North America transformed a raiding style of intercommunity conflict and the varied institutions of peacemaking into new opportunities for emerging leadership positions. A new political and social order was born, and new institutions for cooperation and conflict were forged.

CHAPTER SIX

Cooperation and Conflict in Late Woodland Societies

Clearly the boundary between trading and raiding, enmity and alliance, was a shifting and fluid one.

(Hantman 2001:122)

Profound and critical transformations took place in domestic, economic, political, religious, and social relations throughout eastern North America in the centuries following the florescence of Middle Woodland tribal societies and prior to the rise of Mississippian chiefly polities in the early second millennium (Emerson et al. 2000; Koldehoff and Galloy 2006; Nassaney 2001). Late Woodland was a time of regional culture change and variability, which culminated in a series of remarkable cultures, including Algonquian speakers of the Mid-Atlantic Coast and Northeast; Caddoan, Natchezan, and Tunican speakers of the Transmississippi West; Iroquoian speakers of the Northeast; Muskogean speakers of the Southeast; and Siouan speakers of the Midsouth and Midwest. Although mortuary ceremonialism was unspectacular, prompting some archaeologists to see the Late Woodland period as a kind of social dark age, economic and political organization was clearly developing rather than stagnating (Kerber 1986).

The beginning of the Late Woodland period is traditionally set at the time when Middle Woodland local groups were substantially transformed into fundamentally different tribal organizational forms. Late Woodland societies exhibit great temporal variability throughout eastern North America. For example, in the American Bottom region of the Central Mississippi Valley, the

Terminal Late Woodland period ended around AD 1050; while in the Great Lakes, Mid-Atlantic Coast, and Northeast regions, Woodland cultures continued well into the European colonial period.

Hallmark features of many Late Woodland societies in eastern North America, as compared to Middle Woodland groups, include dramatic changes in intersocietal cooperation and conflict, mortuary ceremonialism, prestige-goods exchange, settlement patterns, and subsistence practices. During the Late Woodland period populations grew, settlement strategies changed, regional communication subsided, and in some areas "relations deteriorated to the point of outright warfare" (Milner 2004:106).

Variability in Late Woodland cultures can be seen in marked contrasts among well-documented archaeological cultures such as Weeden Island on the southeastern Gulf Coastal Plain (Milanich et al. 1997), the various Late Woodland phases of the American Bottom region in the Central Mississippi Valley (Koldehoff and Galloy 2006), the Algonquian polities of the Mid-Atlantic Coast (Potter 1993), the Langford tradition of northern Illinois (Emerson 1999), and the Algonquian and Iroquoian groups of the Northeast (Engelbrecht 2003). These regional expressions of Late Woodland cultural transformations show marked variation over time and space, and in the ways in which they integrated social institutions and coped with intersocietal conflict.

One of the best documented prehistoric Late Woodland areas of eastern North America is the American Bottom region of the Central Mississippi Valley (Koldehoff and Galloy 2006). Late Woodland in the American Bottom, as was the case with much of the Eastern Woodlands, was a period of technological innovation and increasing social complexity (Emerson et al. 2000). Societies with specific regional identities emerged in the American Bottom (Fortier and Jackson 2000), as community patterns transformed domestic relations, population levels dramatically increased, and premaize subsistence practices increasingly underwrote the economy (Fortier et al. 2006).

In the fourth century AD, local groups throughout the Midwest and Midsouth had ventured into the uplands, but only sporadically. After the fourth century, the pace of social interaction among tribal groups began to slow down as "various regions of the Midwest pursued individual and non-lineal cultural paths" (McElrath et al. 2000:16). Demographic, domestic, economic, political, and social changes brought about a general restructuring of midcontinental societies, as the intricate and widespread Middle Woodland exchange systems collapsed. With greater reliance on food production, the expansion of riparian gardens, and improved subsistence storage systems, gradual economic changes brought about population and settlement realignments in many areas of the Eastern Woodlands.

Hilltop Enclosures
Ritual or Defense?

Rock shelters and hilltop enclosures in the Midwest during the Late Woodland period have been interpreted as domestic sites, ritual enclosures, and defensive positions. For example, the presence of habitations in defensive locations, especially rock shelters, during early Late Woodland times in eastern Kentucky suggests to some archeologists that defense, in addition to protection from the weather, may have been a strong consideration in the choice of settlement. The defensive locations of many early Late Woodland sites may indicate real or perceived threats.

From eastern Kentucky into southern Illinois, large construction projects put up low rock walls that partially or completely encircled the crests of hills. Often referred to as "hill forts," they were built in remote places, far from habitation areas. Although the stone constructions have been suggested to be defensive enclosures, their remoteness and poor access to water make them unlikely to have been used for defense. In addition, the large numbers of people that would have been required to defend them make it doubtful that these were true fortifications. Hilltop enclosures seem to have been located between local-group boundaries or settlements, rather than within polity boundaries. Thus, they seem to have been used seasonally as social or ritual spaces. The walls and steep slopes delineating such ritually important places resemble earlier Middle Woodland hilltop ceremonial enclosures.

Increased seasonal population movement and shifts in community location appear to have been hallmarks of the Late Woodland period. The shift from Middle to Late Woodland witnessed a decrease in long-distance exchange, cemetery monumentality, and local ceramic heterogeneity, but an increase in conflict resulting from territorial defense. Kerber (1986:172) notes that the "social necessities of active territorial defense—leadership, allegiance, continuity—provided a new context of overtly political competition both within and between communities, and it was probably this context of competition rather than its antecedent conditions which was most responsible for the net increase in the political complexity of Woodland groups between 400 and 1000 A.D."

At the close of the Middle Woodland period, the uplands and floodplain of the sparsely populated American Bottom region were briefly unoccupied; but regional resettlement occurred in the early portion of the Late Woodland period, especially in the uplands by expanding pioneer populations characterized by shifting patterns of settlement based on slash-and-burn horticulture

(Fortier et al. 2006:191). This expansion was fueled by indigenous agriculture and improved seed processing and preparation techniques (McElrath and Fortier 2000). The initial stage of frontier settlement represents a resettlement of the American Bottom region by small and dispersed pioneering populations who probably emigrated from areas adjacent to the Central Mississippi Valley (Koldehoff and Galloy 2006).

Large-scale settlement and cultivation in the uplands was based on Eastern Agricultural Complex indigenous seed crops composed of starchy and oily seeds of several native cultigens, as well as gourds, squash, and tobacco—all of which would have been grown with minimal labor investment. Starchy and oily seeds had become an essential part of the diet in many places by Late Woodland times (Fritz 1990:416–24; Simon 2000:42–46, 48, 52). Maize, although present, is poorly represented in archaeological samples. Substantial plant-food storage or caching suggests that settlements were seasonally occupied and frequently abandoned. Typical of many Late Woodland groups across much of eastern North America was a practice of scheduling farming, fishing, gathering, and hunting activities with respect to changing seasonal cycles. These forager-farmers routinely used fire to clear fields and encourage plant and animal habitats important for fishing, gathering, hunting, and swidden agriculture. Mortuary procedures were simple and unobtrusive, leaving behind neither cemeteries nor burial mounds. There is also scant evidence of ritual paraphernalia, indicating lack of consensus-building and community-integrating activities (McElrath and Fortier 2000:115). Likewise, leadership positions were weakly developed above the household or hamlet level.

McElrath and Fortier (2000:115) suggest that the "primary mechanism for dealing with intragroup stress would have been community fissioning. The lack of clearly recognizable formal religious or political paraphernalia may be directly attributable to the fact that dispute adjudication and conflict resolution were not priorities as long as there was a frontier available to accept discontented groups." Fissioning provided adequate stress reduction for local-group farmers until population density increased to the point that other social-integrating and conflict-resolution mechanisms had to be implemented.

Immigration, population growth, and settlement expansion continued to take place from AD 650 to 900 in the American Bottom, during a time of regional "filling-in." Population expanded and local groups occupied and filled the frontier uplands, a process fostered by shifting cultivation of indigenous and tropical seed crops. Some settlements routinely used maize in conjunction with native cultigens (Simon 2000), representing the first marked reliance by Midwestern populations on maize. As semisedentary foragers, farming groups continued using forest-fallow swidden agriculture at prominent landscape features situated on or near key resources or landmarks.

Two spheres of farmer-foraging settlement mobility have been postulated. One is the seasonal or periodic abandonment and reoccupation of habitation areas composed of small, scattered, seasonal camps, each including two or three circular houses. The second is the complete abandonment of a settlement after one or two years of continuous use, followed by its reoccupation after about twenty years as part of a cyclical land-use pattern (Koldehoff and Galloy 2006). Both large and small settlements were spread across the uplands and the Mississippi floodplain as local groups amalgamated and fissioned. These farmers and foragers distributed themselves across the region by annually and seasonally relocating villages and dispatching task groups. Village locations, while frequent, were probably limited geographically and occupied for several years by no more than a few dozen people (Milner 2004:114). The typical residential group may have circulated within a territory covering at most twenty-five square kilometers (Koldehoff and Galloy 2006).

Subsistence strategies and mortuary practices continued in much the same fashion as before, but important changes and innovations took place during the 250 years prior to AD 900. New social-integrating mechanisms appeared, regional interactions among communities increased, and the egalitarian nature of society changed. Although widespread prestige-goods exchange was minimal, interregional similarity in ceramics and the rapid dispersal of the bow and arrow indicate the presence of broad-scale interaction. In the seventh century, the bow and arrow was adopted throughout the midcontinent, bringing about changes in alliances, hunting, and raiding (Nassaney and Pyle 1999). Population increased greatly after the adoption of the bow and arrow, suggesting an increased efficiency in hunting and territorial defense.

The appearance of discoidals, discs, pipes, and supernatural "animal" effigies on pipes and ceramic vessels suggests an intensification of intragroup and intercommunity interaction at upland focal points (Fortier and Jackson 2000:139–40), coupled with the diffusion of, or local innovations in, cosmology and ritual. The presence of clay and stone discoidals may represent early forerunners of the chunkey game, which provided an important means of interaction in the following centuries.

Ceramic discs may have been used in games of chance or skill, but they also encode early artistic references to Above World and Middle World cosmic powers in the use of rayed circle and cross iconographic motifs. The rayed (sun) circle motif identifies the Above World, while the cross motif references the symbolic logs of the sacred fire of the Middle World. The two together form "a vertical axis, demonstrating an important uniting principle of the cosmos" (Lankford 2007:21). The "concept of a holy fire identified with the sun and fed by four symbolic logs oriented to the four cardinal points is the most widespread and basic ceremonial concept in the Southeast" (Waring 1968:33).

The use of tobacco and the increased occurrence of pipes reflect the intensification and renewed emphasis of ritual behavior and the sacred aspects of tobacco use as early as the eighth and ninth centuries AD. The portrayal of supernaturals, perhaps spirit companions, on ceramic pipes further underscores an emphasis on otherworldly concerns. Bird imagery emphasizes coherence with Above World sources of power, while frogs and turtles incorporated in ceramic art suggest connections to the Beneath World. The presence of ceramic bowls, found for the first time in the Late Woodland period, may signal early forms of feasting and an emphasis on preparation and communal consumption of ritual medicines. Public feasting and community libation rituals may have taken place in large communal buildings located at focal points in the upland forests. Feasts, rituals, and other integrative mechanisms that evidence indicates were present from AD 650 to 900 formed the basis for cosmological, domestic, economic, ideological, and political transformations and elaborations of the tenth century.

The new integrating mechanisms may have been responsible for, or may have been brought about by, the arrival in the region of immigrants, who appear to have been accepted into local populations with no obvious signs of conflict. Few skeletal remains have been found, however, making it difficult to gauge the degree of violence that might have taken place during the "filling-in" process. As regional population levels rose, "the landscape was now likely divided into defended territories" (Galloy 2002:436). Perhaps conflict resulting from intercommunity discord could no longer be dampened by local group fissioning.

The "filling-up" period in the American Bottom region ended about AD 900. Continued population increase brought about violent conflicts and caused new conflict-reducing mechanisms to evolve. Violence, often in the form of feuding, is commonplace among swidden farmers (Sahlins 1968; Vayda 1961). Once the uplands could no longer accommodate more populations, intergroup conflict and the mechanisms that attempted to dampen it become apparent in the archaeological record. Local-group leadership positions which may have been only weakly developed were now beginning to gain increasing authority. The power of regional leaders, evident by the middle of the eleventh century, probably had its beginnings in the evolving political dynamics of the eighth through tenth centuries.

The tenth century and first half of the eleventh century were marked by intensification and innovation in ideology, settlement, and subsistence. For example, settlement patterns were reorganized, farming was intensified, and village life became increasingly sedentary and focused on the Mississippi River floodplain. Reoccupation of the floodplain was greatly accelerated (Fortier and Jackson 2000) as populations in the American Bottom region began consolidating in large communities as part of a general movement out of the uplands. Intensive cultivation of maize was now established in alluvial settings, and maize agriculture began to reshape the physical landscape and human society for the first time. Land was increasingly and routinely cultivated, and its products integrated into the diet (Koldehoff and Galloy 2006:294).

Sometime between AD 800 and 1100, maize was rapidly adopted by people throughout much of the Eastern Woodlands (Fritz 1990:398, 408–9; Smith 1989:1570), but its use varied from one area to another. In the midcontinent, maize was grafted onto well-established plant cultivation practices, while in other areas, such as the Northeast, it was adopted without being preceded by a long tradition of growing native cultigens (Milner 2004:118).

The role of maize as a major dietary item suggests some degree of agricultural intensification (Simon 2000). Maize demands construction of formal fields, constant care, concentration of settlement to the most fertile and sustainable soils, reduced individual mobility, and increased labor investment (Koldehoff and Galloy 2006:294). Maize agriculture may have underwritten feasting events, specialized crafting, and community rituals that served as the social and political glue for emerging political aggrandizement, alliance networks, interregional exchange, and social hierarchies (Pauketat 2004:60).

One aspect of crafting is found in Late Woodland weaponry. Symbolic war clubs, manufactured from exotic stone, were exchanged in various forms throughout much of the midcontinent by the tenth century. Their widespread use points to the transformation of conflict and its incorporation in ritual and artistic representation in eastern North America. The use of iconic images of heroic supernaturals, wearing combat regalia and brandishing maces or crownform clubs, is richly illustrated by examples at Missouri's Picture Cave, a site dating to the tenth century AD (Diaz-Granados 2004:145–48; figure 6.1). These images clearly indicate the adoption of symbolic weaponry and mundane war clubs in the tenth century as burgeoning political competition and rivalry manifested itself among emerging elites.

Figure 6.1.   The Black Warrior at Picture Cave I, Missouri (photo by James R. Duncan, reproduced with permission).

By the early eleventh century, evidence for the construction of formal maize fields, interregional exchange networks based on utilitarian goods as well as prestige items, and nucleated, structured communities indicates the emergence of strong leadership positions (Fortier and McElrath 2002; Pauketat 2004). Tribal leaders of the early eleventh century wielded more power and authority than their ancestors of the ninth century. Between AD 1050 and 1100, formal cemeteries appeared for the first time at Cahokia and across the countryside (Emerson et al. 2003). The uplands were resettled in a new and dramatic way: large nodal settlements and mound centers were established, primarily along transportation and exchange corridors.

Sedentary, nucleated villages did not come into being in the American Bottom region until approximately AD 900–1050, a time of dramatic cultural heterogeneity and rapid change, which took place in tandem with the appearance of maize agriculture and the bow and arrow, and regional resettlement of upland populations into floodplain and bluff-top villages. As already noted, large-scale cultivation of maize on alluvial soils served to transform the physical as well as the sociopolitical landscape (Fortier et al. 2006). Dramatic increases in the overall density, size, and social complexity of the population took place in conjunction with agricultural intensification (Schurr and Schoeninger 1995).

Evidence from other areas of the Eastern Woodlands also indicates that regional cultural changes were taking place. In the Upper Midwest, effigy mounds built between the eighth and twelfth centuries included animal-like figures. Some mounds appear to have been shaped like war clubs or reptiles (see Milner 2004:fig. 73). The association of reptiles with symbolic weaponry has a long tradition in the Eastern Woodlands.

The effigy-mound builders were dispersed hunters and gatherers who interred a few individuals in the mounds. Maize and other domesticated plants were consumed in minor amounts, but the diet was primarily based on game and wild plants. Camps were small and were moved intermittently. Debris left near the mounds suggests that mortuary rituals were conducted in their vicinity. Effigy mound rituals

> provided opportunities to arrange marriages and to establish cooperative relations with the members of other groups. A few dozen people working for several days could have thrown up a mound while participating in the festivities that accompanied such gatherings. Perhaps social groups identified by totemic markers built the mounds to establish claims to particular areas. (Milner 2004:108)

Earthen burial and effigy mounds functioned as local integrating mechanisms (Mallam 1976) in the Upper Mississippi basin.

During the last half of the first millennium, the Southeast witnessed major population growth, heavier reliance on stored cultivated foods, greater regionalism, and a decline in interregional interaction. Accompanying these changes was an increase in the severity of warfare, several centuries prior to the rise of fortified Mississippian towns and chiefly political and social organization. By the eleventh century, increases in the intensity and level of warfare, and changes in its nature, were accompanied by new forms of symbolic weaponry, increased levels of skeletal trauma, substantial fortifications, and heroic warrior iconography. Greater frequency of intergroup conflicts may have been partially sustained by increasing emphasis on field cultivation, storage of plant foods, and increased use of the war club. The bow and arrow was becoming a significant military weapon.

Along the southeastern Gulf Coastal Plain in the post-Hopewell era, the Weeden Island culture (Milanich et al. 1997) witnessed the rise of religious practitioners who conducted elaborate mortuary rituals focused on charnel houses built atop platform mounds in sacred, ceremonial precincts. The religious leaders provided links to the supernatural and achieved special social status through the development of outside contacts, manipulation of long-distance exchange, and coordination of interlineage activities. While social organization lay between the egalitarian structure of family groups and hierarchical regional polities, these groups indicate the increasing political authority of religious specialists, who assumed ever-greater importance as coordinators of interpolity alliances and world-renewal rituals. The lack of evidence for Weeden Island warfare may be explained by the emphasis on cooperative alliances, sustained diplomacy, and peace-promoting rituals.

In addition to being a time of economic, social, and technological change, the Late Woodland period was a time of rapid global cooling in the Northern Hemisphere. The major impact of the Vandal Minimum cold spell took place around AD 500 (Berglund 2003). A number of societies throughout the world experienced some degree of changes in land use; depopulation; increased levels of warfare; large-scale relocation; and reductions in organizational complexity (Baillie 1999; Broecker 2001; Gunn 2000). In parts of the Eastern Woodlands, such as the Midsouth, Midwest, and southern Appalachians, cultural change is evident at the middle of the first millennium; while in the western part of the Lower Southeast along the Gulf Coast and Lower Mississippi Valley, there is little evidence of disruption, underscoring the variable nature of climate and its effect on human populations.

From AD 700 to 1200, the Medieval Warm Period, or Medieval Optimum, may have promoted field agriculture over much of the Eastern Woodlands (Anderson 2001). A general climatic warming took place in some areas when temperatures increased over the earlier Vandal Minimum cold episode. The warmest period, from AD 950 to 1045, may have had temperatures equal to those of today (Esper et al. 2002). Between AD 800 and 1000 there was adequate rainfall in the Upper Midwest, along with relatively long, warm summers and cool, dry winters (Brose 2001:51).

Some populations continued to be scattered over the landscape; but, for the first time in many areas, nucleated villages began to be occupied for much if not all of the year, replacing an earlier pattern of occasional nucleation by dispersed populations around mortuary events and associated monumental-construction efforts. Intensive agriculture based on local domesticates appears to have been practiced in some areas, and this may have resulted in the emergence of complex tribal forms, if not chieftaincies. Maize and other storable crops assumed an increasingly significant and important role in the diet. Population nucleation, settlement fortification, and stored-food surpluses may be visible archaeological correlates of more complex political organization (Anderson 2002). While there is little evidence for nucleated settlements prior to the Late Woodland period in most parts of the Eastern Woodlands, after AD 800 large aggregated settlements, sedentary communities, and fortified towns appeared in many areas (Anderson and Mainfort 2002; Nassaney and Cobb 1991). Settlement patterns and scale of political organization varied appreciably over the region. For example, in some areas, such as the Mississippi, Ohio, and Tennessee river valleys, settlement nucleation was widespread; while in other areas, such as the Appalachians and South Atlantic Slope, populations of small groups of "mobile, part-time horticulturalists" remained dispersed until much later (Cobb and Nassaney 1995:206).

With settlement nucleation, intermittent monumental construction no longer fostered group identity among dispersed hunters and gatherers. Where mound building continued, it was related to the maintenance and legitimation of the power and authority of chiefly elites. After AD 900, when maize agriculture had become well established in the floodplains of river valleys, a competitive social environment arose, as villages became more protective of territorial boundaries.

Late in the first millennium, in the southern part of the Eastern Woodlands and especially in the Central to Lower Mississippi Valley, mounds were incorporated into village layouts, as a type of site plan emerged that consisted of a centrally located plaza surrounded by mounds and domestic buildings.

Platform mounds supported houses of elite rulers, as well as temples or charnel houses containing the bones of the elite's ancestors. The Toltec site, for example, located on the Arkansas River in central Arkansas, has eighteen mounds accompanied by two plazas, habitation areas, and an embankment and ditch (figure 6.2). Some of the mound summits have produced evidence of feasting (Milner 2004:110).

By the end of the first millennium, chiefdoms emerged in the Central and Lower Mississippi Valley. In areas where intensive maize agriculture was practiced, civic-ceremonial centers characterized by temple and mortuary mounds were arranged around plazas, the hallmark of chiefly centers. These ritual and political centers occurred widely across the Eastern Woodlands in the succeeding centuries. Principal sites with mounds and plazas tended to be inhabited by large numbers of people for as long as several generations, or in some cases for centuries. Dependence on corn—an increasingly significant component of the diet—and other crops profoundly changed the nature of warfare. When food is stockpiled, it inevitably becomes a key objective of raids. Once dependence upon stored food is a feature of the economy and warfare becomes a common economic interest, then buffer zones, defensive fortifications, larger residential aggregations, population movements, and territorial changes begin to develop. Intersocietal conflict at this point is transformed, because the residential or territorial group is occupied with protecting stored subsistence

Figure 6.2.   Mound A, Toltec Mounds, Lonoke County, Arkansas (© 2008 David H. Dye).

resources, rather than seeking kin-group vengeance. Kelly (2000:68) observes, "a new phase of the coevolution of war and society is triggered by substantial reliance on food storage."

Eastern Woodland archaeology reveals a sharp increase in violence by the end of the first millennium (Milner 2007). With elevated levels of strife and violent death, warfare placed increased stress on populations. Settlement nucleation, skeletal trauma, unoccupied or lightly occupied buffer zones, symbolic weaponry, and fortifications with bastions are clearly evident in the archeological record by approximately AD 1000 (Milner 2000). Social and political relations among local groups had begun to deteriorate by this time. People shot with arrows, presumably victims of violence, have been identified in many skeletal collections (Milner 1999:122). Bows and arrows were ideal weapons for warriors who attacked their enemy's settlements or ambushed individuals or small groups of people around their villages. Perhaps increases in defensive measures reflect the kind of society beginning to emerge in the southern Eastern Woodlands (Milner 2004:121).

The initial construction of fortifications at political centers signals periods of heightened hostilities among neighboring polities. Increased conflict may have resulted from competition over stored food surpluses in above-ground corncribs. Visible signs of chiefly largess would have been vulnerable to envious or hungry neighbors. The shift from below-ground storage pits to aboveground corncribs in the Terminal Late Woodland may have been made difficult with the earlier introduction of the bow and arrow. In addition, chiefly political organization, with its ability to mobilize warrior militias, would have given tactical advantage to societies with better coordinated forces. The initial construction of fortifications in the Terminal Late Woodland period marks early efforts to protect ancestral powers, chiefly munificence, and symbols of authority. In response to threats of interpolity raiding and thievery of storable surplus, defensive palisades become a practical necessity.

Around AD 900–1000, offensive posturing is evident in areas of the Midsouth, where populations responded to aggressive behavior by placing sites in defensive positions, erecting palisade walls, and digging ditches to enclose settlements, to protect the inhabitants from neighboring polities. Areas that had previously been settled were now abandoned, creating buffer zones of otherwise habitable real estate among competing polities, while other areas coalesced for protection into a few relatively large villages in politically crowded floodplains. These efforts arose in response to heightened levels of hostilities that culminated in endemic warfare (Knight and Steponaitis 1998:11; Little 1999).

Osteological analysis also suggests that lethal intergroup conflicts increased in frequency late in the Woodland period (Bridges et al. 2000; Milner 2007) after the introduction of the bow and arrow, which spread rapidly over the Eastern Woodlands in the seventh century AD (Nassaney and Pyle 1999). Coupled with use of the bow and arrow and war clubs, raiding had the potential to become widespread and increasingly lethal. For example, at Site 1Pi61, a Late Woodland site in Pickens County, Alabama, 8 percent of the burial population had embedded arrow points (Bridges et al. 2000:38), 25 percent had upper body fractures, and 16 percent had lower body fractures, presumably due to blows from war clubs. Some of the individuals were buried in mass graves (Bridges et al. 2000:42–43, table 3.1). The manner in which the mass burials were interred leads researchers to believe that the graves held captives (Hill 1981). At this site, the two sexes had roughly equal mortality rates from violence, a ratio that would soon change in the succeeding Mississippian period.

Warfare at the Woodland/Mississippian transition was fundamentally altered, as the political authority of community leaders became increasingly centralized. Dependence on corn, use of the war club and bow and arrow, and chiefdom-like political forms caused intersocietal conflict to become progressively institutionalized. The rise of chieftaincies (Carneiro 1998; Redmond 1998) began in the Late Woodland period, if not earlier. The social and political environment of chieftaincies is one in which leaders gradually acquire increasing amounts of limited authority based on emerging hierarchies. Positions of permanent leadership are created in essentially nonhierarchical, noncentralized tribal societies. Leadership and authority positions become increasingly hereditary, institutionalized, and hierarchical under the conditions of warfare (Carneiro 1998).

The wielders of ritual authority have the necessary sanctity and moral voice to convince their followers that the extension of their control over other leadership functions will be beneficial and for the common good. Ritual sanctity enables leaders to preside over an emergent simultaneous hierarchy, which as we have seen is generally associated with more permanent regional leadership. Emerging elites also begin to promote their ancestors as powerful intermediaries with the supernatural world. The construction of shrines which house sacred bundles and ritual paraphernalia embodies the authority and presence of their ancestors whose remains lie in repose.

Chieftains are short-term leaders who achieve status in an intermittently situational hierarchy. Leaders compete with one another for prestige, which is acquired through one's prowess, talent, and success as an ambassador or diplomat, athlete, hunter, orator, or warrior. A man cannot aspire to a leadership position in a chieftaincy unless he possesses prestige, and upon becoming a chieftain he can only continue to function as a leader through the exercise of prestige. Chieftains can wield power based on the support of their followers, generally in the context of a council. Hierarchical, centralized leadership may confer selective advantage upon such groups, thus increasing the efficiency of decision making. In the face of consistent hostile threats, hierarchical leadership positions may become permanently institutionalized as hereditary offices in an emerging regional polity (Redmond 1998:6).

Chiefdoms, or regional polities, are made up of subordinate villages under the permanent control of a chief, who consolidates the villages within a region (Carneiro 1981:45). The chief occupies a formal office at the top of a regional administrative hierarchy of local village chiefs, in a "simultaneous decision making hierarchy" (Johnson 1982:396). Most leadership functions are centralized in the institutionalized, hereditary office of the chief. To reduce potential sources of disruption in the intergenerational transfer of chiefly authority, the development of chiefly-control hierarchies is usually accompanied by the development of institutionalized social ranking and status differentiation (Johnson 1978:101).

Theories about the emergence of complex societies in the Eastern Woodlands have emphasized the importance of population pressure, intensive agriculture, warfare, and control over the exchange of "prestige goods" (Milner 1998a; Pauketat and Emerson 1997). Theories concerning chiefdom development often center on competitive emulation (Clark and Blake 1994) or warfare (Carneiro 1994). The military advantage a chieftaincy or chiefdom has over a less complex society would prompt defensive reactions and reorganization among its neighbors, who would have to adopt a similar strategy to avoid being incorporated by an aggressive and expanding neighboring polity. Chiefly warfare is based in large part on social ranking and hierarchy. Prior to Mississippian chiefdoms, tribal and chieftaincy forms of social organization emphasized achieved leadership positions based primarily on the exercise of prestige.

Along the Mid-Atlantic Coast, a Late Woodland style of conflict continued among Algonquian speakers until the late seventeenth century. Great enmity existed between coastal Algonquian speakers and the Piedmont and mountain Siouan speakers (Hantman 1993). The two groups feared each other, as well as fearing raids by northern Iroquoians. While skeletal evidence suggests trophy taking (skull-cap removal) and intentional and lethal blows to the head, ethnohistoric documentation reports the capture and killing of war captives. John Smith was told, regarding Indian warfare in Virginia, that they "seldom made warre for land or goods, but for women and children, and principally for revenge" (Barbour 1986:166). Perhaps typical of many Late Woodland groups, "the boundary between trading and raiding, enmity and alliance, was a shifting and fluid one in the Virginia interior" (Hantman 2001:122).

In summary, the Late Woodland period was a time of great change in eastern North America. The primary, late-prehistoric subsistence pattern of corn agriculture had been established by AD 800, as had the use of the war club and the bow and arrow as weaponry. By the early first millennium, symbolic weaponry was an integral component in iconic representations of warriors in ritual regalia. If the sashes worn by the figures in Picture Cave are indicative of warrior societies, then military fraternal interest groups may have been well established by the eleventh century, or even earlier.

The majority of Late Woodland populations, at least in the midcontinent, developed, adopted, or interacted with a Mississippian lifestyle. In some areas, such as the American Bottom region, groups developed a Mississippian way of life. Neighboring polities were more passive recipients of Mississippian cultural expansion, interacting with Mississippian groups or adhering to Late Woodland cultural practices in the presence of intrusive Mississippian populations. In more distant areas, Late Woodland groups developed directly into Upper Mississippian social entities from a non–Late Woodland society. Finally, many Late Woodland groups remained Late Woodland, with little or no change and little or no interaction with Mississippian groups (McElrath et al. 2000:20).

The interaction among Late Woodland groups in the Midwest who either became Mississippian or were influenced by interaction with Mississippian groups is one of the key issues in understanding ethnicity in the Midwest (Emerson 1999), especially the degree of cooperation, social interaction, and violence among the various polities or political groups. The stability allowed by a corn-based economy is exemplified by its continued use well into modern times. Subsistence practices and technology that were forged in the Late Woodland period were basic to many societies in eastern North America. Differences among the various ethnic lifestyles were not a result of divergent economic or technological practices, but rather were "fundamentally social, political, and ideational" (McElrath et al. 2000:20). As Mississippian societies flourished in eastern North America, new institutions and patterns of cooperation were created to mitigate the spiraling violence that arose at the turn of the second millennium AD.

CHAPTER SEVEN

Cooperation and Conflict in the Northeast

Only when grief was forgotten could war end and peace begin.

(Richter 1983:536–37)

The Late Woodland societies of northeastern North America were diverse, complex, and varied in their domestic, economic, political, and social organization. Although there was no one large, regional, homogenous society, two basic economic orientations prevailed throughout the Northeast, corresponding roughly with linguistic groups. One major linguistic affiliation was represented by the Algonquian-speaking forager-gardeners, who virtually surrounded the Iroquoian-speaking farmers (figure 7.1). Many of the Algonquians, unlike their Iroquoian neighbors, grew maize, beans, and squash as dietary supplements rather than as economic staples; but there was great variability in subsistence practices, as well as political organization, among the Algonquian speakers.

Many northeastern Algonquians were mobile, foraging horticulturists who made long-term use of seasonal camps. As patrilineal extended families, these foragers fished, gathered, hunted, and practiced limited horticulture within fairly large, well-defined territorial homelands. Local groups congregated in the summer at social gatherings when rituals, such as mortuary ceremonies, were performed. In the fall they dispersed, in conjunction with seasonal availability of subsistence resources. Flexibility and diversity were overriding organizational principles for Algonquian forager-gardeners with regard to kinship, residence, and social relationships. Men played significant

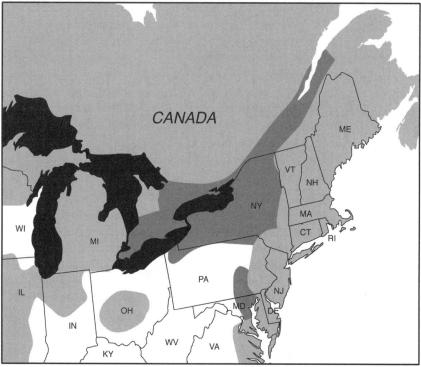

Figure 7.1. Map of Iroquoian (dark gray) and Algonquian (light gray) speakers (adapted from Goddard 1996).

roles throughout the year in providing subsistence, because hunting was such an important component of the diet. Men could not afford to spend extensive amounts of time on raiding expeditions, for fear that their families would face severe food shortages.

The flexible social strategy, mobile settlement pattern, and loose political organization led to a generally peaceful existence among family groups, with the exception of occasional homicides. Maintenance of peaceful relationships is illustrated in the way Algonquians faced potential interpersonal domestic, political, or social violence: individuals or family groups simply moved away from potential trouble. Individuals attempted to dampen or dispel tensions that might otherwise erupt into violent conflicts, but leadership was rare and ephemeral.

An important mechanism for maintaining intersocietal peace can be seen in the symbolic mortuary ritual, the Feast of the Dead. The ritual was shared among some Algonquians and some northern Iroquoians, such as the Huron; the Iroquois proper did not participate. The ceremonial occasion created bonds of fictive kinship between local- and family-group leaders, to promote and reaffirm continuing friendly intergroup alliances and relations (Hickerson 1960). The Feast of the Dead may have survived into the early contact period from a substratum of rituals once associated, throughout much of eastern North America, with Woodland-period mortuary ritual and mound-associated world-renewal ceremonialism. The primary objective of world-renewal ceremonies is to renew nature by repeating the creation acts that took place at the dawn time (Hall 1997).

The Feast of the Dead was based on intergroup concern with mourning and honoring the dead as a context for establishing, consolidating, and maintaining intersocietal alliances, cooperation, friendships, goodwill, linkages, and peace. In addition, these rites also served as opportunities to mobilize and distribute prestigious goods and wealth, which could be exchanged as gifts to strengthen interpersonal and intersocietal relations and to bind groups and individuals with one another. The Feast of the Dead was based on an international etiquette and protocol of intergroup relationships. The ritual embraced a periodic reburial program that created and perpetuated ties among dispersed local groups by displaying bone bundles of the recently deceased, which were later buried in a commonly shared grave.

The ceremony included a set of symbolic acts whose underlying primary function was the staging of imitative magic. For example, the choreographed, ritual dramatization of a war party seeking, discovering, and attacking an enemy would have been performed to recreate events from an earlier, mythic time, "re-actualizing" the past and bringing about combat success in the present world. In another demonstration of imitative magic, competitive pole climbing symbolically aided the spirits of the deceased in their efforts to gain access to the Path of Souls and the Realm of the Dead. Finally, new leaders were "raised up" through symbolic reincarnation of deceased chiefs, in which the names of dead elders and leaders were transferred to the living to perpetuate memories of the departed and their spiritual power. The Feast of the Dead also provided an important context for electing leaders, feasting, mourning the dead, arranging intergroup marriages, dancing, and establishing and strengthening political alliances. Gift-exchange and trade relationships were initiated, discussed, and solidified, all of which served to decrease intersocietal conflict. Thus, the Algonquin Feast of the Dead employed "a shared concern for mourning the dead to establish and maintain intertribal friendships and alliances" (Hall 1997:39).

The Northeast Algonquin political, ritual, and social organization, and the emphasis on peaceful relations, may be responsible for the relative lack of archaeological evidence for intersocietal conflict prior to European colonization (Chilton 2005:150). Despite the paucity of data for warfare, intermittent violence among individuals would be expected to result in some archaeological evidence of homicides or feuding, such as skeletal trauma.

The early seventeenth-century accounts of Northeast Algonquins provide a detailed depiction of indigenous patterns of cooperation and conflict. Malone (1991:9) notes that "frequent conflict and fleeting alliances linked the tribes in a dynamic system of organized violence." Feuds commonly caused conflict, with combat limited to small-scale attacks from ambush. Surprise was critical for success, as was coordination of war parties, but few participants were killed. After European contact, when raiding became commonplace, the motives in warfare were either to enlarge trapping territories or to exclude others from trade (Brasser 1978:86).

The late sixteenth century and early seventeenth century saw intersocietal conflict rapidly escalate for many Algonquian-speaking groups, as they defended themselves from encroachment and competed with other Algonquian-speakers, as well as with Iroquoian groups, over European trade goods and hunting territories. Until the early decades of the seventeenth century, the northeastern Algonquians played a major role in supplying their Huron allies with European wares, and they engaged in increasing commitments to intersocietal violence. In response to rising levels of raiding and warfare, summer camps were moved from major rivers to smaller tributaries to avoid the escalating Iroquoian raids (Day and Trigger 1978:792–93).

Iroquoian speakers, on the other hand, were noted for their relatively peaceful intravillage relations, while sustaining bellicosity and a general propensity for regional intersocietal violence. Iroquoian tribes of the Northeast, virtually surrounded by Algonquian family forager-farmers, were contemporaries of regional-polity Mississippian populations in the Midsouth, Midwest, and Southeast. Iroquoians depended on farming maize, beans, and squash, and on fishing, hunting, and gathering wild plants. They practiced *shifting horticulture*, in which large fields were planted and crops harvested for a few years until the soil eventually played out—at which time villages were relocated to more productive soils, to supply their communities with dependable and sufficient subsistence resources. Harvest, storage, and preparation of cultivated foods demanded a great deal of time on the part of both men and women; but men's agricultural field work was seasonal, which gave them extended periods for long-distance ambassadorial pursuits and raiding.

Iroquoian villagers lived in multiroom, communal longhouses organized around extended families related through women, and governed by clan matrons. A large village might contain as many as a hundred longhouses, each of which could be as long as three hundred feet, accommodating up to twenty families. Most longhouses were smaller, however, and their occupants fewer in number. Estimates for some sixteenth-century villages range from several hundred to two thousand inhabitants (Snow 1996). Villages would be occupied for twenty-five to fifty years at the most, before being abandoned when firewood and prime agricultural soils were finally depleted (Tuck 1978; figure 7.2).

Iroquois domestic and political life was governed in large part by the clan system. Kinship was organized by matrilineal clans, and residence was based on matrilocality. Clan membership defined relationships and decision making at the individual, family, village, tribe, and confederacy level. The clan established the parameters of social behavior, relationships, responsibilities, and obligations among individuals. When there were no kin connections, kinship terms were extended to individuals and to other tribes, thus defining the exact relationships and obligations of one party to the other and the respective roles each would be expected to follow in an egalitarian society lacking formal hierarchical political structures. The clan system and village and intertribal councils were the foundations of Iroquois governance. Matters of concern were brought before the council of matrons who ruled over the longhouses and the clan lineages. Other lineages within the clan would be contacted to determine whether the issue required attention at a higher level. If

Figure 7.2. Community plan of Keffer Village, Ontario (illustration by Ivan Kocsis; courtesy of Museum of Ontario Archaeology, University of Western Ontario).

the heads of the clans and the clan matrons believed that the matter was important enough to bring to the village level, then other clan leaders were informed. The clan matrons were "the soul of the councils, the arbiter of peace and war" (Lafitau 1974:69). The matron leaders in turn notified members of the village moiety about important issues, and the concerned moiety then deliberated until a consensus was reached (Brandão 1997:27–28; 2003).

Women played an important role in these decisions. The matrons, as representatives of their clans, could request that raids be carried out if their clan members had been killed or insulted by an enemy. The matrons could also forestall an attack or request that an attack not be made in cases where war would be detrimental to the tribe or League. However, because of the egalitarian nature of the Iroquois and other tribes in the Northeast, if an individual, family, or, in some cases, tribe of the League wished to ignore the clan matron's or League council's decision, then they could do so, and occasionally did—particularly in the case of a revenge raid (Brandão 1997).

When the topic was war, a clan war leader was invited to participate in the moiety or village deliberations. If the tribal council agreed that the matter under consideration merited the participation of other villages or tribes, clan representatives delivered the agreed-upon message to the confederacy level, where the issue would be taken up. Connecting clan linkages among villages and other tribes was an important component of the business of decision making. "In short, clan leaders, using a complex system of personal contacts, relationships, and diplomacy, ran 'local' and 'national' councils. At village, tribe, and confederacy levels, these councils were the government of the Iroquois" (Brandão 1997:29).

Councils, composed of male village elders and female clan matrons, made decisions to wage war or offer peace in order to carry out political decisions made in the national councils. National, or council-initiated, raids differed from personal or small raiding parties, "petite or private wars," in that requests for personal revenge raids could be made by a clan matron to a warrior or war captain to avenge the death of a relative. The warrior, without council deliberations, was then free to choose the group to attack, and to decide which warriors would be asked to join the raid. Once the council determined war was justified, the war leaders then deliberated among themselves, informing the council of their decision to wage war or not, or to extend peace or not.

The war leaders and peace ambassadors were responsible for the conduct of their missions and for enlisting recruitments. Emissaries might be deployed to other villages and tribes, requesting that their representatives attend the war- or peace-council deliberations. If war was agreed upon, then a date would be set for the raid, and the war leaders would return to their villages or tribes to begin preparations, including the recruitment of volunteers. If peace was agreed upon, then the emissaries would negotiate until the respective parties agreed upon the terms.

Prior to a raid, the war leader feasted the enlisted warriors at his longhouse, where they painted themselves, sang their war songs, danced the war dance, and prayed to the deities and ancestors for divine aid and intervention (Brandão 1997:33). The warrior's "war kit" consisted of a bow and a set of arrows, a war club, a knife, ropes with which to tie captives, extra moccasins, a small pot, a shield, protective armor, and a mat. In the historic period, Iroquois warriors could travel up to fifty miles a day and raid five or six hundred miles away from their town, while hunting, fishing, or gathering along the way. Warriors attacked only when they could surprise their enemies. Attack was initiated by a volley of arrows, after which they rushed into the enemy settlement with clubs for hand-to-hand combat, knives for scalping, and ropes for securing prisoners (Brandão 1997:34–35).

Matrilineal societies, such as the Iroquois, could field large contingents of warriors because of their large population sizes. Warriors could remain away from their village for long periods of time after the spring planting and before the fall harvest, because men were freed from many of the domestic and economic responsibilities. Women spent great amounts of time on domestic activities and on cultivating, tending and harvesting crops, which allowed men to make extended raids away from the village in pursuit of alliances or war (figure 7.3). In conflict with foragers such as the Algonquians, differences in subsistence strategies gave the Iroquois a distinct advantage in warfare, particularly in prolonged conflicts. Military advantage was further enhanced by the potential of tribes to form alliances with defensive or offensive coalition allies, as exemplified in the relatively weak confederations of the Eries, Huron, Iroquois, and Neutrals (Snow 2007). The League of the Iroquois, which formed in the late sixteenth century (Kuhn and Sempowski 2001), was so successful that it had defeated all neighboring tribes and confederacies by the end of the seventeenth century.

Warfare prior to the arrival of Europeans, at least for the Iroquois proper, may have been no less violent than after Western contact (Abler 1989; Brandão 1997). There is archaeological evidence for pervasive conflict beginning in the fifteenth century in the Northeast (Keener 1998:78), as tribal groups fought among themselves and with their Algonquian neighbors. Self-perpetuating, institutionalized feuding prior to European contact was an important element in shaping demographic structure, political orientation, settlement patterns, and social and domestic

Figure 7.3. Keffer Village, Ontario (illustration by Ivan Kocsis; courtesy of Museum of Ontario Archaeology, University of Western Ontario).

organization (Richter 1983; Trigger 1967:154). Raids seem to have been waged primarily for captives, prestige, and revenge (Snow 2007; Williamson 2007).

Escalated raiding or warfare may date to as early as AD 900, with the origin of the Owasco tradition (AD 900–1300; Keener 1998:65). Pre-Owasco sites were widely dispersed across the landscape, as small, seasonal encampments usually situated along streams and rivers. With the onset of the Owasco tradition, the foraging settlement pattern began to change from small camps on major rivers to compact villages on defendable terrain away from major transportation routes, suggesting the rise of warfare at the end of the first millennium (Snow 1995).

Warfare was an important element of the Owasco tradition (Snow 2001), and internecine warfare in the Northeast is believed to have originated at that time, based on archaeological evidence of arrow-riddled burials, cannibalism, defensive palisades, and trophy-taking behavior (Snow 1996). Small-scale raiding dates to an earlier period, as Late Archaic human remains have been found with dart points embedded in them (Milner 1995:232), but conflict increased significantly after AD 900, and reached a high level after AD 1450. Iroquois populations during the Owasco tradition practiced maize agriculture, possessed matrilineal kinship and matrilocal residence systems, lived in large compact villages, and pursued violent warfare that increased in intensity over time (Snow 1994). The growing importance of agriculture (Hart and Means 2002) during the Medieval Warm period (AD 700–1200) (Chilton 2005:145) is associated with palisaded villages and the development of an increasingly sedentary lifestyle. Sedentarization, for Iroquoian populations, "appears to have been a very complex process, slow and asynchronous" (Chapdelaine 1993:201).

While many of the early Owasco settlements were unfortified, the shift to more compact villages, located on defensive terrain away from major transportation routes, has been interpreted as a general concern about external threats (Snow 1994). By AD 1200 most Owasco villages were protected by palisades, some with exterior ditches (Chilton 2005). During the fourteenth century, the frequency of well-planned, heavily palisaded villages increased throughout Iroquoia, as warfare continued to intensify (Snow 1994). Efforts at alliances and peace relations among local groups would have been fostered through diplomacy, feasting, gift exchange, mortuary rituals, and strategic intermarriages to forestall raids or strengthen one's defensive or offensive capabilities. Formerly separate but allied communities began to relocate and amalgamate for defense into fewer and larger settlements (Williamson 2007). Trophy-taking behavior and ritual cannibalism appeared as part of the restructuring and transformation of religious beliefs that gave rise to a highly ritualized system of mourning, revenge, and adoption (Richter 1983:533–34). Sixteenth- and seventeenth-century ethnohistoric accounts augment archaeological evidence for the pursuit of peace and war among Iroquoian speakers, especially the Huron and members of the League of the Iroquois.

The goal of traditional warfare was elimination and total defeat of an enemy; but northeastern tribes prior to the sixteenth century were largely unsuccessful in destroying their enemies, because of strong village fortifications, elaborate alliances, and weak offensive confederacies. Stalemates promoted and intensified the cyclic nature of revenge warfare because enemies were unlikely to be effectively eliminated (Keener 1998:89). With the introduction of European axes and muskets in the mid-seventeenth century, however, the goals of traditional warfare became reality.

Societies reward aggressive, warlike behavior for the useful functions it performs for the social and political group, not for its own sake (Newcomb 1950:320). In Iroquoian society, revenge and prestige were primary motors that drove intersocietal warfare. Based on the important social premise widely shared by Iroquoians that any death was the result of a conscious act by some evil-doer, the appropriate social response was revenge, which had the potential to continue in unabated cycles of violence (Snow 2007). Demands of mourning required the replacement of any individual who had died, even of natural causes. Exceptions were those who had drowned or had been killed in raids. Warriors who carried out successful revenge raids earned praise, prestige, and social advancement:

> Participation in a war party was a benchmark episode in an Iroquois youth's development, and later success in battle increased the young man's stature in his clan and village. His prospects for an advantageous marriage, his chances for recognition as a village leader, and his hopes for eventual selection to a sachemship depended largely—though by no means entirely—on his skill on the warpath, his munificence in giving war feasts, and his ability to attract followers when organizing a raid. (Richter 1983:530)

The prevailing social and political currency in seventeenth-century Iroquoia was prestige, which could be acquired through "generosity, bravery, and diplomatic acumen" (Snow 2007). To marry a desirable young woman in a strongly matrilineal society, or to be selected as a village or council leader, a warrior had to accumulate prestige (Snow 2007), and warfare and raiding for captives were important ways of earning that prestige. Failure to gain honor would result in a loss of prestige, reputation, and respect. For example, young men related by marriage to bereaved clan matrons or lineage relations were obliged to form raiding parties for revenge and capture of captives, or else they would be humiliated by the matrons' scorn and accusations of cowardice (Richter 1983:532).

Warfare before the contact period would have been intermittent, an individual's death sparking a raid to avenge that death. "Warfare was a specific and sporadic response to the death of specific individuals at specific times, a sporadic affair characterized by seizing from traditional enemies a few captives who would replace the dead, literally or symbolically, and ease the pain of those who mourned" (Richter 1983:536). Warfare and the taking of captives was a social integrating mechanism and an integral part of individual and social mourning practices. Precombat rituals illustrate the emphasis placed on captives. The boiling war kettle and subsequent war feast foreshadowed the return of the war party and its cannibalistic rites. During precombat rituals, women who mourned relatives cajoled warriors to bring them prisoners so their grief might be assuaged and their tears dried. During the precombat ritual, allied tribal leaders agreed on the appropriate division of captives among the respective towns (Richter 1983:535).

The mourning war influenced and shaped military strategy and tactics in at least two ways, based on the demands of Iroquoian society. First, a war party's success was determined by its ability to seize prisoners, bring them alive to the village, and distribute them among the mourners. Second, as was the case throughout eastern North America, there were strong sanctions against the loss of lives in combat. Casualties undermined the purpose of the mourning war as a means of restocking Iroquois villages. A warrior killed in a raid, like all who died violent deaths, was believed to be excluded from the Realm of the Dead and doomed to spend an eternity seeking his own form of revenge. The Iroquois considered a warrior who fell in combat to remain apart from his family and friends not only in burial, but also in the next life (Richter 1983:534–35). In light of these considerations, Iroquois war parties minimized fatalities while maximizing success. A war party's failure resulted in social disgrace and humiliation for the war leader and the war party members.

Iroquoian warriors took calculated tactical approaches to increase their chances of survival and ensure success in raids. From an offensive perspective, both large and small war parties relied on ambushes and surprise attacks. They chose smaller-sized groups to attack so they would have the advantage of larger forces. In addition, they carefully avoided frontal assaults on fortified places and engaging the enemy if they were outnumbered. To defend themselves at home, they maintained a network of spies in enemy villages. A matrix of scouts warned of invading war parties, enabling village defenders to attack from ambush. In the event of an attack on their village, the inhabitants retreated behind palisades; but if the enemy appeared too strong for effective resistance, villagers often burned their own settlements and fled into the woods, or to neighboring villages with whom they had previous alliances. When at a disadvantage, they preferred flight or an insincerely negotiated truce to avoid costly stands that would result in unnecessary loss of life (Richter 1983:536).

A small group of five to twenty warriors was the preferred size for a raiding party, but large-scale raids, in which one to five hundred warriors could be involved, were organized on the village, nation, and confederacy levels. In rare cases, a thousand or more warriors would form coalitions of several villages and tribes for joint raids on enemies (Brandão 1997; Trigger 1990). Members of the deceased's household usually did not participate in raids that sought revenge for the deceased (Richter 1983:532).

Preferred combat weapons included bows, war clubs, and knives. Wooden body armor was effective against flint arrow points, but was quickly abandoned upon European contact when metal arrow points and particularly muskets made armor obsolete. When attacking an enemy, warriors used bows and arrows first; this was followed by hand-to-hand combat with war clubs; and, finally, knives were employed for scalping and dismemberment. Raiders fought until one group fled, surrendered, or was wiped out. In the first decade

of the seventeenth century, Champlain noted relatively bloodless battles between massed confrontations of warriors. Battles composed of large numbers
of warriors were quickly but momentarily abandoned, however, in favor of re-
doubled emphasis on small-scale raids and ambushes once muskets were introduced into the suite of weaponry (Richter 1983:538).

When warriors returned with captured men, women, and children,
mourners selected a prisoner for adoption to replace a recently deceased individual. Or, if they desired, the family might vent their rage through torture,
execution, and cannibalism. The fate of prisoners captured by Iroquois warriors was decided by family members (Brandão 1997; Keener 1998:81). Upon
seizure the captive might be killed immediately and either beheaded or
scalped; but with the emphasis on population replacement, this option might
take place only if more captives were taken than could be safely returned to
the home village. If kept alive, captives would be brought back and exhibited
in the victorious village as war trophies. The face and hair of captives and
the scalps of victims alike were painted red to symbolize their physical and
spiritual adoption, respectively. Captives could either be adopted to maintain
population levels or tortured to satisfy family members and war deities. If
they were tortured as a sacrifice to a supernatural, then the ceremonial per-
formance resulted in dismemberment and ritual cannibalism.

Wallace (1972:101) summarizes the victim's possible modes of treatment
upon defeat and subsequent capture:

> The common aim of all war parties was to bring back persons to replace the
> mourned-for dead. This could be done in three ways: by bringing back the
> scalp of a dead enemy (this scalp might even be put through an adoption cer-
> emony); by bringing back a live prisoner (to be adopted, tortured, and killed);
> or by bringing back a live prisoner to be allowed to live and even to replace in
> a social role the one whose death had called for this "revenge."

Human remains resulting from trophy taking and cannibalism have been
found in archaeological midden deposits. Ritual cannibalism, perhaps signaling the beginning of "mourning warfare" in the archaeological record in the
fourteenth century, involved the consumption of a victim's flesh or organs as
a way to acquire the courage, power, and strength of an enemy warrior (Trigger 1990). Cannibalism, as an important component of Iroquois prisoner sacrifice, resulted in split, cut, and cooked human bones (Abler 1980; Engelbrecht 2003). By the sixteenth century, as warfare accelerated, village
middens contained substantial quantities of human bone and artifacts manufactured from human bone.

Iroquois Ambassadors

To establish and maintain alliances and peaceful relations, the Iroquoians appointed men held in high esteem to serve as peace ambassadors. These men, who possessed great prestige and had garnered high respect through their service and bravery, served their villages and confederacies as representatives, traveling unarmed and unprotected into enemy villages. Peace ambassadors were chosen as emissaries because of their importance as leaders within Iroquoian society; because of the prestige, respect, and danger inherent in the role; and to convince the enemy of the sincerity of the efforts at peace. Important leaders had to be involved in the peace process to make agreements binding.

To kill an Iroquois peace representative was a serious affront that could spark a war or, if warfare was ongoing, intensify attacks against the transgressors. Every major conflict during the second half of the seventeenth century was either initiated or intensified by the capturing or killing of Iroquois peace ambassadors. Unarmed Iroquois emissaries provided easy targets for revenge, and their murder served to make the Iroquois lose face among the community of warring tribes. The loss of well-respected leaders would be a crucial blow to any village. Hence, the Iroquois rarely mistreated peace representatives from other groups.

In eastern North America, trophy-taking behavior was chartered through myths that told of great power awarded by supernaturals to deserving warriors if they followed the supernatural's dictates to obtain human trophies. In the case of Iroquoian speakers, the supernatural Oscotarach (Pierce-Head) occupied a lodge on the Path of Souls, the route taken by souls to reach the Realm of the Dead. Oscotarach drew the brains out of the heads of the dead and kept them (Thwaites 1896–1901, 10:147).

Trophy-taking behavior, manifested in the taking of heads and other body parts, began in about AD 1000 and intensified around AD 1300 (Williamson 2007). Taking heads and scalps is a form of soul capture (Hammel cited in Engelbrecht 2003:43). A widely held belief in eastern North America maintained that "the spirit of a slain warrior was controlled by his slayer" (Hall 1997:134). As live enemies were adopted and acculturated into the matriclans, so too were enemies' spirits adopted through their body parts, especially heads and scalps. Potential adoptive captives, the scalps of dead enemies, and the status of the dead family member being mourned were all equated symbolically through the use of red paint in adoption rituals (Hall 1997:34).

Taking captives was especially important for the renewal of spiritual power. When a person died, especially an important leader such as a clan matron, village leader, or council ambassador, the spiritual power of the lineage, clan, and nation was reduced in proportion to the spiritual strength of the person who had died or who had been killed. In an effort to replenish the depleted power resulting from the death, the Iroquois conducted mourning raids to find suitable candidates for potential adoption. Vacant positions in Iroquois families and villages literally and symbolically remained unoccupied until they were replaced by captives taken in such raids. Transference of the departed's spiritual energy, embodied in the individual's name, to a captive insured that the continuity of Iroquois society was safeguarded, the tears of the mourners were dried, and the social role and spiritual strength of loved ones were assured (Richter 1983:530–31). As population levels plummeted in the mid-seventeenth century, the Iroquois desperately fielded war parties in efforts to replace family members and to maintain the status quo of household, clan, and village spiritual strength.

Warfare was endemic in the Northeast beginning at the turn of the first millennium, and warriors had to be prepared to defend their villages and territory. In addition, they had to have the capability of repelling attacks. Iroquoian society dictated that warriors were expected to be fearless, self-reliant, and uncomplaining. They had to carry out the requests of the clan matrons for revenge raids and be unyielding in their pursuit of captives. Warfare provided warriors with opportunities for social and political currency, prestige, honor, leadership, and revenge (Brandão 1997; Snow 2007). Traditional Iroquoian warfare was complex, being based on many intertwined goals and motives that reinforced and complemented one another (Keener 1998).

The Iroquois strove to maintain peace, but tribal raiding could be initiated based on perceived provocations, real or imagined slights, public insults, trespassing on Iroquois territory, or the taking of Iroquois members as prisoners or hostages. If a warrior was insulted by a member of a tribe with whom the Iroquois were at peace, he was within his rights in killing the person, even if it meant the dissolution of the peace agreement (Brandão 1997). Large-scale raids and attacks could also be initiated by killing a single individual, particularly if the person were a well-respected clan matron, council ambassador, or tribal leader. While peace could be negotiated and established with a long-time enemy, Iroquois warriors "remembered every past transgression and the slightest insult or misunderstanding could result in the renewal of hostilities" (Keener 1998:82).

Iroquois peace negotiations began, and frequently consisted entirely of, condolence ceremonies and gift exchange to assuage the grief of family and tribal members. Peace was possible only when war ended and grief was forgotten (Richter 1983:536–37). The League of the Iroquois was known as the "Great Peace" because the original five participating nations, symbolically considered as five families occupying compartments in a longhouse of five fires, were encouraged to settle homicides by negotiation and compensation (Hall 1997:39). Blood revenge prompted by homicides would easily escalate to unremitting cycles of feuding and violence. Several Iroquoian tribes attempted to curtail the potential for intertribal conflict and violence by forming a league in the late sixteenth or early seventeenth century (Kuhn and Sempowski 2001). In a cultural pattern that predated European contact, violence and warfare were conceived as the natural state of the world; peace had to be constantly tended and repeatedly renewed if it was to prevail (Snow 2007). Iroquois restraint is evident on several occasions in the post-European contact period, when they attempted to maintain peace, even after being attacked (Keener 1998:82).

There were few opportunities for peace in Iroquois society. It was not until all the grief suffered by the various families was assuaged and all the tears from their eyes had dried that peace could prevail. Demands for revenge based on the social premise that deaths were the result of an enemy's evil actions not only explains the high frequency of violence as compared to the maintaining of trade and diplomatic relations (Snow 2007), but also underscores the inability of even the most gifted ambassadors to stop blood feuding among tribal societies (Otterbein 1994).

Two major aspects of European contact pushed Iroquoian warfare in new directions in the seventeenth century: European-induced disease, and the introduction of firearms and hatchets. After the 1620s, sustained European contact dramatically transformed the role of warfare in Iroquois culture. As thousands died from epidemic diseases, ever-growing numbers of captives were required for Iroquois families who desperately sought to replace their losses. Mourning wars of unprecedented scale loomed ahead. Warfare in the seventeenth century became "a constant and increasingly undifferentiated symptom of societies in demographic crisis" (Richter 1983:537). Demands for captives, requests for revenge, and requirements for war honors and warrior prestige combined to produce a "paroxysm of warfare" (Snow 2007). Although Iroquois warfare was based on defensive reactions to the aggression of their enemies, once a conflict was initiated the Iroquois adopted an offensive warfare strategy (Keener 1998:214).

The period from 1640 to 1660 was a critical time in northeastern tribal warfare. Traditional defenses, weapons, and warfare strategies were affected by new technology and ideas. New and effective weapons included iron axes, muskets, counterpalisades, and shields, as well as unique assault tactics designed to destroy villages and capture or kill the inhabitants. A rapid escalation in warfare tactics also took place. The Iroquois of the 1640s and 1650s bore new weapons and used various new battle tactics in attacking their foes, whom they put on the defensive, launching an ever-increasing barrage of effective attacks (Keener 1998:215). Through the military successes of the 1650s and 1660s, the Iroquois greatly expanded their territorial claims. The unintentional but devastating impact of Eastern Hemisphere diseases further brought about changes in the pursuit of war and peace.

The first epidemic diseases introduced from the Eastern Hemisphere spread across Iroquoia in the fourth decade of the seventeenth century. The initial recorded smallpox epidemic killed approximately 60 percent of the inhabitants in the villages it reached in 1634, triggering a sudden burst of grief and revenge that prompted a backlash of death, destruction, and captive taking. In retaliation, the Iroquois destroyed the Huron and Petuns by 1651, defeated the Neutrals by 1653, and vanquished the Eries by 1656 (Snow 1994:115–16). In 1675, the Susquehannock were forced from Pennsylvania south into Maryland. Those who were not tortured and killed as scapegoats for the epidemics were incorporated into Iroquois communities as replacements for lost relatives. Captives who could acculturate quickly, especially women and children, became Iroquois citizens who repopulated the decimated villages. Through the process of forced acculturation of captives, the Seneca, for example, were able to maintain a population level of approximately four thousand individuals throughout the seventeenth century (Snow 1994:110). By the mid-1660s French priests estimated that two-thirds or more of the people in many Iroquois villages were captive adoptees (Richter 1983:541). Iroquois warriors were so successful in war, and captured so many prisoners who were later adopted, that they were able to recoup their losses from diseases. The Iroquois continued raiding in order to reduce enemy populations while attempting to stabilize their own (Keener 1998:94).

By the 1640s, most enemies of the Iroquois lived in fortified villages out of fear born of recent attacks and capture of inhabitants. In order for the Iroquois to defeat or disperse their enemies in the mid-sixteenth century, they had to attack and breach village defenses. The tactical Achilles' heel in attacking a village was the approach to the defensive wall, during which the offensive force could incur unacceptably high casualties in the "field of fire" (Brice 1984), the cleared area around a fortified village, which provided defenders unobstructed aim at attackers (Bradford 1988:166). In response to these heavy casualties, the Iroquois developed new tactics that helped reduce mortalities during assaults on fortifications. In the 1650s they constructed moveable barrier walls and protective shields, so warriors would be safe from musket fire during the approach and breach of the outer wall. The protective walls and defensive shields were constructed of thick pieces of wood capable of withstanding musket fire. These devices were successful when the enemies fortified their settlements with oval walls without flanking bastions.

When flanking bastions were added to a village's defensive fortifications, the Iroquois again changed their tactics, by avoiding fortified towns and concentrating attacks outside the village: laying sieges, deploying hit-and-run raids, destroying unprotected settlements, burning crops, disrupting supply lines, and ambushing reinforcements. These attacks caused the enemy to be in a constant state of defense and terror, severely limiting their offensive capabilities. Targeting crops was a deliberate strategy to destroy an enemy's food supply and promote submission through starvation. Small raiding groups stationed themselves along transportation routes and attacked inside enemy territory. They killed from positions of ambush, taking as many captives as possible—a signature strategy of the Iroquois throughout the seventeenth century (Keener 1998:93–96).

One of the most important items traded to the Iroquois may have been the iron hatchet, which came to be an invaluable weapon for attacking strongly built wooden palisades. The Iroquois utilized two hundred to one thousand warriors in massed attacks storming village fortifications. To reduce "field of fire" casualties, they breached the outer wall as quickly as possible. Once the outer wall was reached, warriors fired through loopholes into the interior of the village, while other attackers hacked at the base of the palisade with sharp-edged European hatchets to create an opening. Once the wall had been breached, warriors then rushed in to kill or capture the defenders (Keener 1998:90–91).

Guns quickly augmented Iroquois use of bows and arrows, as muskets provided considerable advantage over enemy forces who possessed few if any firearms. Iroquois proximity to Dutch traders and trade goods gave the Iroquois a critical advantage over their enemies in acquiring weaponry. By the 1640s, the Mohawk had approximately three hundred guns, and within some twenty years all Iroquois tribes and many Algonquians were armed with muskets. Once the Iroquois became well armed and proficient with guns, they demonstrated the gun's inherent superiority over traditional weaponry. For example, the Iroquois had great success in using muskets in surprise attacks against Algonquian and Huron canoe fleets that traveled the Ottawa and St. Lawrence Rivers (Otterbein 1964).

The introduction of guns and metal arrow points greatly increased the chances of death in combat and led to a major reorientation in Iroquois tactical warfare (Richter 1983:538). Guns provided two advantages over bow-and-arrow technology: penetrating power and shock value. When guns were used as shock weapons against warriors unfamiliar with them, musket fire could have a devastating impact on an opponent's morale. Native wooden armor, while protective against stone-tipped arrows, could be pierced by musket balls and metal arrow points. Muskets nullified the defensive strategy of "dodging the arrow" witnessed by early French observers (Abler 1989:274–75).

Throughout the 1640s, the Iroquois were successful in attacks against their traditional enemies. Iroquois confidence rose as their enemies suffered great losses, resulting in their capture, destruction, or dispersion. Only enemies armed with muskets and well-constructed, flanked village defenses could effectively defend themselves against Iroquois attacking forces. Territorial claims were greatly enlarged between 1650 and 1684 as a result of the military successes provided by new tactics, metal hatchets, and muskets (Kenner 1998:208).

In the mid-seventeenth century the Iroquois Confederacy had acquired new weaponry and tactics, and this set member tribes apart from other Iroquoian groups in how they conducted warfare; but the motives for warfare still remained fundamentally the same as in the precontact period (Keener 1998:213). The Iroquois utilized more successful and more flexible warfare strategies than their opponents, and developed unique battle tactics that their enemies did not emulate, including organizing and coordinating small ("petite") and large ("national") war parties that could engage in hit-and-run attacks as well as assaults on heavily fortified villages (Otterbein 1979).

The new technology and tactics were employed with deadly efficiency. As the Iroquois destroyed one enemy village after another through direct assaults and harassing hit-and-run raids, the enemy's morale over time was weakened, eroded, and finally shattered. As Iroquois confidence increased, so too did their attacks, resulting in the ultimate destruction of their enemies. Once the opportunity presented itself, the Iroquois could not resist the temptation to fulfill their ancient desires for revenge and increased opportunities for prestige and respect (Keener 1998).

Unlike traditional warfare, where raids typically took place in the summer and early fall, the Iroquois intensified their attacks to harass their enemies throughout the year. Hit-and-run raids by small numbers of warriors were augmented by direct attacks of five hundred to one thousand warriors against fortified villages, which placed the enemy under constant stress. The Iroquois, unlike other Iroquoian communities, were able to organize and coordinate large groups of warriors from all tribes of the League for year-round offensive campaigns. The Huron, on the other hand, were unable to field large numbers of warriors because of tribal divisions and population losses from diseases that were not recouped by captives (Trigger 1990).

War parties had to range ever further in their quest for captives because the tactical advantage provided by guns more or less evaporated by the 1660s and 1670s, as firearms came into general use throughout Iroquoia. By 1675, European diseases and firearms had produced new patterns of conflict that threatened to derange the traditional functions of the mourning war. By the 1680s, Iroquois opponents became better armed with muskets; and the incorporation of new fortification tactics such as flanking walls enabled them to defend or defeat Iroquois forces more frequently. Some of the lands the Iroquois had formally conquered were regained as a result of enemy successes (Keener 1998:97).

The mourning war complex, however, was beginning to unravel by the late 1670s. Warfare was failing to maintain a stable population through captives, and traditional "customs regarding the treatment of prisoners were decaying as ritual degenerated into chaotic violence and sheer murderous rage displaced the orderly adoption of captives that the logic of the mourning-war demanded" (Richter 1983:543). In the decades from 1680 to 1701, the Iroquois were involved in devastating warfare throughout Iroquoia against French forces, Canadian militia, and their Native allies.

By 1700, the Anglo-French struggle for control of the continent made warfare as the Iroquois were practicing it dangerously dysfunctional for their society. Iroquois warfare and culture at the end of the seventeenth century had reached a turning point. Up to about 1675, despite the impact of disease and firearms, warfare still performed functions that outweighed its costs; but thereafter, the Anglo-French struggle for control of North America made war disastrous for the Iroquois. The mourning war was no longer even symbolically restocking the spiraling population decline. The heavy death toll of the previous decades had robbed the Iroquois of many respected headmen and clan matrons to whom the people had looked for guidance and arbitration of disputes. Mourning wars were no longer socially integrative, nor functionally viable (Richter 1983:551).

In "The Grand Settlement of 1701" and other treaties in the first decade of the eighteenth century, the Iroquois agreed to keep peace and acknowledged their inability to prevail militarily over their French and their allied Native American enemies (Havard 2001). The peace settlement lasted for the next forty years, but even by the 1720s hit-and-run raids were again binding Iroquois families and villages together as renewed conflict "provided enough captives for occasional mourning and condolence rituals that dried Iroquois tears and reminded the Five Nations of their superiority over their enemies" (Richter 1983:559).

CHAPTER EIGHT

Cooperation and Conflict in the Upper Midwest

As we know, social systems both create and resolve hostility; we need to be sure we know which side of the process we are on as we interpret the remains of prehistory.

(Brashler et al. 2000:569)

A variety of distinct Late Woodland groups began to appear throughout the Upper Midwest by around AD 700, gradually adopting key cultural characteristics that enable archaeologists to distinguish one local or tribal-like group from another. Societies with Upper Mississippian characteristics emerged from a Late Woodland base, as maize agriculture was intensified and added to existing native eastern North American garden crops. In addition, social organization changed as these mobile hunters and gatherers increasingly became sedentary agriculturists.

Upper Mississippian societies had a broadly shared, generalized culture, characterized by shell-tempered pottery and dependence on field agriculture. Unlike Middle Mississippian polities to the south, Upper Mississippian archaeological sites do not have ritual centers, great plazas, or temple mounds (Hall 2004:98). By European contact, Upper Mississippian groups were distributed over a wide area of the Upper Midwest, from northern Illinois to southwestern Minnesota, and westward to the central Missouri valley (Henning 1998). Site composition varied from hamlets of a few wigwamlike dwellings to large villages. Political and social organization was relatively egalitarian: each village or community had the same level of power and influence, unlike in Middle Mississippian societies, whose hamlets, villages, and towns were ranked under one polity.

Profound cultural changes began to take place in the Upper Mississippi Valley between AD 900 and 1150, when a number of distinctive groups began to exhibit increased levels of social interaction and military competition. One of these culture complexes, Oneota, formed around AD 1000 and is identified primarily by the presence of characteristic shell-tempered pottery. Settlements thrived alongside numerous and diverse Late Woodland groups (Oversteet 1995), with generally small sites that were sometimes fenced or lightly palisaded, and occupied by only a few families. Subsistence, although with increased dependence on corn, was a continuation of earlier Late Woodland practices.

After AD 1000, during the Medieval Warming, summers grew warmer and somewhat moister in the Upper Midwest, and winters increasingly drier, extending the agricultural season (Brose 2001:51). Increased agricultural productivity in the early second millennium was a function not only of warmer climates, but also of individual and corporate-group decision-making policies, information sharing, field-allocation procedures, and responses to demands for increased surplus.

From the middle of the twelfth century to the end of the fourteenth century, Oneota societies underwent a period of expansion and encroachment throughout the Upper Midwest (figure 8.1). Villages remained comparable in size to earlier settlements and were seasonally relocated, being positioned near a diversity of resources (Gibbon 1982). Many Upper Midwest local groups experienced violent conflict or the threat of violence, as Oneota groups spread throughout the Eastern Plains and Midwest, encroaching into territories of their neighbors.

Oneota expansion varied according to the ways in which each culture-contact situation played out, but it was usually associated with some form of conflict conducted over relatively short distances. Over time, local groups gradually invaded, acquired, and settled neighboring territories. Some of these groups were eventually absorbed by their expanding neighbors, while others fled and some stood their ground. These latter populations were destroyed, pushed out, or absorbed. Military strategies ranged from violence and intimidation to acculturation and alliance building. Intersocietal conflict from the middle of the twelfth century to the end of the fourteenth century might be described as a kind of *encroachment conflict*. The nature of the conflicts and the responses of the belligerent groups differed by region and the historical and cultural circumstances of each contact situation (Hollinger 2005).

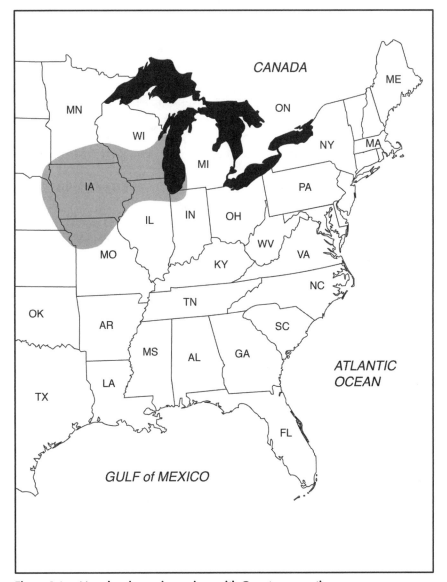

Figure 8.1. **Map showing major regions with Oneota occupation.**

Late in the twelfth century, Aztalan and related sites of eastern Wisconsin were abandoned by Middle Mississippian populations, perhaps because of conflict with nearby Oneota groups. Aztalan was heavily fortified with a substantial bastioned and plaster-covered palisade, and the interior was compartmentalized by a complex arrangement of secondary palisade lines (Birmingham and

Goldstein 2005). Evidence for conflict is seen in cannibalism and trophy-taking behavior, and the conflagration of large sections of the palisade, some of the houses, and a charnel structure. Charnel houses or ancestor shrines were favored targets in Mississippian warfare, and their conflagration is often associated with palisades destroyed by fire and burned houses in village areas (Dye and King 2007). By AD 1200, the Middle Mississippian and Late Woodland inhabitants of eastern Wisconsin appear to have been forced out or absorbed: "Warfare . . . soon led to merging of Late Woodland groups for defense against expanding Oneota populations who finally drove Woodland peoples from Wisconsin by A.D. 1200," and "eastern Wisconsin was securely in the hands of Oneota peoples by A.D. 1300 and Late Woodland and Middle Mississippian populations had abandoned the region" (Hollinger 2005:142).

Sites in the Upper Mississippi valley, such as the Wever site (AD 1250–1350) located in eastern Iowa (Hollinger 2005), have produced human remains found in refuse pits. Hollinger believes the remains are those of males and females who were executed captives, as village residents would have been buried in cemetery areas. Isolated bones, also recovered from refuse pits, reveal evidence of cultural modification and trophy-taking behavior, such as scalping and tooth removal. Also at this time, materialized ideology associated with warfare is seen in ceramic motifs that depict the Thunderers (Benn 1989). The representations of Thunderers on ceramics "reveals a deeply rooted, widely accepted ideology that was dominated by supernatural beings associated with war" (Hollinger 2005:122) (figure 8.2). These vessels may have been used for the preparation of ritual medicines used in ceremonies associated with alliances, diplomacy, and warfare.

By the end of the twelfth century, Fort Ancient, Iroquois, Middle Mississippian, Langford, and Oneota populations had developed materially identifiable cultural traditions and were expanding at the peril of their neighbors. Although social groups contemporaneous with Oneota settlements shared many of the same economic, political, and social characteristics, only a few had a flexible organization that "promoted their survival by either displacing or incorporating their neighbors from frontier zones" (Brose 2000:110). The flexibility of the Oneota cultural pattern gave them a decided advantage over their more socially or economically specialized competitors. Oneota society was relatively broad based and generalized, providing the flexibility to adapt to varying economic, environmental, and social situations. Such adaptability facilitated the formation of new political alliances and the practice of intense warfare (Hollinger 2005).

Groups who opposed aggression either yielded territory by withdrawing from conflict, or stood and fought for their territory and villages. Those latter

Figure 8.2. Bison scapula tool with engraved human image missing feet, hands, and head, Correctionville site (13WD6–2), Woodbury County, Iowa (courtesy of Dale R. Henning).

communities fortified their villages, a process involving significant invest-
ments of resources and labor. Warriors might respond to the fortified villages
of their enemies by shifting their tactics to ones that stressed mobile attacks.
The majority of such engagements involved ambushing work parties some distance from village "safe zones" (Milner 1998a). Massacres of village populations sometimes took place during opportune moments when defenses were
momentarily down or populations were debilitated through starvation or disease (Willey 1990; Willey and Emerson 1993). Successful raiding could
weaken an enemy while strengthening attackers, as warriors increased their
prestige and social status through military victories. Captives could be
adopted, replacing individuals who had recently died or had been killed or
captured through raiding, or they could be killed through torture and mutilation (Starna and Watkins 1991).

During the thirteenth century, Oneota communities expanded throughout the eastern plains, midwestern prairies, and northern woodlands of the
Upper Mississippi Valley, replacing or displacing non-Oneota peoples. Archaeological evidence of intersocietal conflict associated with these expan-
sions includes evidence of alliance formation, burned settlements, combat
symbolism, fortified villages, massacres, shifts in settlement patterns, skeletal
trauma, and trophy taking. From southeastern Minnesota, southwestern Wisconsin, northwestern Illinois, and perhaps the central Illinois valley and
other areas in the tenth century, Oneota populations had expanded by the
fourteenth century to an area reaching from central Indiana to north-central
Kansas, and from west-central Illinois to Michigan's Upper Peninsula
(Hollinger 2005).

Oneota expansion and encroachment into neighboring, non-Oneota territories often had disastrous consequences for the Oneota and their neighbors. For example, an Oneota village along the central Illinois River in east-
central Illinois documents the devastating effects of repeated ambushes on a
"front-line" population by neighboring Middle Mississippian populations
(Milner et al. 1991a, 1991b; Milner 1999). The Norris Farms 36 Oneota
cemetery and village (Santure et al. 1990) was occupied for only a few
decades around AD 1300, but it documents the high level of conflict and violence in the early fourteenth century.

Many of the individuals buried in the village cemetery mound had died violent deaths. Of the 264 individuals interred in the cemetery (about 16 percent of the total population), approximately one-third of the adults, including males and females, show signs of having died violent deaths. The trauma
rate among adults is 34 percent. Evidence of arrow points embedded in bone,
blunt-force trauma, decapitation, and scalping are clearly seen in the human

remains. Many of the victims had been struck with heavy weapons, such as war clubs, on their backs, fronts, and sides; or they had been shot with arrows. Some people seem to have been facing their attackers, while others were wounded in an attempt to escape. Some victims are examples of overkill, having been struck many more times than was necessary to cause their deaths. Warriors other than the killer or killers may have struck blows to share in the kill and to gain prestigious war honors. This excessive violence may have been motivated by strong emotional feelings of revenge. Bodies were often mutilated by decapitation, removal of limbs, and scalping as part of the widespread pattern of trophy taking.

It is not known whether the victims were killed away from the village, or whether they were attacked in the village. Those villagers fled who could do so, not to return until some time later. In any case, the remains of the deceased were left exposed and were scavenged by carnivores before returning inhabitants or neighbors could bury them in the village cemetery (Milner and Smith 1989).

All but two of the Norris Farm victims were over fifteen years old, as is consistent with the idea that most of the raids were against small task groups who had traveled beyond the safe zone of the village (Milner 1998a:73). About equal numbers of men and women were recovered from the cemetery, suggesting that women were not abducted to be taken back to enemy villages as captives (Milner and Smith 1990). The majority of casualties represented by the nearly complete skeletons show signs of debilitating conditions that would have impaired these individuals' ability to escape or defend themselves. "These were truly opportunistic killings; victims tended to be the people who were least able to save themselves" (Milner 1999:115). The evidence suggests a pattern of almost continuous raiding over the course of the life of the village.

The Norris Farm population had a comparatively low level of health, suffering from iron-deficiency anemia and various infectious diseases. In the area of health, they were a "highly stressed population" relative to other, comparable prehistoric peoples (Milner and Smith 1990:148). As Emerson (2007:139) points out, "Perhaps the major impact of such long-term, chronic violence is its destabilization of a society's subsistence strategies, political and social patterns, and general lifeways. This pattern of low-scale, continuous, and persistent violence can destroy or entirely transform a society long before it kills large numbers of the society's members."

At about the same time as the Norris Farm attacks or slightly later, a single, catastrophic, large-scale massacre took place at the Crow Creek site, a fortified village on the Missouri River in South Dakota (Willey 1990; Willey and Emerson 1993). The site was surrounded by a ditch that formed part of the village's defensive works. The massacre seems to have occurred as the village fortifications were being replaced, which would have been a time of unusual vulnerability for the inhabitants (Willey 1990:5–6; Willey and Emerson 1993). The Crow Creek inhabitants, like those living at the Norris Farms site, were suffering from poor community health and diet.

When the village was attacked, its inhabitants were indiscriminately killed and mutilated, then left exposed for a long period of time before being buried. Many of the bodies had been mutilated or dismembered: noses, hands, and feet were sometimes cut off; teeth were smashed; and heads were removed and mutilated (Willey 1990:106–52). The scale of the attack suggests that most of the village inhabitants—men, women, and children—were killed and scalped, and their bodies mutilated. Most of the five hundred massacre victims were dumped into the village's fortification ditch (Willey 1990:14, 61; Willey and Emerson 1993). The village's total population is not known, but it is likely that a large fraction died during the attack, as more bodies are known to exist in the makeshift ditch grave and in the site's burned houses. The villagers appear to have been clubbed to death while fleeing their attackers, as there are no arrow points in the bodies. Presumably, survivors eventually returned, or members of neighboring villages undertook the grisly task of burying the scattered and mutilated remains.

Individuals with healed injuries indicate that the massacre was not an isolated act of hostility and aggression. Based on healed injuries, including scalping, it appears that some Crow Creek villagers had survived repeated previous ambushes (Willey 1990:113, 178). Each raid may have produced only a few victims, but some of the survivors lived long enough to be killed in the massacre. The violence at Crow Creek seems to have been the culmination of long-standing tensions and repeated raids that finally erupted into a catastrophic confrontation. Non-Oneota groups may have been responsible for the attacks.

By the first half of the fourteenth century, Oneota groups had reached their maximum expansion. At almost the same time, other neighboring groups, such as the Iroquois and Fort Ancient, were expanding in similar fashion. Buffer zones, lacking any substantial or long-term occupations, began to increase in number and size as violent confrontations took place among comparably organized groups. When stalemates were reached, buffer zones became dangerous areas of resource acquisition, hunting, and raiding.

Alliance-forming and peacemaking rituals, such as the Calumet Ceremony (Blakeslee 1981; Hall 1997), appear in the archaeological record of the Midwest among Oneota communities around AD 1400, along with regional growth in fortified villages, widespread prestige-goods exchange, and long-distance raids by large war parties. Disk pipes, presumably tied to the Calumet Ceremony or similar alliance or adoption rituals, spread throughout much of the Upper Midwest and Eastern Plains, representing rituals that facilitated interregional diplomacy, exchange, peace, and stability. The Calumet Ceremony, perhaps similar in form to that seen at European contact, evolved from earlier rituals and protocols long established for building alliances. As warfare changed, so did the nature of alliances and the rituals upon which they were constructed. With the rise of alliance rituals, individuals could achieve status and prestige through their ability to establish and maintain peace as well as war (Hollinger 2005:327). Although warfare did not slack off at any point prior to Western contact, the rise of Calumet-like ceremonialism may have brought about some degree of relative peace in parts of the Midwest. In response, interregional exchange began to thrive, as practices instituted for peacemaking and alliance building spread.

Warfare shifted in scope and tactics to emphasize long-distance raids by small-scale contingents of warriors. Individual warrior needs and interests could be fulfilled through the acquisition of war honors and personal prestige. Although conflict continued, alliances, communication, and exchange increased. Ritual peacemaking mechanisms, such as the Calumet Ceremony, allowed leaders to establish peace, build alliances, promote exchange, and establish fictive kin relationships through ritual adoption.

At about the same time, subsistence insecurity was aggravated in the Upper Midwest and the Great Lakes region by the onset of the Little Ice Age (Milner 2000:68). By AD 1450, in the aftermath of territorial expansion through conflict, the periphery of Oneota cultures and neighboring territories began contracting (Gibbon 1974). Oneota populations consolidated at large, nucleated centers located on major riverine trade routes, from which they controlled communication and exchange. Some of the centers, such as Blood Run and Utz, were established along the peripheries by AD 1500 and continued to be occupied until around AD 1700. Other groups adopted similar settlement patterns, with large population centers separated by vast unoccupied buffer zones.

Villages appear to have been occupied throughout much, if not all, of the year (Henning 1995), supported by increased production of corn, beans, and squash (Riley and Freimuth 1979; Sasso et al. 1985). Maygrass and little barley had earlier been added to the diet, along with sumpweed, sunflower, and squash. North American domesticates continued in importance (Hollinger and Pearsall 1994), and bison were occasionally hunted by ambush and stalking. A change from small, square, or oval houses to large, longhouse structures may reflect a shift from patrilocal to matrilocal postmarital residence patterns (Hollinger 1995).

Matrilocal Warriors

Documenting changes in residence patterns is important for the study of co-operation and conflict. For example, matrilocality arises in dominant, aggressive societies that are expanding into territories of hostile but subordinate groups. Analysis of matrilineal/matrilocal societies suggests that they are successful "predators" when competing with neighboring hunting-and-gathering groups. Matrilineal/matrilocal systems break up fraternal males, a practice that suppresses feuding and internal warfare. Large numbers of unrelated men are concentrated for defense and offense, a pattern not feasible among hunting-and-gathering societies.

Ultimately, foragers are thus at a disadvantage when in competition with segmental matrilineal/matrilocal groups. As social organization shifts, matrilocality facilitates external warfare and alliances while dampening internal feuds and promoting internal peace. The large, multifamily houses of matrilocal societies served as contexts within which unrelated men were socialized into more effective fighting and diplomatic forces. Not surprisingly, war parties and ambassadorial contingents were gone for long periods of time in order to strike enemies at great distances or establish mutually beneficial alliances. Typically, alliances and raids took place after the spring planting and prior to the fall harvest. Thus, warriors were often absent from their villages for long periods of time, raiding distant enemies, trading with allies and relatives, or engaging in multinational diplomacy in faraway communities.

Although generally vacant, large peripheral territories remained under the control of centralized populations. Interregional hostilities were episodic, alternating with peaceful interactions that allowed communication, exchange, and alliances to take place. In comparison with earlier times, there was an increased emphasis on iconography that emphasized aggression and power, as well as the exchange of prestige goods in the context of rituals that allowed alliances to be brokered by negotiating parties.

As Oneota groups consolidated, they distanced themselves from non-Oneota people. Peace and war in the late fifteenth and early sixteenth centuries differed from earlier intersocietal conflict in that alliances and raiding were conducted at much greater distances from home villages than had previously taken place. From AD 1400 to 1650, major Oneota settlements were separated from friends and enemies by hundreds of miles. The most significant abandonment by a large Oneota population seems to have taken place on the La Crosse terrace (Henning, personal communication 2008).

Skeletal remains from McKinney Village (AD 1550–1640), an Oneota site located atop a bluff overlooking the confluence of the Iowa River with the Mississippi in eastern Iowa, reveal that the inhabitants were engaged in interpersonal violence (Hollinger 2005). Isolated human remains found in trash pits, middens, hearths, and communal roasting pits represent trophies taken from enemies and captives brought back to the village who were subsequently tortured, mutilated, and discarded. The trophies, taken from all sexes and ages, were carefully cleaned, decorated, and crafted, then intentionally broken and burned in a communal roasting pit. Hollinger (2005:124) notes that "whether taking captives for return to one's village or taking human body parts as trophies, the process was about power." Warriors gained prestige through trophy taking and the capture and adoption of either live enemies or, through taking scalps or other body parts, their spirits. The inhabitants of the McKinney site were engaged in intensive agriculture, and participated in interregional exchange. Investment in increased interregional exchange occurred at the same time that changes were taking place in social organization.

In the early seventeenth century, new transformations altered Oneota and other populations of the upper Midwest. The global economy, international politics, and continent-wide pandemics introduced from Europe wrought devastation and massive cultural reorganization. Prior to direct contact with Europeans, and perhaps before the influx of European trade goods, the impact of new forces began to be felt. Disease spread throughout the Midwest, rapidly decimating populations concentrated in densely populated centers. Warfare may have further spread virulent diseases. In such a scenario, raiding parties may have descended upon their weakened enemies and in turn contracted the diseases, carrying them to their homes, their allies, or other enemies. While proof presently does not exist that this in fact took place, the spread of disease through warfare is a likely model for the rapid movement of eastern North American pandemics. For example, pandemic disease and war parties from the east have been forwarded as reasons for the La Crosse terrace abandonment around AD 1650 (Dale R. Henning, personal communication 2008).

European products, at first incorporated directly into existing Native exchange systems, were later supplied directly by European traders. The traditional subsistence economy over time was reoriented toward fulfilling European demands. Existing antagonistic relations became exacerbated as new forces, including alliances, diseases, and weapons technologies, shifted power balances and fueled conflicts. Working in concert, disease, starvation, warfare, and economic pressures brought about changes in traditional domestic organization, exchange patterns, settlement patterns, social organization, subsistence practices, and technology. The archaeologically documented Oneota and other Midwestern cultures became the ethnohistoric and ethnographic "tribes" of the colonial period. The Oneota fell victim to changes in the processes that had enabled them to control the Midwest for almost five hundred years, as they became victimized by more powerful tribes who proved to be more successful at exploiting the changes brought on by European contact (Hollinger 2005).

Beginning in the early seventeenth century, midcontinent populations were destabilized by the indirect effects of European contact. Racing ahead of European settlements, disease decimated heavily populated centers located on major exchange routes. With new weapons, such as firearms and metal axes, old enemies took advantage of each other's weaknesses, brought on by disease and famine, to wage wars of annihilation. Algonquian and Iroquoian tribes pushed westward, driving other tribes ahead of them or exterminating them completely, if possible. For the Oneota, large territories were abandoned in favor of defensive strategies that included new alliances with former enemies and amalgamation into multiethnic refugee settlements. Ultimately, Oneota peoples succumbed to the aggressive practices that had allowed them to thrive for almost seven hundred years (Hollinger 2005).

Warfare in the Upper Midwest from the mid-seventeenth century to the end of the eighteenth century varied in form and scale. The style of long-distance raiding characteristic of the previous two centuries continued according to traditional warfare. Small raiding parties traveled great distances to raid their enemies, accumulating personal war honors and earning social prestige. Tribes encroached on the territories of others as they were pushed further west by inhabitants to the east, who were being annihilated by disease, starvation, and devastating raids. In the early seventeenth century, for example, members of the Iroquois League set about destroying their traditional enemies, whom they blamed for the massive population losses they had suffered. Those who survived Iroquois League depredations and were not incorporated within the league moved westward into territories claimed by others.

Disruption of a sociopolitical situation that had been relatively stable for more than two hundred years was caused by European contact, which was felt long before Europeans were actually present among these communities. New diseases devastated Native American population centers, warfare increased, and economic systems were modified, causing reorientation of subsistence practices and settlement patterns. Traditional technologies were abandoned or modified in favor of new weapons and tools derived from Europeans. Social organization was transformed in response to the economic changes and new social pressures. Entire populations were absorbed, assimilated, displaced, or dissolved, creating new ethnicities. Long-distance conflict continued, but encroachment conflict reemerged as power balances shifted and motivations expanded to include the politics of European polities. Large villages were often composed of ethnic groups banded together for mutual defense and trade. Diseases struck down huge segments of indigenous populations, eliminating vast bodies of traditional knowledge held by elders and ritual specialists. Iconography however, continued to stress appeals to supernatural beings (figure 8.3).

Agriculture may have become less important relative to other food sources. Complex field systems were replaced by less labor-intensive hilled-field systems (Gallagher 1992). The demands of the fur trade pressured groups into more regular seasonal rounds, as local groups reorganized into smaller family units for winter hunting. These local groups were increasingly pulled into the world economy. Communal bison hunting became an important part of the seasonal round (Michalik 1982), and the introduction of the horse and the gun facilitated increasing exploitation of bison.

Intense raiding raged in the midcontinent during the mid- to late seventeenth centuries. Men, women, and children were killed, or they were captured and then sold into slavery or tortured and mutilated. Longhouses and small circular residences, found contemporaneously in the same sites, indicate that postmarital residence patterns were shifting from matrilocal back to patrilocal, which suggests that Midwestern populations were undergoing depopulation from disease and war (Hollinger 1995). Members of the Iroquois Confederation continued attacking people to the west, and this exacerbated the chronic warfare. Oneota groups documented archaeologically in the early seventeenth century became the tribal groups known historically as Chiwere speakers—including the Ioway, Missouria, Otoe, and Winnebago (Mott 1938); and perhaps components of the Dhegiha-speaking Kansa, Omaha, Osage, and Ponca, as well as the Mdewakanton Dakota (Birk and Johnson 1992; Henning 1993). By the late seventeenth, a *Pax Oneota* (Henning 2003) had become a time of negotiations that allowed some Ioway the opportunity to trade across northern Iowa and into the Green Bay area for a brief period of time.

In summary, intergroup conflict in the midcontinent was prominent throughout the eleventh to eighteenth centuries, peaking in intensity around AD 1300 and again during the 1600s (Hollinger 2005). Warfare against enemies and efforts to establish alliances with neighboring local groups and polities characterizes some one thousand years of Upper Midwestern Oneota societies. In contrast to Late Woodland tribes of the late first

Figure 8.3.   Bird Man, New Albin Tablet, Allamakee County, Iowa (from *Missouri Archaeologist* 25:fig. 23; courtesy of Missouri Archaeological Society, Inc.).

millennium in the Upper Midwest—who were characterized by low levels of conflict, small population size, hunting and gathering, and mixed farming— Oneota communities between AD 1000 and 1150 exhibited increased levels of regional social interaction and military competition. From AD 1150 to 1400, Oneota populations witnessed some 250 years of expansion and encroachment upon neighboring groups. Emerson (2007:140) notes that "the late prehistory of the northern midcontinent was marked by periods of chronic intergroup hostility and episodic hostilities that totally devastated communities." Between AD 1400 and 1650, Oneota local groups carried out raids and created exchange relationships over long distances. During the European contact period, from AD 1650 to 1800, small raiding parties continued to travel great distances to trade and raid, but encroachment reappeared and continued to increase in frequency. Historic groups vied to control larger territories as they became increasingly involved in economic and political relationships with European powers.

CHAPTER NINE

Cooperation and Conflict in the Lower Midwest and Southeast

Without a doubt, humans have the latent potential to unleash violence against other humans, just as humans have the potential for amicable cooperation.

(Emerson 2007:132)

With the end of the Late Woodland period, community life, religious institutions, and social organization underwent significant alterations across the midcontinent, as regional political hierarchies emerged and settlements became increasingly nucleated and protected through ditches, embankments, and palisades. Fortified great towns, in place throughout much of the Lower Midwest and Southeast between AD 1000 and 1200, were vivid reminders, to the Mississippian people who lived within the confines and protection of their walls, of strained political relations, aggressive enemies, and potential expectations of intergroup violence (figure 9.1). A critical change was taking place in the political landscape at the turn of the first millennium, and that change was evident in the way neighboring polities cooperated and fought with one another.

The largest of the great Mississippian mound centers was Cahokia in east-central Illinois (Emerson 1997; Hall 2004; Milner 1998b; Pauketat 1994, 2004; Pauketat and Emerson 1997; figure 9.2). As the premier and unequaled Mississippian political, religious, and social center of eastern North America, Cahokia occupied some 16 square kilometers and contained over 120 earthen mounds. The inner sanctum, which included the Grand Plaza and Monks Mound, was enclosed by nearly three kilometers of a twenty-thousand-log central

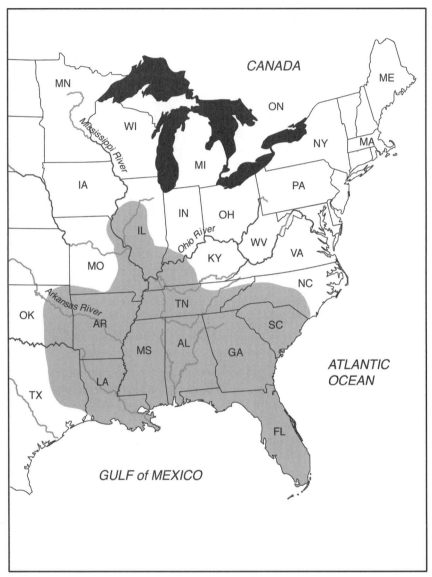

Figure 9.1.   Mississippian culture in eastern North America.

palisade wall, replete with bastions, that was rebuilt at least four times (Dalan et al. 2003). Monks Mound, the largest earthen monument to be built in prehistoric North America north of Mexico, is 30.5 meters tall and has a footprint of some 6.5 hectares (figure 9.3). Proliferation in mound and plaza construction at Cahokia signaled the initial sanctification of an emerging elite ideology, linked

Figure 9.2. Cahokia site, Madison and St. Clair Counties, Illinois (© 2004 S. N. Patricia, RA).

to a legitimizing iconography (Brown 2004b; Pauketat and Emerson 1991), that had profound ramifications throughout eastern North America.

While a general change from a Woodland to a Mississippian lifestyle is evident in many areas of the Eastern Woodlands, it should be remembered that there was a great deal of variability across the region. Significant diversity is seen in domestic, economic, ideological, political, and social organization, as well as in community plans, craft production, settlement patterns, cooperation, and conflict, throughout the Mississippian world (Wilson et al. 2006).

Mississippian people followed an economic schedule that took advantage of regular cycles of food abundance. In addition to domesticated maize, beans, squash, and sunflowers, several weedy cultigens, and a variety of wild nuts, greens, and fruits, Mississippian peoples consumed terrestrial and aquatic animals, primarily deer, turkey, and fish. Food production was intensified to create surplus comestibles, critical for feasts that functioned as political, ritual, and social events. Feasts served to promote and cement adoption ceremonies, alliance building, ceremonial exchange, and tributary payments, in addition to a variety of intragroup and intergroup relations (Dye 1995; Kelly 2001; Knight 2001; Pauketat 2002).

Feasting assumed increased importance with the spread of maize agriculture between AD 800 and 1200, as new forms of food production were grafted onto preexisting horticultural practices, promoting elevated population growth and

Figure 9.3. Monks Mound, Cahokia Mounds, Madison and St. Clair Counties, Illinois (© 2004 David H. Dye).

renewed interregional relations. In some areas settlement nucleation continued, while in other regions dispersed homesteads were the rule. Accompanying these changes were unprecedented rates of interpolity cooperation, conflict, and exchange.

Prior to AD 800, tribal-level raids based on feuding behavior took place in response to kin vengeance, prestige enhancement, and resource competition; but by late in the first millennium or early in the second millennium, institutionalized forms of warfare began to emerge. The organization of Mississippian chiefly warfare was based on advisory councils, inherited hierarchical leadership positions, and the rise of warrior societies in the form of sodalities or cultic institutions. As warfare became commonplace across the region, diplomatic structures arose to establish diplomatic alliances. Throughout the midcontinent at the end of the first millennium, chiefly conflict and cooperation spread rapidly, as evidenced in an array of archaeological evidence.

War and measures to establish alliances and peace both transformed and were transformed by the evolving chiefly forms of political organization (Dye 2006a).

The expansion of Mississippian culture from about AD 800 to 1200 corresponds to the Medieval Warming (Neo-Atlantic; Broecker 2001), a favorable time for field-based horticulture, with temperatures in the Northern Hemisphere comparable to or only slightly less warm than those at present (Crowley 2000). Paleoclimate data indicate that periods of good climate are frequently associated with relative tranquility, while periods of worsening climate are associated with social and political unrest. Long-term climate change has significant, direct effects on land-carrying capacity, which in turn affects food supply. A shortage of food resources increases the likelihood of armed conflicts, famine, and migrations (Zhang et al. 2007:19214), while abundant food supplies will give rise to population growth.

The intimate relationship of climate and culture reflects the importance of variable agricultural harvests and chiefly abilities to generate, and appropriate if necessary, surplus food supplies (Anderson 2001:166). In the American Bottom region from AD 900 to 1150, for example, the archeological record reveals a proportional increase in less-palatable acorns to preferred hickory nutmeats, which may indicate the heightened pressure of exponentially increasing human populations upon diminishing foraging yields (Delcourt and Delcourt 2004:126). For societies dependent on agriculture, repeated crop failures brought on by prolonged bad weather could have disastrous effects. Mississippian societies appear to have developed elaborate cropping and storage strategies to reduce the effects of drought, but they were not always successful, even in periods of optimum climatic conditions (Anderson et al. 1995).

Despite the relatively favorable climate, a new era of social conflict is seen in the rise of fortifications between AD 1050 and 1200 (Milner 1999:123). The intensity of attacks is reflected in the strength of these fortifications, with their equally spaced bastions, well-planned palisades, and adjoining ditches and embankments. Perhaps with the need to protect stored surpluses of subsistence resources, new forms of intersocietal conflict arose. Attacks against fortified towns probably included storming palisades by large numbers of warriors, whose aim was to seize storable surplus, dominate social labor, exact tribute, and destroy an enemy chief's sources of legitimation, especially mortuary shrines and their contents (Dye and King 2007). Anderson (1999:228) notes that "low intensity warfare, which occasionally gave way to major episodes of apparent conquest or extermination, was a way of life" among Mississippian polities. Palisades constructed around settlements can be viewed as evidence for heightened expectations of attack, and for threats of armed conflict of increased intensity and severity. Throughout much of the Lower Midwest and Southeast, strongly fortified villages accompanied the rise of Mississippian societies (Milner 2000; Milner and Schroeder 1999:104). In some areas populations nucleated, while in other areas households and hamlets remained dispersed, with people seeking refuge in fortified centers during times of increased conflict and hostilities.

Fortified towns often arose prior to efforts in bringing about regional political consolidation of adjacent regions, signaling the initial appearance of chiefly polities. The construction of ditches, embankments, and bastioned palisades reinforces the idea that Mississippian emergence involved some degree of intrusion, competition, or conflict with respect to neighboring triballike or chiefly polities. Once consolidation had been achieved, defensive measures could be relaxed, as nearby groups had now been incorporated, suppressed, driven out, or subjugated (Anderson 1999:221–22). The early phases of political consolidation, and its continued maintenance, were predicated on a polity's potential for warrior mobilization (Milner 1999:120).

Palisades were built not only to guard a chiefdom's staple and wealth finance, but also to withstand attacks from bow-and-arrow warfare and protect the sources of chiefly authority, legitimacy, and power often housed in the ancestor shrines. The bow and arrow fundamentally transformed the competitive advantage in intergroup conflict (Blitz 1988:124), restructured the scale and organization of warfare (Nassaney and Pyle 1999:260), brought about an increase in mortality (Bridges et al. 2000:56), and prompted population movements (Seeman 1992) throughout the Eastern Woodlands, but especially in the Mississippian world. Specialized arrows for raids and social display of warrior valor are evident by AD 1000 throughout much of the midcontinent. The bow did not immediately necessitate construction of fortified communities, but the fortifications that arose around AD 1050 were designed specifically as a direct response to bow warfare: tall, plastered palisade walls; closely spaced bastions (ca. 30 m); constricted entrances; embankments; and deep ditches (Milner 2000). Plastered Mississippian palisades may have been a response to the use of fire-tipped arrows by massed warriors (DePratter 1983:47), and closely spaced bastions allowed archers to overlap their firepower.

Regional consolidation in chiefly societies often involved the transition from dispersed to nucleated settlements. One primary political benefit of nucleated populations was that this practice provided chiefly elites with social labor necessary for monumental construction projects and aggrandizement strategies. Constructing monumental architecture, including mounds, plazas, palisades, and shrines; training warriors for chiefly militias who could carry out elite mandates of conquest and raiding; and encouraging craft specialization that included highly skilled manufacture of symbolic weaponry, such as maces, paved the way for hierarchical chiefly organization and its legitimation (figure 9.4). Thus, it is not surprising that regional consolidation and population nucleation were accompanied by large-scale labor projects, elevated status differences, and increases in the production of symbolic weaponry and alliance paraphernalia employed in war and alliance rituals.

Figure 9.4. Crownform mace, southeastern Kentucky (© 2004 David H. Dye, courtesy of Tennessee State Museum, Gates P. Thruston Collection of Vanderbilt University).

Strong defenses appear to have been built during initial regional political centralization and consolidation at Mississippian sites. The construction and maintenance of elaborate wooden walls and the vacant land that lay between polities are testimony to the need for heightened military security; but they are also an important indication of the strength and authority of leaders who could mobilize construction labor, coordinate relatively large warrior forces, and deploy diplomatic negotiators.

Mississippian palisade construction and buffer zones signaled initial regional political consolidation of a polity's hinterlands. Although defensive palisades were built to guard staple and wealth finance and to withstand attacks during bow-and-arrow warfare, buffer zones would have created a protective no-man's-land around the polity (Hally 1993). The political impetus of these forces was born in chiefly aggrandizement and the ability of chiefs to mobilize formidable militias and cement binding alliances with potentially devastating capabilities and results.

Offensive posturing is evident where populations responded to aggressive behavior by placing sites in defensive positions, such as prominent elevations and islands. Palisade walls and ditches enclosed settlements to protect the inhabitants from other polities, perhaps their neighbors. Areas that previously had been settled were now abandoned, creating buffer zones of large areas of habitable real estate among polities (Hally 1993). Populations appear to have coalesced into a few relatively large villages in response to endemic warfare (Knight and Steponaitis 1998:11).

Associated with the rise of intersocietal conflict and the construction of fortifications is the increase in skeletal trauma and trophy-taking behavior. Scalping and dismemberment occupied a dominant role in intergroup conflicts throughout the Eastern Woodlands (Axtell and Sturtevant 1980; Milner 1995; Owsley and Berryman 1975). The nature of settlement defense is directly related to the types and severity of violent trauma. Mortality rates and traumatic injuries are at their greatest levels in small- to medium-site contexts (Bridges et al. 2000). Undefended hamlets, for example, exposed individuals to attack by arrows and consequently reveal high percentages of human remains with embedded arrow points. On the other hand, mid-sized sites with defensive features such as palisades, and those located on islands, have high mortality from upper-body and cranial injuries due to axes and war clubs, but rarely from arrow points. The largest and best defended sites, which would have been overwhelmingly formidable to invaders, were largely secure from warfare except under unusual circumstances (Bridges et al. 2000:60).

Evidence for rituals and mythology with themes of heroic supernaturals in mortal combat is associated with the rise of chiefly combat late in the first millennium, accompanied by considerable mortality, as well as aggregation and population spacing. Historical trajectories of individual Mississippian polities differed as a result of varying power strategies by ruling elites, who expanded, consolidated, and entrenched their political control as they sought to protect their interests and sources of authority. The archaeological record documents more frequent use of warfare symbolism once chiefs began to mobilize labor and goods for defensive and offensive strategies. Competition over resources, especially social labor, generally brought about restructuring of the ideological, political, and social geography. The transformation of the Mississippian geopolitical world resulted in large part from competition among chiefly elites who sought to consolidate neighboring polities into ever-larger political formations. Their successes and failures affected the emergence, florescence, domination, and collapse of regional polities in a complex matrix of political change. Political power waxed and waned within relatively limited confines, however.

Pauketat (2007:156) has postulated that a *Pax Cahokiana* existed throughout much of the Mississippi Valley from AD 1050 to 1200 as "part and parcel of a political-religious cult emanating from the American Bottom." His argument is based on the presumed presence of Cahokians at these sites, along with their gifts: decorated ceramic vessels, Cahokia-style gaming stones, distinctive arrow points, special ear ornaments, red stone figurine smoking pipes, and marine-shell beads. Many of these prestations have been found at sites both north and south of Cahokia. In addition to Cahokian ambassadors and their gifts, warriors from Cahokia and their allies "maintained peace and order in the Upper Mississippi Valley between A.D. 1050 and 1200 through tactical strikes against populations who might have, from a Cahokian viewpoint, stepped out of line. They perhaps did likewise down-river, at least to the confluence of the Ohio and Mississippi Rivers and into southeastern Missouri" (Pauketat 2007:156).

Another avenue for alliances and peaceful interactions was the transformation of the earlier Woodland stage burial-mound ceremonialism into a world-renewal ritual known as the New Fire ceremony around AD 1050 (Brown 2004a, 2004b:119). At the heart of the ritual was the rekindling of the sacred fire in the temple or ancestor shrine (Hall 1997:147–48); but adoption, a mechanism used for the previous Hopewellian interactions, apparently continued to aid Mississippian interactions (Hall 1997:147). "The dissociation of mound construction from World Renewal ritual could have led to the replacement of mound construction by cemetery burial for the general population and in time to the emergence of the Sun Dance and Calumet ceremony from elements previously associated with burial mound ceremonialism" (Hall

1997:167). Thus, the Green Corn ceremony, the Sun Dance, and the Calumet ceremony may all have emerged from elements previously associated with Woodland-stage burial mound ceremonialism. Hall (1997:120) notes that the "calumet served to mediate a symbolic rebirth as part of an adoption ceremony to create fictional bonds of kinship between unrelated individuals and hence, indirectly, the social groups to which they belonged." The adoption ritual "related to a symbolic reincarnation but also in ritual to affirm alliances" (Hall 1997:121).

Fire-clay figures, manufactured between AD 1050 and 1150, were retooled as sacred pipes. The fact that "they were found far from Cahokia, their point of origin, strongly suggests that these pipes may have functioned in ways similar to the historic-period calumet ceremonies" (Reilly 2004:135–36). Reilly adds, "Perhaps, through the act of retooling these flint clay figurines into pipes and distributing them to certain, select outlying elites, the rulers of Cahokia were visually and ritually 'adopting' other groups by transferring objects that expressed commonalities of belief, thus strengthening long-distance alliances" (2004:136).

By AD 1200, warfare and alliance rituals were a fundamental part of the invocation to spiritual powers necessary for successful military operations. Rituals and myths chartered the institutionalization of warfare, and the authority, cooperation, organization, purpose, unity, and appropriate behavior required of warriors who were successful in combat. By the middle of the thirteenth century, figural art portraying combat and symbolic weapons as accoutrements of ritualized aggressive action was widespread (Brown and Kelly 2000). Figural art and symbolic weaponry rapidly became crucial to the rituals of warfare, as priestly warriors gained increasing authority over warfare ceremonies connected with combat (Dye 2004).

The representation of severed body parts is visible in the iconography of special elite goods, perhaps corresponding with initial efforts by Mississippian chiefs at creating, demonstrating, and legitimizing regional political consolidation. Elite status and wealth are marked by columella pendants, marine shell cups, and pearl beads. Engraved shell cups and gorgets, for example, suggest a number of themes relating to warfare, including heroic warriors brandishing weapons (Phillips and Brown 1978:plate 10) and severed heads (Brown and Dye 2007; Phillips and Brown 1978:plate 17).

War prisoners and human-body-part trophies were portrayed in iconographic form and served as implements of elite rituals associated with warfare and chiefly office. War trophies and combat weaponry were dominant themes of the chiefly cult organization (Brown 1985; Knight 1986). The connection of war-trophy symbolism with elite behavior and the pursuit of war honors reinforced the role of warfare by conferring honor and prestige upon those individuals who demonstrated personal military success, thereby gaining them preeminent political and ritual positions.

Used to seal alliances, to obtain success in battle, and to garner war honors, human-body-part trophies connected the spirits of slain enemies with the successful warrior's relatives, enabling the slain enemy to accompany deceased relatives on their journeys along the Path of Souls or spirit trail (Hall 1997). Trophy imagery then became a key source of power for warriors in their connection with the ancestors, the celestial realm, and the deities who resided in the Other World (Dye 2004). Myths that promoted and legitimized trophy-taking behavior in the Mississippian world were widespread, and elements of these mythic charters survived into the nineteenth century, especially on the Eastern Plains (Bowers 1965).

Individuals in regional societies sought social and political recognition as great warriors based on their personal achievements, documented by the possession of human trophies. In Mississippian societies, the acquisition, public display, and presentation of trophies was vital for the functioning of chiefly office. The association between trophies and chiefly positions was manifested in their use as prestige items, symbolizing a chief's military efficacy. These trophies, or their iconographic representations, were wealth markers, status emblems, and rank signifiers (Chacon and Dye 2007). Severed human heads continued to play a prominent role in Mississippian art during the late thirteenth century and throughout the fourteenth. Perhaps the most distinctive iconographic trophy motif was the severed agnathous human head (Brown and Dye 2007), which served as an element of regalia for a highly specific, elite Mississippian headgear: the high-crest feather headdress (Sampson and Esarey 1993:469).

The classic expression of Mississippian art, ritual, and status paraphernalia reached a peak in elaboration with the acquisition, manufacture, use, and entombment of copper in the late thirteenth and early fourteenth centuries. The continued emphasis on war-trophy symbolism in Mississippian art took place as preeminent members of Mississippian society further associated elite status with military prowess and with connections to supernaturals of the celestial realm. The incorporation of hawk markings in dress and body decoration emphasized success in combat as a measure of social standing (Brown and Kelly 2000:475). Elite status was displayed through the entombment of symbol-laden copper emblems that associated ceremonial regalia, condensed wealth, ritual weaponry, and war trophies with specific high-ranking individuals.

Heroic Warriors

During the late twelfth and early thirteenth centuries, the Braden art style exhibited a range of themes, including those of Chunkey Player and the Birdman. The latter theme had roots in Late Woodland societies in the Midwest. These thematic images, engraved on pottery from AD 1100 to 1200 at Cahokia, often emphasized severed heads of supernatural heroic warriors. Maskettes representing Long-Nosed Gods, markers of the horizon, were worn by elite males as earrings and had a broad distribution during the eleventh through the thirteenth centuries. They were used in adoption rituals for war captives.

These marine-shell maskettes have been identified with a Siouan epic myth cycle whose mythological hero was a Thunderer known as Red Horn. Thunderers were associated with supernatural powers and leadership in warfare. In the Winnebago Red Horn Hero Cycle, the supernatural hero is also known as "He-who-wears-human-heads-as-earrings," the name conferred upon him at creation. The twelfth-century Long Nosed God maskettes may represent the severed heads of supernaturals mentioned in the Red Horn Hero Cycle.

Mississippian combat imagery was crafted and exchanged in a broad area of the Eastern Woodlands, from the Appalachians to the Ozarks and from the Gulf Coast to the Midwest (figure 9.5), and it is found in the major political and ceremonial towns. Three key artifact genres illustrate figural heroic-warrior art: engraved marine-shell cups, engraved marine-shell gorgets, and repoussé sheet-copper plates. Pictorial themes on symbolic artifacts consist of complex images connected to the warrior elite in which ax-, mace-, sword- or war-club-wielding supernaturals are dressed in ritual regalia.

The elaboration of heroic warrior symbolism was manifest at Mississippian regional centers once chiefly efforts at political consolidation had taken place. Mississippian warfare art comprised a limited set of beliefs concerning a specific religious cult whose subject matter was the otherworld—especially the celestial strata of a tiered cosmos where mythic warrior heroes, existing in mythic time, performed supernatural exploits—rather than the mundane themes of earthly warfare (Knight et al. 2001:133).

By AD 1200, death by violence was approaching 11 percent of mortality among adults at middle-sized palisaded sites such as Lubbub Creek in northwest Mississippi (Bridges et al. 2000:44). Handheld weapons had proliferated into several forms by this time, ranging from sticks and staffs to war clubs. In general, more males were dying than were females, presumably because males were being killed in the context of raids and ambushes. At the Koger's Island site in northwest Alabama, for example, there was a dramatic increase in mortality of young males (Bridges et al. 2000:57), and males at Moundville in west-central Alabama display more fractures than females (Powell 1988:194). However, at the Orendorf site in the central Illinois valley, the interpersonal trauma rates for females and males are roughly equal (Steadman 2008:59).

Successful military campaigns were often based on a chief's ability to forge effective alliances through war councils. Alliances allowed a chief to create forces larger than a single polity could effectively field and to concentrate and coordinate multipolity attacks against specific towns. Successful assaults on fortified towns signaled the ability of principal chiefs to aggregate fighting forces in overwhelming numbers, through alliances with neighboring chiefs, to combat their common rivals. In the spring of 1543, for example, De Soto thwarted a coalition of some twenty chiefs and their respective polities who were planning a massive, coordinated attack on the fortified Spanish settlement at the Lower Mississippi river town of Aminoya (Hudson 1997:384).

A long dry spell in the middle of the twelfth century and a second one between AD 1276 and 1297 may have affected outbreaks of intersocietal conflict among farming communities in the Eastern Woodlands (Benson et al. 2007; Ollendorf 1993:175). The onset of the Little Ice Age after AD 1300 disrupted agrarian cultures throughout much of the world (Fagan 2000; Grove 1998; Zhang et al. 2007), and many Eastern Woodland farming communities may have been affected by these climatic changes (Anderson 2001; Stahle et al. 2007). Benson et al. (2007:346), however, believe the "major reductions in prehistoric Native American habitation sites/population occurred during anomalously warm, not cold, climatic phase."

Warfare and settlement nucleation increased as heroic-warrior iconography, long-distance exchange, and monumental construction decreased. Milner (1999:125) documents a substantial increase in fortified settlements in the upper Midwest and Northeast, attributing the defensive buildup to climatic-induced stress on crop yields when droughts worsened and became more frequent. Territorial conflicts often arose from the need to raid vital stored food surpluses.

Decline in the overall size of Mississippian towns is documented between AD 1300 and 1550. In fact, there were no large centers during this time (Holley 1999). Many of the great centers such as Moundville had shrunk so from their former political eminence that their hereditary paramountcy lacked any real political power (Knight and Steponaitis 1998:23). Etowah was abandoned by the end of the fourteenth century, perhaps because of a devastating attack, never to gain its regional importance and preeminence (King 2003). A number of Mississippian chiefdoms throughout much of the Midsouth and Midwest collapsed in the early fifteenth century, leaving the area vacant for four hundred years. Abandonment may have been part of the reaction to a changing climate, resulting in large-scale, simultaneous migrations from the "vacant quarter" as a consequence of climatic deterioration that "exacerbated a competitive and often hostile political climate" (Cobb and Butler 2002:637).

By the late fourteenth century, much of the Mississippian world had changed, bringing about the cessation of combat rituals and iconography. Chiefly legitimizing strategies were transformed after the fourteenth century, when they had been based on appeals to the supernatural world and the exchange of exotic, highly crafted, and symbolically laden goods. In contrast, post-fourteenth-century Mississippian chiefs employed power strategies that emphasized "more secular measures, including the overt use of force" (Anderson 1994b:137).

By AD 1400, emphasis placed upon supernaturally charged prestige goods was replaced by regional political-military competition. As the importance of competition among elites in the larger region increased, a competitive landscape resulted wherein chiefs were in constant competition with their neighbors as they jockeyed between alliance and warfare to extend or break free from political domination (King 2006:83).

A pattern of population dispersal in some areas and coalescence in others is reflected in the dramatic and fairly widespread episode of decline and abandonment prior to the arrival of epidemic diseases and European settlers (Smith 1996:316). Throughout much of the Eastern Woodlands, warfare had developed into a well-orchestrated pattern of offensive and defensive strategies and tactics. Regular surprise raids and ambushes were carried out in conjunction with episodic large-scale attacks across broad and extensive buffer zones between neighboring polities. Early European accounts document chiefly forces composed of allies who organized large militias that were equally agile on land and water (DePratter 1983:49–55).

The fifteenth and early sixteenth centuries witnessed increased tensions and strife across much of the Eastern Woodlands. Frequent and perhaps intense warfare is reflected in weapons trauma on skeletal remains (Anderson 1999:224). Decline of the widespread prestige-goods exchange and deteriorating climate almost certainly are linked to the increase in conflict, as reduced alliance formation, elite interaction, and exchange relations curtailed the ability of chiefs to ameliorate hostilities with neighboring polities.

Fisher-Carroll (2001) documents the cascading effects of an epic North American late sixteenth-century mega-drought (Stahle et al. 2000) as it was manifested in the northern portion of the Lower Mississippi Valley. The severely diminished subsistence base proved to be catastrophic for the populations living in the region, resulting in wide-scale depopulation at the peak of the drought between 1570 and 1580. Response to food shortages typically occurs in three sequences of events during severe famines: alarm, resistance, and exhaustion (Longhurst 1986). During the resistance and exhaustion stages, hostility, political unrest, theft, and competition intensify. During the stage of resistance from 1560 to 1570, "interpersonal violence certainly would have increased, probably between competing groups to begin with, but may have progressed to intergroup social breakdown" (Fisher-Carroll 2001:242).

Early French and Spanish expeditions provide first-hand accounts of Mississippian warfare. Fortified towns dotted the landscape in some regions; in other areas, they were noticeably absent. Scalping and dismemberment are frequently mentioned. The objectives of success in warfare seem to have been primarily political, revolving around legitimizing dominance and authority, resolving chiefly grievances, and expanding and consolidating one's polity (Dye 2002:130). These remarkable ethnohistoric descriptions provide only tantalizing hints, however, and must be used in conjunction with archaeological evidence.

Associated with depopulation in the early sixteenth century was the strong desire to avoid losing warriors in battle. War chiefs went to great lengths to safeguard their warriors' lives and to avoid kin retribution and loss of prestige, respect, and social standing. Because of the increasing concern about loss of productive members, warfare rituals may have placed even greater emphasis on amulets, medicine bundles, portable shrines, and spiritual aid for military success. While rituals and associated warfare paraphernalia promoted the principal chief's sanctity of office in the precontact period, by the seventeenth century emphasis had shifted to the individual warrior's safety—and his protection by the war chief—and to a greater dependence on individual symbolic objects such as personal medicine bundles.

In the sixteenth century, French and Spanish explorers witnessed scenes of Mississippian preparations for war. Flemish engraver Theodor de Bry's 1590 copper plates illustrate European perceptions of these stages of war rituals. The French colonizers describe and illustrate deliberations on important affairs, such as warfare, and the ceremonies performed both before an expedition went against the enemy and on their return from combat. Preparations prior to military campaigns included war feasts, sorcery, and declarations of war. French colonists saw chiefs heading their warrior militias, and consulting with priests on the chances of success in combat. They witnessed the military expedition's order of march, the way in which towns were fortified, and how the settlements were set on fire by their enemies. They also observed the way in which warriors treated the slain enemies; the exhibition of trophies; and the ceremonies conducted after a victory, with thanks given to the sun.

The political dimensions of chiefly warfare seem to have given rise to several warfare styles, as documented by European observers. There is clear documentary evidence of two basic, interrelated styles of offensive, chiefly warfare (Anderson 1994a; DePratter 1983; Dye 1990): guerrilla raids/ambushes and formal battles. Guerrilla raids took the form of hit-and-run attacks and ambushes. Successful raids depended on intelligence, mobility, surprise, and knowledge of the topography where the attack would take place. Although limited in their effectiveness, raids and ambushes were well suited to "reduce the effectiveness of an enemy force, demoralize a fixed population, reduce the flow of supplies, capture towns for short periods of time, or demonstrate that certain targets, such as villages and civic centers, are vulnerable" (Steinen 1992:135). Raiding parties aided in the control of a tributary polity. Raiders tried to penetrate an enemy's territory, surprise the enemy with a quick strike, and then withdraw with minimal losses and maximum gains. To lose warriors in combat indicated a lack of ritual purity and supernatural support, and poor leadership. Effective raids were executed swiftly and conducted with maximum surprise and unremitting violence.

When principal chiefs perceived that they had an advantage over their rivals, they may have engaged them in mutually agreed-upon formal battles, composed of militia-based armies of several hundred to several thousand warriors maneuvering under, and coordinated by, a chain of command. Organized battles were probably of short duration, because of supply and transportation problems, but foods such as pemmican could be prepared in advance to offset logistical problems (DePratter 1983:64–66).

A particularly effective offensive technique was to shoot fire-tipped arrows over palisade walls to ignite roof thatch. Yet hand-to-hand combat with war clubs was the preferred mode of fighting. Shock weapons such as war clubs possess greater striking power and accuracy over fire weapons such as the bow and arrow (Gabriel and Metz 1991:56–75; Keeley 1996:49). The ubiquity of war clubs in Eastern Woodland iconography and as symbolic weaponry, beginning in the tenth century, attests to their central role in warfare and warrior prestige and valor. The war club was the preferred weapon of combat and was its primary symbol (Hudson 1976:245).

For chiefs to be successful they had to have a well-coordinated military organization. Chiefly combat organization was based on hierarchical structure and formal institutions. The kin-based, hierarchical nature of Eastern Woodland political organization provided chiefs with a ready-made structure for the organization of their warrior militia. Hierarchical structure provided the organizational capability to create effective chains of command based on graded military ranks. In between the chiefly commander and the lowest warrior lay the graded warrior ranks.

At the upper end of the ranks, experienced warriors sat on war councils, serving as military advisors. Their status was probably ascribed and achieved, whereas lower-ranking warriors' status was clearly achieved through military success. Elite warriors helped plan attacks and served as leaders of militia subunits. French and Spanish leaders, in accordance with European military systems, referred to these individuals as "captains." These "captains," in fact, probably served Native military roles in much the same way as their European counterparts did in their system. The responsibilities of "captains" within the overall command structure were important for relaying orders and maintaining discipline.

Hierarchical structure provided Mississippian chiefs the authority to issue orders to subsidiary chiefs, who relayed commands to their principal warriors. These people, in turn, passed them on to their warrior constituents. A multi-tiered command structure, based on graded ranks, enabled chiefs to command large numbers of warriors through an efficient and effective chain of command. The command structure allowed chiefly commanders to maintain discipline through punishment of disobedient, recalcitrant, or careless warriors, based on the support from chiefly supporters. Chiefs compelled obedience through the sanctity, authority, and power of their office (Carneiro 1992:35). Principal chiefs, in conjunction with their war councils, marshaled militia forces composed of the polity's able-bodied males. Militia mobilization took place at the principal chief's command, throughout the polity's hamlets, villages, and towns. Rapid mobilization and deployment of chiefly militias could be carried out by ruling elites in defense of their towns, and in offensive attacks against their enemies.

The precipitating factors of warfare found in the mid-sixteenth century—facilitation of chiefly financial expansion and control, legitimation of chiefly authority, and resolution of chiefly grudges—had undergone considerable alteration by the late seventeenth century (Dye 2002). The power of the hereditary paramount, whose office was still evident, had by the early eighteenth century, "dwindled away to nothing" (Nairne 1988:38) in many areas. Warfare no longer served to legitimize the authority of the principal chief, whose office had now been devalued and restricted to civil matters. However, it directly enhanced the authority of the war chiefs who "earned these Honors by the greatness of their actions" (Nairne 1988:41). Seventeenth-century war chiefs wielded considerable authority, but only under the conditions of warfare. Once they were back in their towns, warriors could ignore their war chief's dictates. The war chief's authority grew in the political vacuum created after the hereditary paramount's authority and control dwindled at the end of the sixteenth century.

The institutionalized, hierarchical political structures and formal institutions associated with chiefly warfare had changed considerably by the seventeenth century, but some structures remained relatively intact. Some degree of hierarchy is still evident, although the chain of command had weakened considerably. The war organization of most Mississippian polities continued to be stratified by hierarchical ranks. Warriors worked their way through the various military grades through the accumulation of war deeds and honors. The seventeenth century Apalachee, for example, had a ranked series of achieved military statuses (Scarry 1992:171–72). In addition to the commander or "captain," there were four warrior ranks. The Creek (Hudson 1976:225) and Natchez (du Pratz, cited in Swanton 1911:129) also had war ranks. The Cherokee's five warrior ranks served under a series of war officials, including "four beloved men with esoteric knowledge necessary for war, war priest, speaker for war, and surgeon" (Gearing 1962:26). The men elected by the warriors in turn appointed some eight officers. In addition, there was a seven-man war council. The command structure, while hierarchical, was rudimentary. In actual practice, the militia "captains" directed their own warriors.

Another area of military continuity was the hierarchical and spatial organization of the war council and war camp. The structure of the typical war camp corresponded to Nairne's (1988:42) early eighteenth-century description of a Chickasaw camp, in which "social distinctions were formally expressed in a spatial idiom" (Knight 1998:57). Their camp was in the form of a crescent, with the chief officers' "lodge" in the center. In front of the officers' fires were red "targets," upon which were placed their individual "amulet" bags or medicine bundles. No one was allowed to light a fire until the officers lit theirs and delivered some of the fire to their attendants, whose fires were in front of the officers. The other "Captains" and their attendants likewise established a line of fires in front of the officers. All of these fires were considered sacred. After the front fires had been made, the remaining warriors lit their fires and established camps behind the officers.

War councils were an important feature of seventeenth-century town life; but their power over the various militia leaders seems problematic, as the war council's authority was changed from that of an elite, policy-advising body to one having limited power to enforce its hold over individuals. The warfare cult "lost its former intimate connections with the sanctity of political aristocracy" (Knight 1986:682) by the first third of the seventeenth century. Nevertheless, "definite warfare related cult institutions persisted in many of the same societies during the Colonial era" and they "manipulated appropriate *sacra* conforming in many respects with the earlier warfare/cosmongony complex" (Knight 1986:682). The resilience of the warfare-cult institution—incorporating stylized nonutilitarian war clubs and copper axes—suggests that some aspects of late prehistoric ritual behavior continued into the seventeenth century. The war club, as one example, remained a potent symbol of military prowess and success. The Chickasaw sacred "ark," a portable shrine, also suggests continuity with earlier Mississippian rituals.

The style of warfare in the seventeenth century also showed marked changes over earlier forms of intersocietal conflict (Dye 2002). Whereas formal battles are evident, utilizing hundreds of warriors, guerrilla raids or small-scale, kin-based militia warfare became the preferred mode of fighting (figure 9.5). Another aspect of warfare was the beginning of long-term

Figure 9.5.   Theodor de Bry, after an original painting of 1564 by Jacques Le Moyne de Morgues, *Outina's Order of March*, 1591 (from *America*, 1st ed., Frankfurt-am-Main, 1591, pt. 2, pl. 14; courtesy of Birmingham, Alabama, Public Library, Prints and Map Collection).

associations with Europeans who led, organized, and instigated Native military forces, sometimes in alliances with their own forces. Slave traders may have been typical of Europeans who led Native war parties in raids against enemy forces. The objectives of these Europeans included heading and organizing slave raids, pacifying frontiers, and destroying, disrupting, and weakening their rivals' allies. The use of Natives as mercenaries laid the ground for inciting one polity against another.

Mississippian societies had various structural poses with their neighbors and distant polities. While a community might be building or maintaining alliances with one set of local groups, it could be negotiating disputes with another set, and engaging in hostile actions against yet a third. Numerous examples abound in the ethnohistoric literature of cases where groups were developing alliances, arbitrating disputes, and sending out war parties simultaneously to different polities. As is the case with modern nations, Native societies in eastern North America were engaged in a dynamic interplay of complex external relations that required a great deal of political and ritual effort on the part of leaders and their councils.

Both political life and religious conceptions were characterized by formalized and structured balance in the dualistic conception of peace and war. There were formal, named dual divisions: the White (peace) and Red (war) structures (Dye 1995; Hudson 1976:234-237; Lankford 2008:73–97). The Red side, composed of warriors, war chiefs, and other officials (such as the primary war chief's assistant and the war speaker), organized and carried out warfare; its sphere of political action was directed outside the polity. The Red side conducted rituals that prepared warriors for battle, maintained their state of sanctification, and incorporated them back into society. The White side, on the other hand, was composed of primary council leaders who managed both internal and external political activities by dominating the domestic affairs of their towns and villages and hosting visiting diplomatic delegations from neighboring polities. White-side rituals involved efforts at alliance construction, arbitration/negotiation, and warfare termination.

The relationship between White and Red organizations was not simple and straightforward (Lankford 2008:73–97). Peace embassies were sent by village councils, but the Red division usually made up the contingent. In arbitration rituals, for example, White negotiating councils sent the council speaker, the Red organization's warrior mediator, as an envoy who headed the delegation that deliberated with the community in question. Political actions were complex and elaborate, being implemented through rituals organized by White and Red leaders and their administrators in a complex web of intermeshed networks.

In order to facilitate political action, often based on religious intent, a widespread protocol based on tightly structured etiquette existed for leaders throughout eastern North America who wished to pursue interpolity negotiations (Brown 2006; Drooker 1997; Dye 1995; Hall 1997; Lankford 2008). Rituals associated with the business of establishing peace and welding alliances were complex, elaborate, and symbolic (figure 9.6). Alliance rituals may have had their origins in the rise of tribal groups of the Late Archaic period, if not earlier. By Middle Woodland times, negotiation rituals would have become highly elaborated and intermeshed with mortuary ceremonialism. European accounts from the sixteenth to eighteenth centuries provide rich ethnohistoric details of stately processions, metaphoric speeches, obligatory feasting, prestige-goods exchange, ritual dancing, offerings of tobacco, cleansing through smoking and medicinal drinks, displays of status, mock combat with symbolic weaponry, and adoption of leaders as fictive kin.

Negotiation rituals were a point of intersection for many aspects of community life (Hall 1997:156–57). On the political level, the rites established and maintained peaceful relations among unrelated groups by creating fictions of kinship between leaders. On the economic level, the ceremonies

Figure 9.6.   Theodor de Bry, after an original painting of 1564 by Jacques Le Moyne de Morgues, _A Council of State_, 1591 (from _America_, 1st ed., Frankfurt-am-Main, 1591, pt. 2, pl. 29; courtesy of Birmingham, Alabama, Public Library, Prints and Map Collection).

cushioned towns, villages, or bands against risks, such as crop failures or changes in game availability. Exchange and alliances could be established with neighbors who would provide aid and comfort in stressful times. On the social level, negotiation rituals provided a means by which capable and worthy individuals could gain higher status through personal achievements.

Although trade or exchange is often cited as the primary component of negotiation ceremonies, an additional function was the establishment of military alliances. Military aspects of negotiation, greeting, and adoption rituals included mock-combat displays, with prestigious warriors brandishing symbolic weaponry and ritual paraphernalia. Martial-arts skills were demonstrated in these orchestrated events, which emphasized the use of various types of war clubs, the recitation of war honors, and the striking of the war post. The playing of flutes had military overtones as well. Flutes, often crafted in the form of an atlatl, were widely employed in eastern North America to recruit warriors to join war parties (Hall 1997:118).

A primary objective of diplomatic negotiations was an individual's adoption into an unrelated family as fictive kin—a metaphoric act which defined the relationship and obligations between two leaders and their respective communities or polities. A standardized, international set of established rules, employed by strangers to avert violence and to weave alliances, incorporated ritual adoption, which was based on earlier mortuary ceremonialism and spirit adoption. The key to proper protocol for "well-mannered" visitations was a complex set of highly symbolic ritual behaviors, the ultimate goal of which was to establish and maintain peaceful relations or to form the foundation for forging political and military alliances.

Lankford (2008) outlines three basic stages in the international diplomatic protocol between polity leaders: the *approach*, the *preliminary council*, and the *main council*. The basic diplomatic protocol was widespread throughout eastern North American and had numerous regional and local variations. The rituals were complex and involved, often lasting several days.

In the first stage, the approach, the visitors, if not already detected by the host village, halted a short distance from the community, sending a diplomatic vanguard forward to announce their arrival. Envoys carried flutes in the Southeast, calumets in the Midwest, and wampum belts in the Northeast as symbols of their diplomatic intent and status. The host village leader or town chief came out in a procession to parley with the emissaries. The chief or the chief's representative bore material evidence of their social and political rank and status, such as emblematic regalia. Displays of status made the visitors aware of the rank and authority of specific individuals with whom they hoped to establish some type of binding arrangement, such as an alliance or an exchange partnership. Indications of status might include large retinues of warriors in full regalia; flute players; painted deerskin robes as apparel; or possibly specific rank identifiers, such as copper or shell gorgets, symbolic weaponry, tattooing and body painting, headdress regalia, mantles, and sacred bundles. Likewise, visiting ambassadors who sought political negotiations or alliances usually held the rank of chief or chief's proxy, dressing and carrying themselves in a manner appropriate to their station in society.

Upon meeting the visitors, the host leader and his entourage caressed them and offered them food. Caressing was sometimes combined with weeping, and often included a smearing or wiping of bodily fluids, such as tears, saliva, or mucus, on the visitors. In some areas of eastern North America, the hosts raised their hands toward the sun, thereby absorbing the sun's rays and power, which could then be transferred to their bodies and those of their guests. The hand raising, or "cosmic salute," may have also served as a solicitation to the sun to serve as witness to the proceedings and negotiations. The visitors, in turn, bestowed gifts on the hosts, informing them of their peaceful intentions and perhaps initially outlining their requests. At the conclusion of the approach, the combined party of hosts and advance visiting emissaries returned to the main body of visitors who waited nearby.

The second stage, the initial or preliminary council, took place between the host chief and his emissaries and the visiting leader and his entourage. The hosts advanced toward the visitors in an impressive assemblage of nobles and chiefs. The visitors and hosts were ritually cleansed and purified by mutual censing through smoking, usually tobacco, and the consumption of special medicinal libations, such as the black drink. The preparation of medicinal drinks was widespread throughout eastern North America; they were brewed in pottery jars and served in bottles and bowls encoded with sacred motifs (Dye 2006b). The guests were caressed or stroked again by the hosts, who once more rubbed bodily effluvia on the visitors as a mark of respect.

The host chief, when conferring with a visiting delegation away from the town, was supplied with an artificial lodge, or arbor, for the occasion. A temporary leafy arbor was constructed to provide a shady, cool locale for negotiations. In addition, it was sanctified by priests, to maintain the proper state of ritual purification which had been earlier achieved through the smoking ceremony and the consumption of medicinal libations. The visitors were seated upon layers of cane and tree boughs covered by woven mats or animal skins. Gifts were exchanged to reflect the new relationship of the participants. The hosts offered food to the visitors, even if they were not hungry. Feasting served as a critical element of the ritual and the rules of hospitability dictated that food must be offered. Neglecting to extend sustenance and refusing to consume proffered food would have been egregious offenses.

After explaining the purpose of the visit, the guests requested the host's hospitality, as a signal to move to the next stage of negotiations, which would take place in the village or town. If the visitors' assurances and explanations were considered sincere and acceptable to the chief, the visiting leader and his entourage would be invited into the town to continue the dialogue. As the assembled dignitaries repaired to the village or main town, the visiting group's leader was transported on a litter, the host's shoulders, or an animal skin.

As the participants were ritually purified or sanctified, they had to be carried to the arbors, leaders' lodges, or council houses to maintain their present state of purity. Where platform mounds were constructed, mound summits were the settings where negotiations typically took place. Mound summits represented the celestial realm or Upper World (Lankford 2008). The "lifting of the guests was a way of assisting them to undergo transformation from their dual state into people ritually purified for entrance into the celestial world of order, peace, social structure, and so on" (Lankford 2008:135).

The third stage of international diplomatic protocol was the main council, which was convened once the visitors entered the town and their leader was transported either to a council house or an arbor in the open, depending on weather conditions or season of the year. The assembled warriors and chiefs sat on woven cane mats or animal skins throughout the rituals. Woven mats also provided a proper repose for gifts; ritual paraphernalia, including symbolic weaponry; calumets; and sacred bundles.

In situations where the calumet was employed, beginning sometime after the late fourteenth century in the Midwest, the participants smoked the calumet pipe in complex ritual sequences. First, smoke from the calumet was offered to the sun (celestial realm), earth (lower realm), cardinal directions (Thunderers), and other world forces. Second, visitors were censed with sacred tobacco smoke to maintain their state of purity and balance. Third, the hosts took turns dancing the calumet. The dance was open to individual interpretation to some degree and was performed by warriors who used raptor-like movements with the calumet in hand. These were formal, public performances where warriors transformed themselves into supernatural heroic warriors such as Morning Star, the Twins, or Thunder, and asked for power from supernaturals such as the Great Serpent. In ritualized sequences, one or two warriors demonstrated their martial prowess, warrior status, and combat skills through use of the war club pitted against the calumet, which was wielded as a weapon. Symbolic weaponry was employed in mock combat, suggesting one function of archaeologically recovered symbolic war clubs, such as maces, swordform bifaces, and monolithic axes. War clubs were a primary symbol of cosmological power and possessed supernatural attributes and symbolic associations, particularly with the sun and thunder deities. War clubs represented chiefly divine origin and the authority of ruling elites (Van Horne 1993:160–62).

The mock combat was concluded by "striking the post" with a war club, a symbolic act also found in war rituals. In greeting or negotiation rituals, warriors recounted their war honors as a way of introducing themselves to their visitors and stating their status. If all the warriors struck the war post and recounted their war honors, the calumet dance could last for several days. Throughout the ritual events, the visitors were attended to and feted.

Eventually, the two parties arrived at the heart of the negotiations and delivered speeches to one another in highly stylistic, metaphoric, and symbolic phrases detailing their intentions and the advantages which would come about if their proposals were accepted. The negotiations defined the nature and extent of the proposed economic, kinship, political, and social relationships between the parties, with each side clarifying the boundaries of its agreement to the other's proposals. Existing relationships of alliance or enmity, and preexisting commitments with other groups, would be taken into account in building the new relationship.

A critical component of the negotiation ritual was the visiting chief's adoption into one of the host's lineages or clans. For many eastern North American societies, adoption served to replace a recently deceased leader. The adoptee, because of his rebirth, might be fed as if he were a small child or rocked as though he were an infant. As part of the adoption ritual, new clothing appropriate to the new role in the family would be provided. Reclothing was part of the symbolism associated with the reincarnation of a deceased leader, as well as an indication of the visitor's new status. "Strangers were not only symbolically reborn but figuratively reclothed with mantles of honorary leadership, reprising in their persons roles earlier filled by members of a cast of honored dead" (Hall 1997:41). Reclothing of the adoptee in garments belonging to the deceased was part of the symbolism of the reincarnation of the deceased (Hall 1997:163).

The visiting leader was usually adopted as a brother of the chief, generally an elder brother who would be "a generous provider, concerned with the welfare of his larger family, and would be expected to defend them with his abilities as a warrior" (Lankford 2008:111). The "child" honored "was symbolically reconceived, physically reclothed, socially redefined, and made a new link in a chain of simulated kinship connecting two otherwise unrelated bands or villages" (Hall 1997:41). The adoption component of the negotiation ritual was presumably the denouement of the discussions and proceedings. The prototype for the ceremony was a requickening rite to raise a deceased chief symbolically in the person being honored (Hall 1997:82). The purpose of the negotiation ceremony was "the promise of children, long life, and plenty," to create bonds of kinship between two otherwise unrelated groups of people, and to facilitate intertribal trade (Hall 1997:83).

Rituals of negotiation and feuding/warfare evolved in eastern North America during an early period of prehistory and almost certainly were in place in some form whenever exchange took place between non-kin-related local groups. The exchange of highly crafted, exotic items would have entailed diplomatic negotiations and discussions that allowed goods and people to move throughout much of eastern North America.

CHAPTER TEN

The Paths of War and Peace
in Eastern North America

It ain't as much the things we don't know that gets us into trouble. It's the things we know ain't so.

Artemus Ward

Three broad patterns or types of lethal aggression may be identified in Native eastern North America: self-redress homicides, feuds, and warfare. In self-redress homicides, individuals settle disputes through their own aggressive actions. Feuds may result if blood revenge follows a homicide, but feuds are usually limited to one or two killings at a time and generally lack political objectives. Warfare, on the other hand, is organized violence that affects the balance of power between independent political groups or communities, and it often has clear political objectives.

Organized violence in eastern North America underwent a series of transformations, from absence of warfare to the chiefly warfare documented at European contact. From about 11,000 to 5000 BC, violence among simple, unsegmented hunter-gatherers typically would have been restricted to self-redress homicides. As simple foraging societies began to develop social segmentation, feuding became more prevalent. In time, chiefly warfare, based on raiding, incorporated formal, hierarchical institutions and inherited offices as part of elite aggrandizement.

In this book, I suggest that these three types of lethal aggression are apparent in prehistoric and early historic eastern North America from approximately 11,000 BC to around AD 1700. The first type is characterized by self-redress

homicides and appears to have been the predominant mode of justice seeking from the Paleoindian to the latter part of the Middle Archaic period (ca.
11,000 to 5000 BC). Feuding may have been the prevalent form of retaliatory
justice during the Late Archaic through Late Woodland periods (ca. 5000 BC
to AD 1000). The third pattern or type of lethal aggression is warfare, which
may have been typical of Mississippian and related regional polities (ca. AD
1000 to 1700). Each of these aggression types is associated with other broad
trends in domestic, ideological, political, settlement, social, and subsistence
organization.

Archaeologists take a variety of stances in their interpretations of evidence for lethal aggression in eastern North America. Some point to the
paucity of evidence and propose that there was little, if any, violence in the
past, especially feuding and warfare. Others look at the evidence for violence,
interpret it as minimal, and attribute it to nonfeud/war activities such as
hunting or sports-related accidents. Still others see violence in the form of
feuding and warfare as endemic in prehistory. How do we reconcile these varied and conflicting positions? In this chapter I argue that each stance has its
merits, depending on the time period, the type of sociopolitical organization,
and the region of eastern North America.

To understand cycles of violence and cooperation, and the institutions
used to curb violence and promote cooperation, one must distinguish between interpersonal violence and intergroup violence. Interpersonal violence is physical aggression between people, often triggered by the desire to
interfere with the activities of another person or to avenge some real or imagined wrong. Such grudges are sometimes resolved by self-redress homicides or
feuding and may result in killing. While interpersonal violence is not war, it
may lead to war under certain conditions. Intergroup violence is conflict mobilized to fuel grievances between social groups. Such violence is considered
war when it "involves entire groups organized as political communities,
and—intentionally or unintentionally—its outcomes affect the balance of
power between such social groups and communities" (Wolf 1987:129).

In virtually every society, some kind of fighting or violence takes place, in
spite of those institutions that maintain positive relations, promote cooperation, and quell violence. In this book I argue that the three modes of violence
coevolved with political and social organization. That is, there are linkages
among peace, levels of aggressive behavior, and sociopolitical organization. As
shown by archaeological examples from eastern North America—especially
the Northeast, Midwest, and Southeast—sociopolitical complexity and the
nature of peace and lethal aggression are intertwined in complex but patterned ways. Haas (2001:343) cautions that complexity is not a cause of war:

"The higher frequency of warfare in states and chiefdoms is not necessarily a product of organizational complexity; rather, the economic and demographic conditions that are conducive to warfare also are conducive to the development of complex, centralized polities." Researchers have noted the correlation between conflict and social complexity (Fry 2006; Haas 2001; Kelly 2000). Haas (2001:343), for example, notes that "the level, intensity, and impact of warfare tend to increase as cultural systems become more complex."

Fry (2006:112–13) proposes a model of the patterns of lethal conflict and justice seeking in relation to social organization. He concludes that "patterns of fighting, conflict management, and justice seeking all relate to social organization" (2006:113). Each pattern of conflict is associated with a level of sociopolitical complexity. Self-redress revenge homicide is typical of nomadic hunter-gatherers, feuding is typical of tribes, and warfare is typical of chiefdoms (Fry 2006:table 8.4). Fry's model reflects the central tendencies in the relation of lethal aggression to social organization and has relevance to eastern North America.

Nomadic hunters and gatherers in the past employed a variety of violent and nonviolent solutions to resolve conflicts and to seek justice. In self-redress revenge homicide, a person with a grievance takes aggressive unilateral action to punish another individual or to prevail in a dispute (Fry 2006:23). Individual self-redress is a coercive approach to settling disputes and may or may not be lethal. Aggrieved individuals take justice into their own hands to seek retribution, but self-redress can lead to increased conflict if not contained through institutions that ameliorate violence and aggression. Vengeance seeking through violent self-redress is an activity that may lead to feuding, if reciprocated.

Lethal, individual self-redress homicides, although not universally present in hunting-and-gathering groups, are usually present among nomadic band societies. Fry (2006:112) notes that individual self-redress homicide as a revenge mechanism is typical of simple nomadic hunter-gatherers, while feuds and warfare are rare. Self-redress steadily decreases and feuding and warfare increase as subsistence patterns incorporate plant cultivation. Feuding increases with the rise of societies exhibiting segmental social systems, such as local groups or tribes. Individual self-redress occurs more frequently than protracted feuding in simple band societies because nomadic foragers tend to lack the well-developed social segments generally present in more complex societies (Kelly 2000).

In unsegmented societies, a homicide is likely to be "perceived and experienced as an individual loss shared with some kin rather than as an injury to

the group" (Kelly 2000:47). In simple nomadic-band societies that lack social segments, justice prevails when the killer, rather than another family
member, is the target of lethal revenge. In foraging groups in which social
segments are weakly developed or altogether lacking, the sense of justice is
often achieved when a killer is killed. Balance is restored between the two
families after the homicide is over, and the families generally put the matter
behind them (Kelly 2000:111). Relative peace is established and maintained
in egalitarian band societies because each individual exercises a high degree
of personal autonomy. Individuals are left to their own devices to pursue personal grievances. Authority is minimal, and leadership is weakly developed;
no one has the authority to adjudicate disputes, hand down enforceable judg-
ments, or call for organized lethal aggression.

One of several factors working against the development of social substitutability and kin-based collective military action among simple nomadic
foragers is the weakness of social segments, such as patrilineal or matrilineal kin units. Individual self-redress is more common in forager bands than
in other types of societies because the former lack lineage development.
The desired targets of self-redress homicides tend to be the perpetrators of
misdeeds (Kelly 2000:113). Thus, homicides are typical of family-level foragers, but social segments are not in place for more organized violence.
"Contrary to the warring over women and territory assumption, disputes
over women, when occurring between members of different bands, tend to
be individual affairs rather than the foundation for intergroup warfare" (Fry
2006:183).

Nomadic foragers emphasize egalitarianism, sharing, and generosity. The
execution of recidivist killers, violent persons, and bullies is pervasively reported for band societies. Execution of individuals who behave too aggressively may be a pattern generalized to nomadic foragers (Boehm 1999:82).
As a result of the high levels of individual autonomy in simple foraging societies, disputes are personal and conflicts are dealt with through avoidance, discussion, homicide, mediation, toleration, and verbal resolution.
Much of the fighting at the family-group level of social organization stems
from sexual jealousy and homicide. Serious aggression tends to result most
typically from "women and corpses" (Fry 2006:229). Rather than fighting
over resources, the "typical pattern is for groups to get along . . . relying on
resources within their own areas and respecting the resources of their
neighbors" (Fry 2006:183). Younger (2005, cited in Dentan 2008:47) suggests, based on computer simulation, that the optimum form of governance
for small-scale human groups such as hunter-gatherers and foragers is
peaceful egalitarianism.

Self-Redress Homicide among Simple Hunter-Gatherers in Eastern North America

Self-redress homicides, as opposed to feuding or warfare, may have characterized early mobile foragers throughout eastern North America. As a means to obtain justice, self-redress homicide would be limited to the killing of a killer or of the killer's immediate kin, and would be most typical when sociopolitical integration was organized at the family group. Cooperation is maintained through family ties, generally bilocal residence, and alliances between nonkin. Feuding and warfare are not typical of simple foraging bands because band societies lack the cohesive kin organizations necessary to sustain violence beyond personal grievances (Knauft 1991:405).

Archaeological evidence of conflict during the period from approximately 11,000 to 5000 BC is lacking for a variety of reasons. The mobility of simple foragers precludes the patterns of evidence generally used to demonstrate violence in the past. Knowledge of skeletal trauma is deficient because cemeteries are rare. Rather, the archaeological signature for conflict resolution is seen in the widespread manufacture and exchange of exotic blades, which are often cached. Large Dalton bifaces, thought to be evidence of alliances, appear in the archaeological record as early as 8500 BC. Earlier caches of hypertrophic blades have been recorded in Clovis contexts outside eastern North America, but the earliest evidence in the Eastern Woodlands of symbolic weaponry is associated with human remains in the northeastern Arkansas Dalton Sloan cemetery (Walthall and Koldehoff 1998).

If it were available, archaeological evidence of human skeletal trauma during the Paleoindian and Early Archaic periods would include individuals killed in retaliation for murder or because of sexual jealousy. In a well-preserved skeletal series, we would expect characteristics of feuding and warfare to be absent: healed fractures, mass graves, mutilation, and trophy taking. Evidence of rodent or carnivore gnawing would also be largely absent, because the victim's kin would presumably have buried the victim shortly after death. Most of those killed would have been males.

To date there is no agreed-upon evidence to assess the nature and degree of peace and violence among early hunter-gatherers in eastern North America. Analogy with modern foragers suggests that for some six thousand years, between 11,000 and 5000 BC, the early hunter-gatherers of eastern North America could have maintained peaceful relationships through avoidance, toleration, discussion, mediation, and verbal resolution. On occasion, recidivist killers would have been dealt with through homicides, resulting in some human remains that would show signs of violent death. With few exceptions, evidence from human remains is lacking. In the Sloan Dalton cemetery, for example, skeletal material is too fragmentary and indistinct to enable assessment of skeletal trauma; but the cemetery does contain the earliest symbolic weaponry in eastern North America, emphasizing the need for maintenance of cooperation and alliance.

Period of Feuding among Complex Hunter-Gatherers in Eastern North America

The six-thousand-year period between 5000 BC and AD 1000, despite considerable cultural variability, appears to have been characterized by justice seeking obtained through feuding, which in turn was fueled by social substitution and social segmentation. Feuding is characterized by "fighting in pursuit of individual or family ends rather than community or societal ends" (Carneiro 1994:6). Feuding is a personal or family matter and may result in revenge raids where kinship ties outweigh political allegiance. A feud is a "situation of reciprocal violence where one grudge precipitates retaliation, which in its turn becomes another grudge that ignites counter retaliation, and so on" (Reyna 1994:38). Feuds are usually "outbursts of unpremeditated, limited hostility" (Pospisil 1994:115) and entail "armed combat between the fraternal interest groups within a political community" (Otterbein 1994:xix–xx).

Feuding differs from war in three basic ways: (1) it is limited to one or two killings at a time, (2) only one side takes the offensive at a time, and (3) there is no clear or necessary political objective beyond the maintenance of individual or family honor (Boehm 1987:221). The amount of pressure to end the conflict that is brought to bear on feuding parties from their own groups increases in proportion to the necessity of cooperation between the two groups (Boehm 1987:157). In feuding, blood revenge typically follows a homicide (Otterbein and Otterbein 1965:1470) and may be considered a patterned form of reciprocal homicide (Fry 2006:86).

Dennen (1995:93) points out that "in war—as contrasted with a feud— violence is relatively 'promiscuous': Anyone of the opposing community may be defined as an 'enemy' and thus be a potential victim. In a feud, the concept of enemy—and potential victim—is more restricted and selective: A particular member or members of a particular kinship group, family or clan." Therefore, self-redress homicides, feuding, and war should be considered patterned themes of lethal aggression. In classic blood feud, both the malefactor and their relatives are considered to be appropriate targets of vengeance. Feuding can be seen as a judicial mechanism in which aggrieved kin groups seek their own justice (Fry 2006:90).

The transition from nomadic, family-level foragers characterized by self-redress homicides to local groups or tribes who may have carried out blood feuds appears to have taken place around 5000 BC (Milner 1999). While self-redress revenge homicide and warfare may be variable occurrences, feuding is the typical means of settling disputes and conflict in segmented social systems. The family hamlet may have characterized some hunter-gatherers around 8000 to 6000 BC. Family hamlets have somewhat higher population densities than family camps, and families tend to cluster into settlement groups or hamlets on a more permanent basis. Feuding may become prevalent among family hamlets as population density gradually increases.

Key evidence for intergroup conflict, such as embedded dart points and trophy taking, appears as early 5000 BC. Skeletal trauma in the form of peri-mortem mutilation associated with trophy taking, and mass burial of individuals with embedded projectile points and broken and fractured bones, are evident some three to four thousand years ago. Modified human bones as grave accompaniments are probably evidence of prestige conferred by trophy taking in raids. Late Archaic buffer zones and territoriality may well have resulted from competition over scarce resources. The initial rise of local groups or tribal societies around 5000 BC may have brought about violence based on kin-based raiding (Anderson 2001). Although many examples of skeletal trauma undoubtedly resulted from interpersonal violence due to self-redress homicides, organized raiding may have occurred periodically. Tribal feuding is based on the organized means of violence carried out by small, informal, and temporary kin-militia groups working under weak chains of command with rudimentary powers of dispersion (Reyna 1994:40–43).

In support of the initiation of a feuding style of conflict resolution, victims of violence begin to appear with regularity around 5000 BC, when embedded spear points, mass graves, overkill, pin-cushioning, and trophy-taking behavior enter the archaeological record (Milner 1999:120). The beginning of tribal organization and social substitution allow a feuding type of conflict settlement to flourish. There is abundant archaeological evidence substantiating claims for feuding as opposed to self-redress homicide or warfare. In contexts where large samples of human skeletal remains are available, feuding based on social substitution is clearly evident.

During the period of feuding, from around 5000 BC to AD 1000, foraging shifts to initial efforts at gardening, and later to well-developed swidden agriculture. What remains essentially the same is the generally mobile character of small-family and local populations, although the degree of mobility is vari-able, with a general trend toward sedentariness through time. In the larger flood plains of the Deep South and along the southern coastal areas, popula-tions became sedentary earlier than those in the more northern areas. Ar-chaeological evidence indicates that feuding developed earliest in these broad flood plains of large rivers and southern coastal areas.

Alliance formation and conflict resolution may have been achieved through mourning rituals that utilized Late Archaic symbolic weaponry in the form of bannerstones, blade caches, and other tokens of exchange and wealth that were widely circulated. The dramatic and spectacular exchange systems of Early and Middle Woodland times may in large part have stemmed from conflict resolution associated with a feuding style of justice seeking. Early and Middle Woodland mortuary ceremonialism may have resulted from innovative ways of forming alliances and institutions of cooperation. With the rise of horticulture, feuding may have escalated, but tensions may have been dampened through the creation and maintenance of extensive ex-change systems based on symbolic weaponry distributed through the context of mortuary ceremonialism. Skeletal evidence of feuding is not found in cemeteries; but mounds include human trophies as burial accompaniments, along with symbolic weaponry, suggesting that the institutions of alliance building and peace maintenance were based on mortuary ritual. The Late Ar-chaic period is also characterized by clear evidence of trophy taking and rit-ual use of symbolic weaponry, which was perhaps employed in the context of funerary ritual.

By 200 BC, trophy taking, symbolic weaponry, and evidence for the earli-est combat iconography are apparent in the archaeological record. Combat iconography came into existence with human forms lacking heads, hands, or feet. Postmarital residence patterns appear to have shifted from bilocal to pa-trilocal during the period of feuding, creating an optimum environment for the creation of fraternal interest groups that may have based their prestige in part on the symbolic representation of trophy taking. Warrior prestige and honors gained in intersocietal conflict appeared during the period of feuding. Peacemaking mechanisms tend to be associated with patrilocal residence and internal warfare (Divale 1984:205). Substantial evidence for violence and the mechanisms for reducing violence are clearly apparent from AD 400 to 1000, when evidence for trophy taking and violence continue to be seen in the archaeological record. Symbolic weaponry was exchanged in the form of stone ax heads, and arrow points are embedded in bodies, signaling a new de-velopment in combat tactics and behavior.

Warfare among Regional Polities in Eastern North America

Regional polities during the period of warfare included chiefdoms and tribes that were bound together by linguistic affiliation, political alliances, and social ties. Warfare developed in the sense that large social groups, whether organized as regional polities or complex local groups, began to pursue "national" policies through organized lethal aggression and alliances. The key administrators of justice sequentially change as social complexity increases from individual self-redress in family groups to feuding among local kin groups, and then, eventually, to public officials in regional polities (Fry 2006:110). Peace in chiefdoms can be kept through a class of legal procedures consisting of duels, juridical fights, and physical punishment, whose purpose is to deliver justice within the polity at a minimal amount of violence (Fry 2006:159); but lethal aggression in the form of torture and death may be meted out to nonkin captured from neighboring regional polities or complex local groups.

Warfare is "organized violence between two autonomous groups that are not part of a more inclusive political structure, the conflict being authorized by their leadership" (Pospisil 1994:114), and includes armed combat between political communities (Otterbein 1994:xix). War is

a group activity, carried on by members of one community against members of another community, in which it is the primary purpose to inflict serious injury or death on multiple nonspecific members of that other community, or in which the primary purpose makes it highly likely that serious injury or death will be inflicted on multiple nonspecified members of that community in the accomplishment of that primary purpose. (Prosterman 1972:140)

These definitions are particularly useful because they clearly exclude individual homicides, on the one hand, and feuding, on the other, from warfare, and clarify war as entailing relatively impersonal lethal aggression organized for political motives between autonomous communities (Fry 2006:91).

Warfare and efforts to ameliorate violence, at least in certain contexts, were widespread and endemic in some areas, especially the mid-continent, during the period from AD 1000 to 1700. Major transformations in domestic life, political and social organization, and subsistence practices took place during this time. Social segmentation increased with the widespread development of matrilocality in much of eastern North America. A shift from patrilocal to matrilocal postmarital residence patterns took place throughout a large area, from the Mississippian Southeast and Lower Midwest to the Upper Midwest Oneota and the northeastern Iroquoian speakers. Matrilocal postmarital residence breaks up the fraternal interest groups associated with patrilocal residence, and promotes militas of unrelated males who are socialized in special men's residences or meeting halls, such as council houses. Matrilocal residence is correlated with warfare, and, when it is present, relations with neighboring societies tend to be unstable, in an atmosphere of external warfare (Divale 1984:205).

Efforts at establishing peace are evident in the form of ceremonial regalia such as pipes and other ritual accoutrements. Symbolic weaponry may denote rituals for promoting and cementing alliances. By approximately AD 1050, the New Fire Ceremony is evident in the Cahokia area, and by around AD 1300 the Calumet Ceremony had developed in the Upper Midwest. Both ceremonies, and perhaps the Sun Dance, became important formal ritual institutions for creating and maintaining social and political alliances, replacing the mortuary-based institutions of feuding—but retaining certain elements, such as adoption of living people to replace the dead.

Changes in subsistence, from swidden agriculture to field agriculture, over a large area of eastern North America early in the second millennium provided storable surplus that was used by elites to fund corporate projects. Settlement patterns shifted, with populations changing from mobile horticulturists to sedentary village or town farmers, who sequestered themselves in many areas of eastern North America in fortified communities located in strategic locales. Consequently, a decline in health took place as a result of poor nutrition and crowded living conditions. Archaeological evidence for warfare is abundant in the form of skeletal trauma; fortified villages and towns; widespread combat iconography; and symbolic weaponry, interred as burial accompaniments, displayed as ritual caches, and portrayed in legitimizing iconography. Prestige accruing from war honors became a critical currency that warriors were mandated to earn and display to be successful, respected, and prosperous members of society. Social advancement, entrance into secret societies, and strategic marriages to desirable spouses may have been largely based on war honors.

Conflict and efforts to seek alliances are well-documented archaeologically in eastern North America beginning with the rise of tribal societies in the sixth millennium BC. Prior to the beginning of feuding, self-redress homicides were the means to justice. The amelioration of conflicts was based on kin connections and exchange relations. The difference between these early, self-redress societies and later, feuding societies with high frequencies of raiding lies in the absence of segmentary systems among the former and the presence of segmentary social units within the latter. Unsegmented societies generally lack permanent extended families and the development of lineages or clans beyond the local group. While they do exhibit capital punishment for homicide and spontaneous conflicts over access to resources, organized group violence is rare. Segmentary social groups, such as tribes and regional polities, exhibit high levels of raiding and death rates per capita; torture; emerging warrior ethos; and trophy-taking behavior. Based on social units that may be divided into subunits, segmentary societies may combine into progressively inclusive units for common interests such as defensive or offensive actions against enemies.

Segmentary societies embrace the principle of social substitutability: the killing of any member of another segment is considered a group offense, and can be avenged by killing any member of the offender's segment. Raiding thus begins as group versus group social action, and can escalate into war as societies grow in organization, scale, and complexity.

Raiding often begins in environments rich in resources, in which societies "can afford to have enemies for neighbors" (Kelly 2000:135). Lack of resources encourages cooperation that is mutually beneficial. As population increases, reliable storage facilities and surplus come into being, bringing about the emergence of segmentary organization and the increased likelihood of feuding and war. With greater use of base camps in highly productive, resource-rich coastal and riverine environments around 5000 BC, evidence for social segmentation and raiding is clearly evident. The causes and transformation of regional polity warfare centered on storable surpluses and the political ambitions of chiefs to consolidate political authority within their polities, as well as to establish external relationships with neighbors through alliances, tribute, or incorporation.

We have seen that peacemaking goes hand in hand with lethal aggression, and that violence and peace have coevolved within Native American society over some eleven thousand years in eastern North America. Peace is not just an absence of war and violence, but rather it is "a different way of living with its own distinctive signatures and practices" (Arkush 2008:564). The capacity for violence is tempered with the potential for highly elaborated peacemaking institutions. While no society is totally devoid of violence, eastern North American Native societies that were highly skilled at warfare also bear witness to the development and establishment of complex rituals and social behaviors designed to ameliorate conflicts, promote cooperation, and reduce aggression.

References Cited

Abler, Thomas S. (1980). Iroquois Cannibalism: Fact Not Fiction. *Ethnohistory* 27:309–16.

Abler, Thomas S. (1989). European Technology and the Art of War in Iroquoia. In *Cultures in Conflict: Current Archaeological Perspectives*, edited by D. C. Tkaczuk and B. C. Vivian, pp. 273–82. University of Calgary Archaeological Association, Calgary.

Adovasio, James M., and David R. Pedler (2005). The Peopling of North America. In *North American Archaeology*, edited by Timothy R. Pauketat and Diana D. Loren, pp. 30–55. Blackwell, Cambridge (MA).

Alley, R. B., P. A. Mayewski, T. Sowers, M. Stuiver, K. C. Taylor, and P. U. Clark (1997). Holocene Climate Instability: A Prominent, Widespread Event 8,200 Years Ago. *Geology* 25:483–86.

Anderson, David G. (1990). The Paleoindian Colonization of Eastern North America: A View from the Southeastern United States. In *Early Paleoindian Economies of Eastern North America*, edited by Kenneth B. Tankersley and Barry L. Isaac, pp. 163–216. Research in Economic Anthropology, Supplement 5. JAI Press, Greenwich (CT).

Anderson, David G. (1994a). Factional Competition and the Political Evolution of Mississippian Chiefdoms in the Southeastern United States. In *Factional Competition in the New World*, edited by Elizabeth M. Brumfiel and John W. Fox, pp. 61–76. Cambridge University Press, Cambridge.

Anderson, David G. (1994b). *The Savannah River Chiefdoms: Political Change in the Late Prehistoric Southeast*. University of Alabama Press, Tuscaloosa.

Anderson, David G. (1996a). Models of Paleoindian and Early Archaic Settlement in the Lower Southeast. In *The Paleoindian and Early Archaic Southeast*, edited by

David G. Anderson and Kenneth E. Sassaman, pp. 29–57. University of Alabama Press, Tuscaloosa.

Anderson, David G. (1996b). Approaches to Modeling Regional Settlement in the Archaic Period Southeast. In *Archaeology of the Mid-Holocene Southeast*, edited by Kenneth E. Sassaman and David G. Anderson, pp. 157–76. University Press of Florida, Gainesville.

Anderson, David G. (1999). Examining Chiefdoms in the Southeast: An Application of Multiscalar Analysis. In *Great Towns and Regional Polities in the Prehistoric American Southwest and Southeast*, edited by Jill E. Neitzel, pp. 215–41. University of New Mexico Press, Albuquerque.

Anderson, David G. (2001). Climate and Culture Change in Prehistoric and Early Historic Eastern North America. *Archaeology of Eastern North America* 29:143–86.

Anderson, David G. (2002). The Evolution of Tribal Social Organization in the Southeastern U.S. In *Archaeology of Tribal Societies*, edited by William A. Parkinson, pp. 246–77. Archaeological Series 15. International Monographs in Prehistory, Ann Arbor (MI).

Anderson, David G. (2004). Archaic Mounds and the Archaeology of Southeastern Tribal Societies. In *Signs of Power: The Rise of Cultural Complexity in the Southeast*, edited by Jon L. Gibson and Philip J. Carr, pp. 270–99. University of Alabama Press, Tuscaloosa.

Anderson, David G., and Robert C. Mainfort, Jr. (2002). An Introduction to Woodland Archaeology in the Southeast. In *The Woodland Southeast*, edited by David G. Anderson and Robert C. Mainfort, Jr., pp. 1–19. University of Alabama Press, Tuscaloosa.

Anderson, David G., Lisa D. O'Steen, and Kenneth E. Sassaman (1996). Environmental and Chronological Considerations. In *The Paleoindian and Early Archaic Southeast*, edited by David G. Anderson and Kenneth E. Sassaman, pp. 3–15. University of Alabama Press, Tuscaloosa.

Anderson, David G., and Kenney E. Sassaman (1996). Modeling Paleoindian and Early Archaic Settlement in the Southeast: A Historical Perspective. In *The Paleoindian and Early Archaic Southeast*, edited by David G. Anderson and Kenneth E. Sassaman, pp. 16–28. University of Alabama Press, Tuscaloosa.

Anderson, David G., David W. Stahle, and Malcolm K. Cleaveland (1995). Paleoclimate and the Potential Food Reserves of Mississippian Societies: A Case Study from the Savannah River Valley. *American Antiquity* 60:258–86.

Arkush, Elizabeth. Warfare and Violence in the Americas. *American Antiquity* 73:560–64.

Arkush, Elizabeth N., and Mark W. Allen, editors (2006). *The Archaeology of Warfare: Prehistories of Raiding and Conquest*. University Press of Florida, Gainesville.

Axtell, James, and William C. Sturtevant (1980). The Unkindest Cut, or Who Invented Scalping? *William and Mary Quarterly* 37:451–72.

Baillie, Mike (1999). *Exodus to Arthur: Catastrophic Encounters with Comets*. B. T. Batsford, London.

Barbour, Philip, editor (1986). *The Complete Works of Captain John Smith (1580–1631)*. 3 vols. University of North Carolina Press, Chapel Hill.

Benn, David W. (1989). Hawks, Serpents, and Bird-Men: Emergence of the Oneota Mode of Production. *Plains Anthropologist* 34:233–60.

Benson, Larry V., Michael S. Berry, Edward A. Jolie, Jerry D. Spangler, David W. Stahle, and Eugene M. Hattori (2007). Possible Impacts of Early-11th-, Middle-12th-, and Late- 13th-Century Droughts on Western Native Americans and the Mississippian Cahokians. *Quaternary Science Reviews* 26:336–50.

Berglund, Birgitta E. (2003). Human Impact and Climate Changes: Synchronous Events and a Causal Link? *Quaternary International* 105:7–12.

Binford, Lewis R. (1980). Willow Smoke and Dogs' Tails: Hunter-Gatherer Settlement Systems and Archaeological Site Formation. *American Antiquity* 45:4–20.

Birk, Douglas, and Elden Johnson (1992). The Mdewakanton Dakota and Initial French Contact. In *Calumet and Fleur-De-Lys, Archaeology of Indian and French Contact in the Midcontinent*, edited by John A. Walthall and Thomas E. Emerson, pp. 203–40. Smithsonian Institution Press, Washington, DC.

Birmingham, Robert A., and Lynne G. Goldstein (2005). *Aztalan: Mysteries of an Ancient Indian Town*. Wisconsin Historical Society Press, Madison.

Blakeslee, Donald J. (1981). The Origins and Spread of the Calumet Ceremony. *American Antiquity* 46:759–68.

Blanton, Dennis B., and Kenneth E. Sassaman (1989). Pattern and Process in the Middle Archaic Period of South Carolina. In *Studies in South Carolina Archaeology in Honor of Dr. Robert L. Stephenson*, edited by Albert C. Goodyear III and Glen T. Hanson, pp. 53–72. Anthropological Studies 9. South Carolina Institute of Archaeology and Anthropology, University of South Carolina, Columbia.

Blitz, John H. (1988). Adoption of the Bow in Prehistoric North America. *North American Archaeologist* 9:123–45.

Boehm, Christopher (1987). *Blood Revenge: The Enactment and Management of Conflict in Montenegro and Other Tribal Societies*. 2nd edition. University of Pennsylvania Press, Philadelphia.

Boehm, Christopher (1999). *Hierarchy in the Forest: The Evolution of Egalitarian Behavior*. Harvard University Press, Cambridge.

Bowers, Alfred W. (1965). *Hidatsa Social and Ceremonial Organization*. Bulletin 194. Bureau of American Ethnology, Smithsonian Institution. (Reprinted, with an introduction by Douglas R. Parks; University of Nebraska Press, Lincoln, 1992).

Bradford, R. D. (1988). *Historic Forts of Ontario*. Mika, Belleville (ON).

Brandão, José A. (1997). *"Your Fyre Shall Burn No More": Iroquois Policy toward New France and Its Native Allies to 1701*. University of Nebraska Press, Lincoln.

Brandão, José A. (2003). *Nation Iroquoise: A Seventeenth-Century Ethnography of the Iroquois*. University of Nebraska Press, Lincoln.

Brashler, Janet G., Elizabeth B. Garland, Margaret B. Holman, William A. Lovis, and Sudan R. Martin (2000). Adaptive Strategies and Socioeconomic Systems in Northern Great Lakes Riverine Environments: The Late Woodland of Michigan.

In *Late Woodland Societies: Tradition and Transformation across the Midcontinent*, edited by Thomas E. Emerson, Dale L. McElrath, and Andrew C. Fortier, pp. 543–79. University of Nebraska Press, Lincoln.

Brasser, Theodore J. (1961). War Clubs. *American Indian Tradition* 7:77–83.

Brasser, Theodore J. (1978). Early Indian-European Contacts. In *Handbook of North American Indians*, Vol. 15, Northeast, edited by Bruce G. Trigger, pp. 78–88. Smithsonian Institution Press, Washington, DC.

Braun, David P., and Stephen Plog (1982). Evolution of "Tribal" Social Networks: Theory and Prehistoric North American Evidence. *American Antiquity* 47:504–25.

Brice, M. (1984). *Stronghold: A History of Military Architecture*. B. T. Batsford, London.

Bridges, Patricia S. (1996). Warfare and Mortality at Koger's Island, Alabama. *International Journal of Osteoarchaeology* 6:66–75.

Bridges, Patricia S., Keith P. Jacobi, and Mary L. Powell (2000). Warfare-Related Trauma in the Late Prehistory of Alabama. In *Bioarchaeological Studies of Life in the Age of Agriculture: A View from the Southeast*, edited by Patricia M. Lambert, pp. 35–62. University of Alabama Press, Tuscaloosa.

Broecker, Wallace S. (2001). Was the Medieval Warm Period Global? *Science* 291:1497–99.

Brose, David S. (1979). A Speculative Model on the Role of Exchange in the Prehistory of the Eastern Woodlands. In *Hopewell Archaeology: The Chillicothe Conference*, edited by David S. Brose and N'omi Greber, pp. 3–8. Kent State University Press, Kent (OH).

Brose, David S. (1994). Trade and Exchange in the Midwestern United States. In *Prehistoric Exchange Systems in North America*, edited by Timothy G. Baugh and Jonathon E. Ericson, pp. 215–40. Plenum Press, New York.

Brose, David S. (2000). Late Prehistoric Societies of Northeastern Ohio and Adjacent Portions of the South Shore of Lake Erie: A Review. In *Cultures before Contact: The Late Prehistory of Ohio and Surrounding Regions*, edited by Robert A. Genheimer, pp. 96–122.

Brose, David S. (2001). Penumbral Protohistory on Lake Erie's South Shore. In *Societies in Eclipse: Archaeology of the Eastern Woodlands Indians, A.D. 1450–1700*, edited by David S. Brose, C. Wesley Cowan, and Robert C. Mainfort, Jr., pp. 49–65. Smithsonian Institution Press, Washington, DC.

Brose, David S., and N'omi Greber, editors (1979). *Hopewell Archaeology: The Chillicothe Conference*. Kent State University Press, Kent (OH).

Brown, Ian W. (2006). The Calumet Ceremony in the Southeast as Observed Archaeologically. In *Powhatan's Mantle: Indians in the Colonial Southeast*, edited by Gregory A. Waselkov, Peter H. Wood, and Tom Hatley, pp. 371–419. Revised and expanded edition. University of Nebraska Press, Lincoln.

Brown, James A. (1979). Charnel Houses and Mortuary Crypts: Disposal of the Dead in the Middle Woodland Period. In *Hopewell Archaeology: The Chillicothe Confer-*

ence, edited by David S. Brose and N'omi Greber, pp. 211–19. Kent State University Press, Kent (OH).

Brown, James A. (1985). The Mississippian Period. In *Ancient Art of the American Woodland Indians*, edited by David S. Brose, James A. Brown, and David W. Penny, pp. 93–145. Harry N. Abrams, New York.

Brown, James A. (1996). *The Spiro Ceremonial Center: The Archaeology of Arkansas Valley Caddoan Culture in Eastern Oklahoma*. 2 vols. Memoirs of the Museum of Anthropology 29. University of Michigan, Ann Arbor.

Brown, James A. (1997). The Archaeology of Ancient Religion in the Eastern Woodlands. *Annual Reviews in Anthropology* 26:465–85.

Brown, James A. (2004a). Exchange and Interaction to A.D. 1500. In *Handbook of North American Indians*, Vol. 14, Northeast, edited by William C. Sturtevant, pp. 677–85. Smithsonian Institution, Washington, DC.

Brown, James A. (2004b). The Cahokia Expression: Creating Court and Cult. In *Hero, Hawk, and Open Hand: American Indian Art of the Ancient Midwest and South*, edited by Richard F. Townsend, pp. 105–23. Yale University Press, New Haven.

Brown, James A., and David H. Dye (2007). Severed Heads and Sacred Scalplocks: Mississippian Iconographic Trophies. In *The Taking and Displaying of Human Body Parts as Trophies by Amerindians*, edited by Richard J. Chacon and David H. Dye, pp. 274–94. Springer, New York.

Brown, James A., and John Kelly (2000). Cahokia and the Southeastern Ceremonial Complex. In *Mounds, Modoc, and Mesoamerica: Papers in Honor of Melvin L. Fowler*, edited by Steven R. Ahler, pp. 469–510. Scientific Papers 28. Illinois State Museum, Springfield.

Brown, M. Kathryn, and Travis W. Stanton, editors (2003). *Ancient Mesoamerican Warfare*. AltaMira Press, New York.

Budinoff, Linda C. (1976). Bioarchaeology of the Drew Cemetery: A Non-Elite, Non-Mound Burial Site at the Adena-Hopewell Transition in Southwestern Ohio. Unpublished M.A. thesis, Department of Anthropology, State University of New York, Binghamton.

Buikstra, Jane E. (1979). Contributions of Physical Anthropologists to the Concept of Hopewell: A Historical Perspective. In *Hopewell Archaeology: The Chillicothe Conference*, edited by David S. Brose and N'omi Greber, pp. 220–38. Kent State University Press, Kent (OH).

Bullington, Jill (1988). Middle Woodland Mound Structure: Social Implications and Regional Content. In *The Archaic and Woodland Cemeteries at the Elizabeth Site in the Lower Illinois Valley*, edited by Douglas K. Charles, S. R. Leigh, and Jane E. Buikstra, pp. 218–41. Research Series Vol. 7. Center for American Archeology, Kampsville Archeological Center, Kampsville (IL).

Caldwell, Joseph R. (1958). *Trend and Tradition in the Prehistory of the Eastern United States*. Illinois State Museum, Springfield.

Carman, John, and Anthony Harding, editors (1999). *Ancient Warfare: Archaeological Perspectives*. Sutton, Stroud (UK).

Carneiro, Robert L. (1981). The Chiefdom: Precursor of the State. In *The Transition to Statehood in the New World*, edited by Grant D. Jones and Robert R. Kautz, pp. 37–79. Cambridge University Press, Cambridge.

Carneiro, Robert L. (1988). The Circumscription Theory: Challenge and Response. *American Behavioral Scientist* 31:497–511.

Carneiro, Robert L. (1990). Chiefdom Level Warfare as Exemplified by the Chiefdoms of Fiji and the Cauca Valley. In *The Anthropology of War*, edited by Jonathan Haas, pp. 190–211. Cambridge University Press, New York.

Carneiro, Robert L. (1992). The Calusa and the Powhatan, Native Chiefdoms of North America. *Reviews in Anthropology* 21:27–38.

Carneiro, Robert L. (1994). War and Peace: Alternating Realities in Human History. In *Studying War: Anthropological Perspectives*, edited by Stephen P. Reyna and R. E. Downs, pp. 3–27. Gordon and Breach, New York.

Carneiro, Robert L. (1998). What Happened at the Flashpoint? Conjectures on Chiefdom Formation at the Very Moment of Conception. In *Chiefdoms and Chieftaincy in the Americas*, edited by Elsa M. Redmond, pp. 18–42. University Press of Florida, Gainesville.

Chacon, Richard J., and David H. Dye, editors (2007). *The Taking and Displaying of Human Body Parts as Trophies by Amerindians*. Springer, New York.

Chacon, Richard J., and Ruben G. Mendoza, editors (2007). *North American Indigenous Warfare and Ritual*. University of Arizona Press, Tucson.

Chagnon, Napoleon (1997). *Yąnomamö*. 5th edition. Wadsworth, Belmont (CA).

Chapdelaine, Claude (1993). The Sedentarization of the Prehistoric Iroquoians: A Slow or Rapid Transformation? *Journal of Anthropological Archaeology* 12:173–209.

Chapman, Jefferson (1995). *Tellico Archaeology: 12,000 Years of Native American History*. Revised edition. University of Tennessee Press, Knoxville.

Charles, Douglas K., and Jane E. Buikstra (1983). Archaic Mortuary Sites in the Central Mississippi Drainage: Distribution, Structure, and Behavioral Implications. In *Archaic Hunters and Gatherers in the American Midwest*, edited by James L. Phillips and James A. Brown, pp. 117–45. Academic Press, New York.

Charles, Douglas K., and Jane E. Buikstra, editors (2006). *Recreating Hopewell*. University Press of Florida, Gainesville.

Charles, Douglas K., S. R. Leigh, and Jane E. Buikstra, editors (1988). *The Archaic and Woodland Cemeteries at the Elizabeth Site in the Lower Illinois Valley*. Research Series Vol. 7. Center for American Archeology, Kampsville Archeological Center, Kampsville (IL).

Chilton, Elizabeth (2005). Farming and Social Complexity in the Northeast. In *North American Archaeology*, edited by Timothy R. Pauketat and Diana D. Loren, pp. 138–60. Blackwell, Malden (MA).

Cioffi-Revilla, Claudio (2000). Ancient Warfare: Origins and Systems. In *Handbook of War Studies II*, edited by Manus I. Midlarsky, pp. 59–89. University of Michigan Press, Ann Arbor.

Clark, John E., and Michael Blake (1994). The Power of Prestige: Competitive Generosity and the Emergence of Rank Societies in Lowland Mesoamerica. In *Factional Competition in the New World*, edited by Elizabeth M. Brumfiel and John W. Fox, pp. 17–30. Cambridge University Press, Cambridge.

Clay, R. Berle (1998). The Essential Features of Adena Ritual and Their Implications. *Southeastern Archaeology* 17:1–21.

Cobb, Charles R., and Brian M. Butler (2002). The Vacant Quarter Revisited: Late Mississippian Abandonment of the Lower Ohio Valley. *American Antiquity* 67:625–41.

Cobb, Charles R., and Michael S. Nassaney (1995). Interaction and Integration in the Late Woodland Southeast. In *Native American Interactions: Multiscalar Analyses and Interpretation in the Eastern Woodlands*, edited by Michael S. Nassaney and Kenneth E. Sassaman, pp. 174–204. University of Tennessee Press, Knoxville.

Conner, M.D., and D.W. Link (1991). Archaeological and Osteological Analysis of Mound 38 at the Albany Mound Group (11-Wt-1). *Illinois Archaeology* 3:23–55.

Cowan, C. Wesley, and Patty Jo Watson, editors (1992). *The Origins of Agriculture: An International Perspective*. Smithsonian Institution Press, Washington, DC.

Cowan, Frank L. (2006). A Mobile Hopewell? Questioning Assumptions of Hopewell Sedentism. In *Recreating Hopewell*, edited by Douglas K. Charles and Jane E. Buikstra, pp. 26–49. University Press of Florida, Gainesville.

Crowley, Thomas J. (2000). Causes of Climate Change Over the Past 1000 Years. *Science* 189:270–77.

Dalan, Rinita A., George R. Halley, William I. Woods, Harold W. Watters, Jr., and John A. Koepke (2003). *Envisioning Cahokia: A Landscape Perspective*. Northern Illinois University Press, DeKalb.

Daniel, I. Randolph (1998). *Hardaway Revisited: Early Archaic Settlement in the Southeast*. University of Alabama Press, Tuscaloosa.

Day, Gordon M., and Bruce G. Trigger (1978). Algonquin. In *Handbook of North American Indians*, Vol. 15, Northeast, edited by Bruce G. Trigger, pp. 792–97. Smithsonian Institution Press, Washington, DC.

Day, J. W., Jr., J. D. Gunn, W. J. Folan, A. Yáñez-Arancibia, and B. P. Horton (2007). Emergence of Complex Societies after Sea Level Stabilized. *Eos* 88(15):169–70.

Delcourt, Paul A., and Hazel R. Delcourt (1987). *Long Term Forest Dynamics of the Temperate Zone: A Case Study of Late-Quaternary Forests in Eastern North America*. Springer-Verlag, New York.

Delcourt, Paul A., and Hazel R. Delcourt (2004). *Prehistoric Native Americans and Ecological Change: Human Ecosystems in Eastern North America since the Pleistocene*. Cambridge University Press, New York.

Dennen, Johan M. G. van der (1995). *The Origin of War*. 2 vols. Origin Press, Groningen (Netherlands).

Dentan, Robert K. (2008). Recent Studies on Violence: What's In and What's Out. *Reviews in Anthropology* 37:41–67.

DePratter, Chester B. (1983). Late Prehistoric and Early Historic Chiefdoms in the Southeastern United States. Unpublished Ph.D. dissertation, Department of Anthropology, University of Georgia, Athens.

Diaz-Granados, Carol (2004). Marking Stone, Land, Body, and Spirit: Rock Art and Mississippian Iconography. In *Hero, Hawk, and Open Hand: American Indian Art of the Ancient Midwest and South*, edited by Richard F. Townsend, pp. 139–49. Yale University Press, New Haven (CT).

Dickel, David N., C. Gregory Aker, Billie K. Barton, and Glen H. Doran (1988). An Orbital Floor and Ulna Fracture from the Early Archaic of Florida. *Journal of Paleopathology* 2:165–70.

Dickson, D. Bruce (1981). The Yanomamo of the Mississippi Valley? Some Reflections on Larson (1972), Gibson (1974), and Mississippian Period Warfare in the Southeastern United States. *American Antiquity* 46:909–16.

Divale, William T. (1974). Migration, External Warfare, and Matrilocal Residence. *Behavior Science Research* 9:75–133.

Divale, William T. (1984). *Matrilocal Residence in Pre-Literate Society*. UMI Research Press, Ann Arbor (MI).

Doran, Glen A., editor (2002). *Windover: Multidisciplinary Investigation of an Early Archaic Florida Cemetery*. University Press of Florida, Gainesville.

Dragoo, Don W. (1963). *Mounds for the Dead: An Analysis of the Adena Culture*. Annals of the Carnegie Museum 37. Pittsburgh (PA).

Dragoo, Don W., and C. F. Wray (1964). Hopewell Figurine Rediscovered. *American Antiquity* 30:195–99.

Drooker, Penelope B. (1997). *The View from Madisonville: Prehistoric Western Fort Ancient Interaction Patterns*. Memoir 31. Museum of Anthropology, University of Michigan, Ann Arbor.

Duncan, James R., and Carol Diaz-Granados (2000). Of Masks and Myths. *Midcontinental Journal of Archaeology* 25:1–26.

Dye, David H. (1990). Warfare in the Sixteenth-Century Southeast: The de Soto Expedition in the Interior. In *Columbian Consequences: Archaeological and Historical Perspectives on the Spanish Borderlands East*, Vol. 2, edited by David H. Thomas, pp. 211–22. Smithsonian Institution Press, Washington, DC.

Dye, David H. (1994). The Art of War in the Sixteenth-Century Central Mississippi Valley. In *Perspectives on the Southeast: Linguistics, Archaeology, and Ethnohistory*, edited by Patricia B. Kwachka, pp. 44–60. University of Georgia Press, Athens.

Dye, David H. (1995). Feasting with the Enemy: Mississippian Warfare and Prestige-Goods Circulation. In *Native American Interactions: Multiscalar Analyses and Interpretations in the Eastern Woodlands*, edited by Michael S. Nassaney and Kenneth E. Sassaman, pp. 289–316. University of Tennessee Press, Knoxville.

Dye, David H. (2002). Warfare in the Protohistoric Southeast: 1500–1700. In *Between Contacts and Colonies: Archaeological Perspectives on the Protohistoric Southeast*, edited by Cameron B. Wesson and Mark A. Rees, pp. 126–41. University of Alabama Press, Tuscaloosa.

Dye, David H. (2004). Art, Ritual, and Chiefly Warfare in the Mississippian World. In *Hero, Hawk, and Open Hand: Ancient Indian Art of the Midwest and South,* edited by Richard F. Townsend, pp. 191–205. Yale University Press, New Haven.

Dye, David H. (2006a). The Transformation of Mississippian Warfare: Four Case Studies from the Mid-South. In *The Archaeology of Warfare: Prehistories of Raiding and Conquest,* edited by Elizabeth N. Arkush and Mark W. Allen, pp. 101–47. University Press of Florida, Gainesville.

Dye, David H. (2006b). Ritual, Medicine, and the War Trophy Iconographic Theme in the Mississippian Southeast. In *Ancient Objects and Sacred Realms: Interpretations of Mississippian Iconography,* pp. 152–73. University of Texas Press, Austin.

Dye, David H., and Adam King (2007). Desecrating the Sacred Ancestor Temples: Chiefly Conflict and Violence in the American Southeast. In *North American Indigenous Warfare and Ritual,* edited by Richard J. Chacon and Ruben G. Mendoza, pp. 160–81. University of Arizona Press, Tucson.

Earle, Timothy (1997). *How Chiefs Come to Power: The Political Economy in Prehistory.* Stanford University Press, Stanford.

Eid, Leroy V. (1985). "National" War Among Indians of Northeastern North America. *Canadian Review of American Studies* 6:125–54.

Ellis, Katharine G., Henry T. Mullins, and William P. Patterson (2004). Deglacial to Middle Holocene (16,000 to 6000 calendar years BP) Climate Change in the Northeastern United States Inferred from Multi-proxy Stable Isotope Data, Seneca Lake, New York. *Journal of Paleolimnology* 31:343–61.

Ember, Carol R., and Melvin Ember (1992). Resource Unpredictability, Mistrust, and War: A Cross-Cultural Study. *Journal of Conflict Resolution* 36:242–62.

Ember, Melvin (1973). An Archaeological Indicator of Matrilocal versus Patrilocal Residence. *American Antiquity* 38:177–82.

Emerson, Thomas E. (1997). *Cahokia and the Archaeology of Power.* University of Alabama Press, Tuscaloosa.

Emerson, Thomas E. (1999). The Langford Tradition and the Process of Tribalization on the Middle Mississippian Borders. *Midcontinental Journal of Archaeology* 24:3–55.

Emerson, Thomas E. (2007). Evidence for Late Pre-Columbian Warfare in the North American Midcontinent. In *North American Indigenous Warfare and Ritual,* edited by Richard J. Chacon and Ruben G. Mendoza, pp. 129–48. University of Arizona Press, Tucson.

Emerson, Thomas E., Eve A. Hargrave, and Kristen Hedman (2003). Death and Ritual in Early Rural Cahokia. In *Theory, Method and Technique in Modern Archaeology,* edited by Robert J. Jeske and Douglas K. Charles, pp. 163–81. Praeger, Westport (CT).

Emerson, Thomas E., and Randall E. Hughes (2000). Figurines, Flint Clay Sourcing, the Ozark Highlands, and Cahokian Acquisition. *American Antiquity* 65:79–101.

Emerson, Thomas E., Randall E. Hughes, Mary R. Hynes, and Sarah U. Wisseman (2003). The Sourcing and Interpretation of Cahokia-Style Figurines in the Trans-Mississippi South and Southeast. *American Antiquity* 68:287–314.

Emerson, Thomas E., Dale L. McElrath, and Andrew C. Fortier, editors (2000). *Late Woodland Societies: Tradition and Transformation across the Midcontinent*. University of Nebraska Press, Lincoln.

Engelbrecht, William E. (2003). *Iroquoia: The Development of a Native World*. Syracuse University Press, Syracuse (NY).

Englebrecht, William E., and Carl K. Seyfert (1994). Paleoindian Watercraft: Evidence and Implications. *North American Archaeologist* 15:221–34.

Esper, J., E. R. Cook, and F. H. Schweingruber (2002). Low-Frequency Signals in Long Tree-Ring Chronologies for Reconstructing Past Temperature Variability. *Science* 295:2250–53.

Fagan, Brian M. (1987). *The Great Journey: The Peopling of Ancient America*. Thames and Hudson, New York.

Fagan, Brian M. (2000). *The Little Ice Age: How Climate Made History, 1300–1850*. Basic Books, New York.

Fagan, Brian M. (2005). *Ancient North America: The Archaeology of a Continent*. 4th edition. Thames and Hudson, New York.

Fairbanks, R. G., C. D. Charles, and J. D. Wright (1992). Origin of Global Meltwater Pulses. In *Radiocarbon after Four Decades*, edited by R. E. Taylor, pp. 473–500. Spring-Verlag, New York.

Faulkner, Charles H. (1996). The Old Stone Fort Revisited: New Clues to an Old Mystery. In *Mounds, Embankments, and Ceremonialism in the Midsouth*, edited by Robert C. Mainfort, Jr., and Richard Walling, pp. 7–11. Research Series 46. Arkansas Archeological Survey, Fayetteville.

Ferguson, R. Brian (1997). Violence and War in Prehistory. In *Troubled Times: Violence and Warfare in the Past*, edited by Debra L. Martin and David W. Frayer, pp. 321–55. Gordon and Breach, New York.

Ferguson, R. Brian, editor (1984). *Warfare, Culture, and Environment*. Academic Press, New York.

Ferguson, R. Brian, and Neal L. Whitehead, editors (1992). *War in the Tribal Zone: Expanding States and Indigenous Warfare*. School of American Research, Santa Fe.

Fiedel, Stuart J. (2001). What Happened in the Early Woodland? *Archaeology of Eastern North America* 29:101–42.

Fisher-Carroll, Rita L. (2001). Environmental Dynamics of Drought and Its Impact on Sixteenth Century Indigenous Populations in the Central Mississippi Valley. Unpublished Ph.D. dissertation, Department of Anthropology, University of Arkansas.

Fontana, Marisa D. (2007). Of Walls and War: Fortification and Warfare in the Mississippian Southeast. Unpublished Ph.D. dissertation, Department of Anthropology, University of Illinois, Chicago.

Fortier, Andrew C., and Thomas E. Emerson (1984). *The Go-Kart North Site and The Dyroff and Levin Sites*. American Bottom Archaeology, FAI 270 Site Report Vol. 9. University of Illinois Press, Urbana.

Fortier, Andrew C., Thomas E. Emerson, and Dale L. McElrath (2006). Calibrating and Reassessing American Bottom Culture History. *Southeastern Archaeology* 25:170–211.

Fortier, Andrew C., and Douglas K. Jackson (2000) The Formation of a Late Woodland Heartland in the American Bottom, Illinois cal. A.D. 650–900. In *Late Woodland Societies: Tradition and Transformation across the Midcontinent*, edited by Thomas E. Emerson, Dale L. McElrath, and Andrew C. Fortier, pp. 123–47. University of Nebraska Press, Lincoln.

Fortier, Andrew C., and Dale L. McElrath (2002). Deconstructing the Emergent Mississippian Concept: The Case for the Terminal Late Woodland in the American Bottom. *Midcontinental Journal of Archaeology* 27:171–215.

Frankenberg, Susan R., D. G. Albertson, and L. Kohn (1988). The Elizabeth Skeletal Remains: Demography and Disease. In *The Archaic and Woodland Cemeteries at the Elizabeth Mound Site in the Lower Illinois River Valley*, edited by Douglas K. Charles, S. R. Leigh, and Jane E. Buikstra, pp. 103–19. Research Series Vol. 7. Center for American Archeology, Kampsville Archeological Center, Kampsville (IL).

Fritz, Gayle J. (1990). Multiple Pathways to Farming in Precontact Eastern North America. *Journal of World Prehistory* 4:387–435.

Fritz, Gayle J. (1993). Early and Middle Woodland Paleoethnobotany. In *Foraging and Farming in the Eastern Woodlands*, edited by C. Margaret C. Scarry, pp. 39–56. University Press of Florida, Gainesville.

Fry, Douglas P. (2006). *The Human Potential for Peace: An Anthropological Challenge to Assumptions about War and Violence*. Oxford University Press, Oxford.

Fry, Douglas P. (2007). *Beyond War: The Human Potential for Peace*. Oxford University Press, Oxford.

Gabriel, Richard A. and Karen S. Metz (1991). *From Sumer to Rome: The Military Capabilities of Ancient Armies*. Greenwood Press, New York.

Gallagher, James P. (1992). Prehistoric Field Systems in the Upper Midwest. In *Late Prehistoric Agriculture:Observations from the Midwest*, edited by William I. Woods, pp. 95–135. Illinois Historic Preservation Agency, Springfield.

Galloy, Joseph M. (2002). Late Woodland Settlement Dynamics and Social Interaction in the American Bottom Uplands, A.D. 650–900. Unpublished Ph.D. dissertation, Department of Anthropology, Harvard University.

Gat, Azar (2006). *War in Human Civilization*. Oxford University Press, New York.

Gearing, Frederick O. (1958). The Structural Poses of 18th-century Cherokee Villages. *American Anthropologist* 60:1148–56.

Gearing, Frederick O. (1962). *Priests and Warriors: Social Structure for Cherokee Politics in the Eighteenth Century*. Memoir 93:1–124. American Anthropological Association, Washington, DC.

Gibbon, Guy E. (1974). A Model of Mississippian Development and Its Implications for the Red Wing Area. In *Aspects of Upper Great Lakes Anthropology*, edited by Elden Johnson, pp. 129–37. Minnesota Prehistoric Archaeology Series No. 11. Minnesota Historical Society, St. Paul.

Gibbon, Guy E. (1982). Oneota Origins Revisited. In *Oneota Studies*, edited by Guy E. Gibbon, pp. 85–90. Publications in Anthropology No. 1. University of Minnesota, Minneapolis.

Gibson, Jon L. (1974). Aboriginal Warfare in the Protohistoric Southeast: An Alternative Perspective. *American Antiquity* 39:130–33.

Gibson, Jon L., and Philip J. Carr (2004). Big Mounds, Big Rings, Big Power. In *Signs of Power: The Rise of Cultural Complexity in the Southeast*, edited by Jon L. Gibson and Philip J. Carr, pp. 1–9. University of Alabama Press, Tuscaloosa.

Gleach, Frederic W. (1997). *Powhatan's World and Colonial Virginia: A Conflict of Cultures*. University of Nebraska Press, Lincoln.

Goddard, Ives, compiler (1996). Native Languages and Language Families of North America (map). In *Languages*, edited by Ives Goddard. Handbook of North American Indians Vol. 17. Smithsonian Institution, Washington, DC.

Graham, Russell W., Ernest L. Lundelius, Mary Ann Graham, Erich K. Schroeder, Richard S. Toomey III, Elaine Anderson, Anthony D. Barnosky, James A. Burns, Charles S. Churcher, Donald K. Grayson, R. Dale Guthrie, C. R. Harington, George T. Jefferson, Larry D. Martin, H. Gregory McDonald, Richard E. Morlan, Holmes A. Semken, Jr., S. David Webb, Lars Werdelin, and Michael C. Wilson (1996). Spatial Response of Mammals to Late Quaternary Environmental Fluctuations. *Science* 272:1601–6.

Greber, N'omi B. (2006). Enclosures and Communities in Ohio Hopewell. In *Recreating Hopewell*, edited by Douglas K. Charles and Jane E. Buikstra, pp. 74–105. University Press of Florida, Gainesville.

Gremillion, Kristen J. (1996). The Paleoethnobotanical Record for the Mid-Holocene Southeast. In *Archaeology of the Mid-Holocene Southeast*, edited by Kenneth Sassaman and David G. Anderson, pp. 99–114. University Press of Florida, Gainesville.

Gremillion, Kristen J. (2004). Seed Processing and the Origins of Food Production in Eastern North America. *American Antiquity* 69:215–34.

Grenier, John (2005). *The First Way of War: American War Making on the Frontier, 1607–1814*. Cambridge University Press, New York.

Griffin, James B. (1961). Some Correlations of Climatic and Cultural Change in Eastern North American Prehistory. *Annals of the New York Academy of Sciences* 95:710–17.

Grove, Jean M. (1998). *The Little Ice Age*. Methuen, London.

Guilaine, Jean, and Jean Zammit (2005). *The Origins of War: Violence in Prehistory*. Wiley, Hoboken (NJ).

Gunn, Joel D. (1997). A Framework for the Middle-Late Holocene Transition: Astronomical and Geophysical Conditions. *Southeastern Archaeology* 16:134–51.

Gunn, Joel D., editor (2000). *The Years Without Summer: Tracing A.D. 536 and Its Aftermath*. British Archaeological Reports International Series 872. Archaeopress, London.

Haas, Jonathan (1996). War. *Encyclopedia of Cultural Anthropology* 4:1357–61. Henry Holt, New York.

Haas, Jonathan (1999). The Origins of War and Ethnic Violence. In *Ancient Warfare: Archaeological Perspectives*, edited by John Carman and Anthony Harding, pp. 11–24. Sutton, Stroud (UK).

Haas, Jonathan (2001). Warfare and the Evolution of Culture. In *Archaeology at the Millennium: A Sourcebook*, edited by Gary M. Feinman and T. Douglas Price, pp. 329–50. Kluwer Academic/Plenum, New York.

Haas, Jonathan, editor (1990). *The Anthropology of War*. Cambridge University Press, New York.

Hall, Robert L. (1997). *An Archaeology of the Soul: North American Indian Belief and Ritual*. University of Illinois Press, Urbana.

Hall, Robert L. (2004). The Cahokia Site and Its People. In *Hero, Hawk, and Open Hand: American Indian Art of the Ancient Midwest and South*, edited by Richard F. Townsend, pp. 93–103. Yale University Press, New Haven.

Hall, Robert L. (2006). The Enigmatic Copper Cutout from Bedford Mound 8. In *Recreating Hopewell*, edited by Douglas K. Charles and Jane E. Buikstra, pp. 464–74. University Press of Florida, Gainesville.

Hally, David J. (1993). The Territorial Size of Mississippian Chiefdoms. In *Archaeology of Eastern North America: Papers in Honor of Stephen Williams*, edited by James B. Stoltman, pp. 143–68. Archaeological Report 25. Mississippi Department of Archives and History, Jackson.

Hamilton, Fran E. (1999). Southeastern Archaic Mounds: Examples of Elaboration in a Temporally Fluctuating Environment? *Journal of Anthropological Archaeology* 18:344–55.

Hamilton, T. M. (1982). *Native American Bows*. Special Publication No. 5. Missouri Archaeological Society, Columbia.

Hantman, Jeffrey L. (1993). Powhatan's Relations with the Piedmont Monacans. In *Powhatan's Foreign Relations*, edited by Helen Rountree, pp. 94–111. University Press of Virginia, Charlottesville.

Hantman, Jeffrey L. (2001). Monacan Archaeology of the Virginia Interior, A.D. 1400–1700. In *Societies in Eclipse: Archaeology of the Eastern Woodlands Indians, A.D. 1450–1700*, edited by David S. Brose, C. Wesley Cowan, and Robert C. Mainfort, Jr., pp. 107–23. Smithsonian Institution Press, Washington, DC.

Hantman, Jeffrey L., and Deborah L. Gold (2002). The Woodland in the Middle Atlantic: Ranking and Dynamic Political Stability. In *The Woodland Southeast*, edited by David G. Anderson and Robert C. Mainfort, Jr., pp. 270–91. University of Alabama Press, Tuscaloosa.

Hart, John P. (2001). Maize, Matrilocality, Migration, and Northern Iroquoian Evolution. *Journal of Archaeological Method and Theory* 8:151–82.

Hart, John P., and Bernard K. Means (2002). Maize and Villages: A Summary and Critical Assessment of Current Northeast Early Late Prehistoric Evidence. In *Northeast Subsistence-Settlement Change: A.D. 700–1300*, edited by John P. Hart and Christina B. Rieth, pp. 345–58. New York State Museum Bulletin 496. Albany.

Hassig, Ross (1992). *War and Society in Ancient Mesoamerica*. University of California Press, Los Angeles.

Havard, Gilles (2001). *The Great Peace of Montreal of 1701*. McGill-Queen's University Press, Montreal.

Henderson, A. G., D. Pollack, and C. A. Turnbow (1992). Chronology and Cultural Patterns. In *Fort Ancient Cultural Dynamics in the Middle Ohio Valley*, edited by A. G. Henderson, pp. 253–79. Monographs in World Archaeology No. 8. Prehistory Press, Madison (WI).

Henning, Dale R. (1993). The Adaptive Patterning of the Dhegiha Sioux. *Plains Anthropologist* 38:253–64.

Henning, Dale R. (1995). Oneota Evolution and Interactions: A Perspective from Wever Terrace, Southeast Iowa. In *Oneota Archaeology: Past, Present, and Future*, edited by William Green, pp. 65–88. Office of the Iowa State Archaeologist, Ames.

Henning, Dale R. (1998). The Oneota Tradition. In *Archaeology on the Great Plains*, edited by Raymond Wood, pp. 345–414. University Press of Kansas, Lawrence.

Henning, Dale R. (2003). The Archeology and History of Ioway/Oto Exchange Patterns, 1650–1700. *Journal of the Iowa Archaeology Society* 50:199–221.

Hickerson, Harold (1960). The Feast of the Dead among the Seventeenth Century Algonkians of the Upper Great Lakes. *American Anthropologist* 60:81–107.

Hill, Mary C. (1981). Analysis, Synthesis, and Interpretation of the Skeletal Material Excavated for the Gainesville Section of the Tennessee-Tombigbee Waterway. In *Archaeological Investigations in the Gainesville Lake Area of the Tennessee-Tombigbee Waterway*, Vol. 4, edited by Ned J. Jenkins, pp. 187–258. Report of Investigations 14. Office of Archaeological Research, University of Alabama, Tuscaloosa.

Holley, George R. (1999). Late Prehistoric Towns in the Southeast. In *Great Towns and Regional Polities in the Prehistoric American Southwest and Southeast*, edited by Jill E. Neitzel, pp. 23–38. University of New Mexico Press, Albuquerque.

Hollinger, R. Eric (1995). Residence Patterns and Oneota Cultural Dynamics. In *Oneota Archaeology: Past, Present and Future*, edited by William Green, pp. 141–74. Report 20. Office of the State Archaeologist, University of Iowa, Iowa City.

Hollinger, R. Eric (2005). Conflict and Culture Change in the Late Prehistoric and Early Historic American Midcontinent. Unpublished Ph.D. dissertation, Department of Anthropology, University of Illinois at Urbana-Champaign, Urbana.

Hollinger, R. Eric, and Deborah M. Pearsall (1994). Analysis of Floral Remains. In *The Tremaine Site Complex: Oneota Occupation in the La Crosse Locality, Wisconsin*, Vol. 2, The Filler Site (47-Lc-149), edited by J. O'Gorman, pp. 105–19. Archaeology Series No. 2. Museum Archaeology Program, State Historical Society of Wisconsin, Madison.

Hudson, Charles (1976). *The Southeastern Indians*. University of Tennessee Press, Knoxville.

Hudson, Charles (1997). *Knights of Spain, Warriors of the Sun: Hernando de Soto and the South's Ancient Chiefdoms*. University of Alabama Press, Tuscaloosa.

Jackson, S., R. S. Webb, J. T. Overpeck, K. A. Anderson, T. Webb III, J. Williams, and B. C. S. Hansen (2000). Vegetation and Environment in Eastern North America during the Last Glacial Maximum. *Quaternary Science Reviews* 19:489–508.

Jacobi, Keith P. (2007). Disabling the Dead: Human Trophy Taking in the Prehistoric Southeast. In *The Taking and Displaying of Human Body Parts as Trophies by Amerindians*, edited by Richard J. Chacon and David H. Dye, pp. 299–338. Springer, New York.

Jacobi, Keith P., and M. Cassandra Hill (2001). Prehistoric Treatment of the Dead: Bone Handling in the Southeastern United States (abstract). *American Journal of Physical Anthropology Supplement* 32:85.

Jefferies, Richard W. (1996). The Emergence of Long-Distance Exchange Networks in the Southeastern United States. In *Archaeology of the Mid-Holocene Southeast*, edited by Kenneth Sassaman and David G. Anderson, pp. 222–34. University Press of Florida, Gainesville.

Jeske, Robert J. (2006). Hopewell Regional Interactions in Southwestern Wisconsin and Northern Illinois: A Core-Periphery Approach. In *Recreating Hopewell*, edited by Douglas K. Charles and Jane E. Buikstra, pp. 285–309. University Press of Florida, Gainesville.

Johnson, Allen W., and Timothy Earle (2000). *The Evolution of Human Societies: From Foraging Group to Agrarian State*. 2nd edition. Stanford University Press, Stanford.

Johnson, Gregory A. (1978). Information Sources and the Development of Decision-Making Organizations. In *Social Archeology: Beyond Subsistence and Dating*, edited by Charles L. Redman, Mary Jane Berman, Edward V. Curtin, William T. Langhorne, Jr., Nina M. Versaggi, and Jeffery C. Wanser, pp. 87–112. Academic Press, New York.

Johnson, Gregory A. (1982). Organizational Structure and Scalar Stress. In *Theory and Explanation in Archaeology: The Southhampton Conference*, edited by Colin Renfrew, Michael J. Rowlands, and Barbara A. Segraves, pp. 389–421. Academic Press, New York.

Johnson, Jay K., and Samuel O. Brookes (1989). Benton Points, Turkey Tails and Cache Blades: Middle Archaic Exchange in the Southeast. *Southeastern Archaeology* 8:134–45.

Johnston, Cheryl A. (2002). Culturally Modified Human Remains from the Hopewell Mound Group. Unpublished Ph.D. dissertation, Department of Anthropology, Ohio State University, Columbus.

Jones, David E. (2004). *Native North American Armor, Shields, and Fortifications*. University of Texas Press, Austin.

Keeley, Lawrence H. (1996). *War Before Civilization: The Myth of the Peaceful Savage*. Oxford University Press, New York.

Keeley, Lawrence H., Marisa Fontana, and Russell Quick (2007). Baffles and Bastions: The Universal Features of Fortifications. *Journal of Archaeological Research* 15:55–95.

Keener, Craig S. (1998). An Ethnohistoric Perspective on Iroquois Warfare during the Second Half of the Seventeenth Century (A.D. 1649–1701). Unpublished Ph.D. dissertation, Department of Anthropology, Ohio State University, Columbus.

Kelly, Lucretia S. (2001). A Case of Ritual Feasting at the Cahokia Site. In *Feasts: Archaeological and Ethnographic Perspectives on Food, Politics, and Power*, edited by Michael Dietler and Brian Hayden, pp. 334–67. Smithsonian Institution Press, Washington, DC.

Kelly, Raymond S. (2000). *Warless Societies and the Origin of War*. University of Michigan Press, Ann Arbor.

Kerber, Richard A. (1986). Political Evolution in the Lower Illinois Calley: A.D. 400–1000. Unpublished Ph.D. dissertation, Department of Anthropology, Northwestern University, Evanston.

Kidder, Tristram R. (2006). Climate Change and the Archaic to Woodland Transition (3000–2500 cal. B.P.) in the Mississippi River Basin. *American Antiquity* 71:195–231.

King, Adam (2003). *Etowah: The Political History of a Chiefdom Capital*. University of Alabama Press, Tuscaloosa.

King, Adam (2006). Leadership Strategies and the Nature of Mississippian Chiefdoms in Northern Georgia. In *Leadership and Polity in Mississippian Society*, edited by Brian M. Butler and Paul D. Welch, pp. 73–90. Occasional Paper No. 33. Center for Archaeological Investigations, Southern Illinois University, Carbondale.

King, James E. (1981). Late Quaternary Vegetational History of Illinois. *Ecological Monographs* 51:43–62.

Knauft, Bruce M. (1991). Violence and Sociality and Human Evolution. *Current Anthropology* 32:391–428.

Knauft, Bruce M. (1994). Culture and Cooperation in Human Evolution. In *The Anthropology of Peace and Nonviolence*, edited by Leslie Sponsel and Thomas Gregor, pp. 37–68. Lynne Rienner, Boulder (CO).

Knight, Vernon J., Jr. (1986). The Institutional Organization of Mississippian Religion. *American Antiquity* 51:675–87.

Knight, Vernon J., Jr. (1998). Moundville as a Diagrammatic Ceremonial Center. In *Archaeology of the Moundville Chiefdom*, edited by Vernon J. Knight, Jr., and Vincas P. Steponaitis, pp. 44–62. Smithsonian Institution Press, Washington, DC.

Knight, Vernon J., Jr. (2001). Feasting and the Emergence of Platform Mound Ceremonialism in Eastern North America. In *Feasts: Archaeological and Ethnographic Perspectives on Food, Politics, and Power*, edited by Michael Dietler and Brian Hayden, pp. 311–33. Smithsonian Institution Press, Washington, DC.

Knight, Vernon J., Jr. (2004). Characterizing Elite Midden Deposits at Moundville. *American Antiquity* 69:304–21.

Knight, Vernon J., Jr., James A. Brown, and George E. Lankford (2001). On the Subject Matter of Southeastern Ceremonial Complex Art. *Southeastern Archaeology* 20:129–41.

Knight, Vernon J., Jr., and Vincas P. Steponaitis (1998). A New History of Moundville. In *Archaeology of the Moundville Chiefdom*, edited by Vernon J. Knight, Jr., and Vincas P. Steponaitis, pp. 1–25. Smithsonian Institution Press, Washington, DC.

Koldehoff, Brad, and Joseph M. Galloy (2006). Late Woodland Frontiers in the American Bottom Region. *Southeastern Archaeology* 25:275–300.

Kuhn, Robert D., and Martha L.Sempowski (2001). A New Approach to Dating the League of the Iroquois. *American Antiquity* 66:310–14.

Kuniholm, Peter I. (1990). Archaeological Evidence and Non-Evidence for Climatic Change. *Philosophical Transactions of the Royal Society of London* 333:645–55.

Kupperman, Karen O. (2000). *Indians and English: Facing Off in Early America*. Cornell University Press, Ithaca (NY).

Lafferty, Robert H., III (1973). An Analysis of Prehistoric Southeastern Fortifications. Unpublished M.A. thesis, Department of Anthropology, Southern Illinois University, Carbondale.

Lafitau, Joseph-François (1974 [1727]). *Customs of the American Indians Compared with the Customs of Primitive Times*, Vol. 48. Champlain Society, Toronto.

Lambert, Patricia M. (1997). Patterns of Violence in Prehistoric Hunter-Gatherer Societies of Coastal Southern California. In *Troubled Times: Violence and Warfare in the Past*, edited by Debra L. Martin and David W. Frayer, pp. 77–109. Gordon and Breach, New York.

Lambert, Patricia M. (2002). The Archaeology of War: A North American Perspective. *Journal of Archaeological Research* 10(3):207–41.

Lambert, Patricia M. (2007). The Osteological Evidence for North American Warfare. In *North American Indigenous Warfare and Ritual*, edited by Richard J. Chacon and Ruben G. Mendoza, pp. 202–21. University of Arizona Press, Tucson.

Lankford, George E. (2007). Some Cosmological Motifs in the Southeastern Ceremonial Complex. In *Ancient Objects and Sacred Realms: Interpretations of Mississippian Iconography*, edited by F. Kent Reilly III and James F. Garber, pp. 8–38. University of Texas Press, Austin.

Lankford, George E. (2008). *Looking for Lost Lore: Studies in Folklore, Ethnology, and Iconography*. University of Alabama Press, Tuscaloosa.

Larson, Lewis H., Jr. (1972). Functional Considerations of Warfare in the Southeast during the Mississippian Period. *American Antiquity* 37:383–92.

LeBlanc, Steven A. (1999). *Prehistoric Warfare in the American Southwest*. University of Utah Press, Salt Lake City.

LeBlanc, Steven A. (2003a). *Constant Battles: The Myth of the Peaceful, Noble Savage*. St. Martin's Press, New York.

LeBlanc, Steven A. (2003b). Prehistory of Warfare. *Archaeology* 56(3):18–25.

LeBlanc, Steven A. (2006). Warfare and the Development of Social Complexity: Some Demographic and Environmental Factors. In *The Archaeology of Warfare: Prehistories of Raiding and Conquest*, edited by Elizabeth N. Arkush and Mark W. Allen, pp. 437–68. University Press of Florida, Gainesville.

Lévi-Strauss, Claude (1943). Guerre et Commerce chez les Indiens de l'Amérique de Sud. *Renaissance* 1:122–39.

Lewis, Thomas M. N., and Madeline Kneberg (1959). The Archaic Culture in the Middle South. *American Antiquity* 25:161–83.

Little, Keith J. (1999). The Role of Late Woodland Interactions in the Emergence of Etowah. *Southeastern Archaeology* 18(1):45–56.

Lizot, Jacques (1991). Palabras en la noche. *La Iglesia en Amazonas* 53:54–82.

Longhurst, Richard (1986). Household Food Strategies in Response to Seasonality and Famine. *IDS Bulletin* 7:27–35.

Mallam, R. Clark (1976). *The Iowa Effigy Mound Manifestation: An Interpretive Model.* Report No. 9. Office of the State Archaeologist, University of Iowa, Iowa City.

Malone, Patrick M. (1991). *The Skulking Way of War: Technology and Tactics Among the New England Indians.* Johns Hopkins University Press, Baltimore.

Marquardt, William H., and Patty Jo Watson, editors (2005). *Archaeology of the Middle Green River Region, Kentucky.* Monograph No. 25. Institute of Archaeology and Paleoenvironmental Studies, Florida Museum of Natural History, University of Florida, Gainesville.

Martin, Debra L., and David W. Frayer, editors (1997). *Troubled Times: Violence and Warfare in the Past.* War and Society, Vol. 3. Gordon and Breach, New York.

McElrath, Dale L., Thomas E. Emerson, and Andrew C. Fortier (2000). Social Evolution or Social Response? A Fresh Look at the "Good Gray Cultures" after Four Decades of Midwest Research. In *Late Woodland Societies: Tradition and Transformation across the Midcontinent,* edited by Thomas E. Emerson, Dale L. McElrath, and Andrew C. Fortier, pp. 3–36. University of Nebraska Press, Lincoln.

McElrath, Dale L., and Andrew C. Fortier (2000). The Early Late Woodland Occupation of the American Bottom. In *Late Woodland Societies: Tradition and Transformation across the Midcontinent,* edited by Thomas E. Emerson, Dale L. McElrath, and Andrew C. Fortier, pp. 97–121. University of Nebraska Press, Lincoln.

Meinkoth, Michael C. (1995). *The Sisters Creeks Site Mounds: Middle Woodland Mortuary Practices in the Illinois River Valley.* Archaeological Research Reports No. 2. Illinois Department of Transportation, Urbana.

Meltzer, David J. (1988). Late Pleistocene Human Adaptations in Eastern North America. *Journal of World Prehistory* 2:1–52.

Meltzer, David J. (1993). *Search for the First Americans.* Smithsonian Books, Washington, DC.

Mensforth, Robert P. (2001). Warfare and Trophy Taking in the Archaic Period. In *Archaic Transitions in Ohio and Kentucky Prehistory,* edited by Olaf H. Prufer, Sara E. Pedde, and Richard S. Meindl, pp. 110–38. Kent State University Press, Kent (OH).

Mensforth, Robert P. (2007). Human Trophy Taking in Eastern North America during the Archaic Period: The Relationship to Warfare and Social Complexity. In *The Taking and Displaying of Human Body Parts as Trophies by Amerindians,* edited by Richard J. Chacon and David H. Dye, pp. 222–77. Springer, New York.

Michalik, Laura K. (1982). An Ecological Perspective on the Huber Phase Subsistence-Settlement System. In *Oneota Studies,* edited by Guy E. Gibbon, pp. 29–53. Publications in Anthropology No. 1. University of Minnesota, Minneapolis.

Milanich, Jerald T., Ann S. Cordell, Vernon J. Knight, Jr., Timothy A. Kohler, and Brenda J. Sigler-Lavelle (1997). *Archaeology of Northern Florida, A.D. 200–900: The McKeithen Weeden Island Culture*. University Press of Florida, Gainesville.

Mills, William C. (1916). Explorations of the Tremper Mound. *Ohio Archaeological and Historical Quarterly* 25:262–398.

Milner, George R. (1995). An Osteological Perspective on Prehistoric Warfare. In *Regional Approaches to Mortuary Analysis*, edited by Lane A. Beck, pp. 221–44. Plenum, New York.

Milner, George R. (1998a). Archaeological Evidence for Prehistoric and Early Historic Intergroup Conflict in Eastern North America. In *Deciphering Anasazi Violence, with Regional Comparisons to Mesoamerica and Woodland Cultures*, edited by Peter Y. Bullock, pp. 69–91. HRM, Santa Fe.

Milner, George R. (1998b). The Cahokia Chiefdom: The Archaeology of a Mississippian Society. Smithsonian Institution Press, Washington, DC.

Milner, George R. (1999). Warfare in Prehistoric and Early Historic Eastern North America. *Journal of Archaeological Research* 7:105–51.

Milner, George R. (2000). Palisaded Settlements in Prehistoric Eastern North America. In *City Walls: The Urban Enceinte in Global Perspective*, edited by James D. Tracy, pp. 46–70. Cambridge University Press, Cambridge.

Milner, George R. (2004). *The Moundbuilders: Ancient Peoples of Eastern North America*. Thames and Hudson, London.

Milner, George R. (2005). Nineteenth-Century Arrow Wounds and Perceptions of Prehistoric Warfare. *American Antiquity* 70:144–56.

Milner, George R. (2007). Population, Food Production, and Warfare in Prehistoric Eastern North America. In *North American Indigenous Warfare and Ritual*, edited by Richard J. Chacon and Ruben G. Mendoza, pp. 182–201. University of Arizona Press, Tucson.

Milner, George R., Eve Anderson, and Virginia G. Smith (1991a). Warfare in Late Prehistoric West-Central Illinois. *American Antiquity* 56:581–603.

Milner, George R., and Sissel Schroeder (1999). Mississippian Sociopolitical Systems. In *Great Towns and Regional Polities in the Prehistoric American Southwest and Southeast*, edited by Jill E. Neitzel, pp. 95–107. University of New Mexico Press, Albuquerque.

Milner, George R., and Virginia G. Smith (1989). Carnivore Alteration of Human Bone from a Late Prehistoric Site in Illinois. *American Journal of Physical Anthropology* 79:43–49.

Milner, George R., and Virginia G. Smith (1990). Oneota Human Skeletal Remains. In *Archaeological Investigations at the Morton Village and Norris Farms 36 Cemetery*, edited by Sharron K. Santure, Alan D. Harn, and Duane Esarey, pp. 111–48. Reports of Investigation No. 45. Illinois State Museum, Springfield.

Milner, George R., Virginia G. Smith, and Eve Anderson (1991b). Conflict, Mortality, and Community Health in an Illinois Oneota Population. In *Between Bands and States*, edited by Susan A. Gregg, pp. 245–64. Occasional Paper No.

9. Center for Archaeological Investigations, Southern Illinois University, Carbondale.

Moorehead, Warren K. (1922). *The Hopewell Mound Group of Ohio*. Publication 211, Anthropological Series Vol. 6, No. 5. Field Museum of Natural History, Chicago.

Morse, Dan F. (editor) (1997). *Sloan: A Paleoindian Dalton Cemetery in Arkansas*. Smithsonian Institution Press, Washington, DC.

Mott, Mildred (1938). The Relation of Historic Indian Tribes to Archaeological Manifestations in Iowa. *Iowa Journal of History and Politics* 36:227–314.

Myer, William E. (1922). Recent Archaeological Discoveries in Tennessee. *Art and Archaeology* 14:141–50.

Nairne, Thomas (1988). *Nairne's Muskhogean Journals: The 1708 Expedition to the Mississippi River*. University Press of Mississippi, Jackson.

Nassaney, Michael S. (2001). The Historical-Processual Development of Late Woodland Societies. In *The Archaeology of Traditions: Agency and History before and after Columbus*, edited by Timothy R. Pauketat, pp. 157–73. University Press of Florida, Gainesville.

Nassaney, Michael S., and Charles R. Cobb, editors (1991). *Stability, Transformation, and Variation: The Late Woodland Southeast*. Plenum Press, New York.

Nassaney, Michael S., and Kendra Pyle (1999). The Adoption of the Bow and Arrow in Eastern North America: A View from Central Arkansas. *American Antiquity* 64:243–63.

Nawrocki, Stephen P. (1997). Analysis of the Human Remains. In *Hopewell in Mt. Vernon: A Study of the Mt. Vernon Site (12-PO-885)*, edited by the General Electric Company, pp. 11–66. General Electric Co., Mt. Vernon (IN).

Newcomb, W. W., Jr. (1950). A Re-examination of the Causes of Plains Warfare. *American Anthropologist* 52:317–30.

Ollendorf, Amy L. (1993). Changing Landscapes in the American Bottom (United States of America): An Interdisciplinary Investigation with an Emphasis on the Late-Prehistoric and Early-Historic Periods (Illinois, Cahokia). Unpublished Ph.D. dissertation, Department of Anthropology, University of Minnesota, Minneapolis.

Olsen, Sandra L., and Pat Shipman (1994). Cutmarks and Perimortem Treatment of Skeletal Remains on the Northern Plains. In *Skeletal Biology in the Great Plains: Migration, Warfare, Health, and Subsistence*, edited by Douglas W. Owsley and Richard L. Jantz, pp. 377–87. Smithsonian Institution Press, Washington, DC.

Osgood, Richard, Sarah Monks, and Judith Toms, editors (2001). *Bronze Age Warfare*. Sutton, London.

Otterbein, Keith F. (1964). Why the Iroquois Won: An Analysis of Iroquois Military Tactics. *Ethnohistory* 11:56–63.

Otterbein, Keith F. (1979). Huron vs. Iroquois: A Case Study in Intertribal Warfare. *Ethnohistory* 26:141–52.

Otterbein, Keith F. (1994). *Feuding and Warfare: Selected Works of Keith F. Otterbein*. Gordon and Breach, Langhorne (PA).

Otterbein, Keith F., editor (2004). *How War Began.* Texas A & M Press, College Station.

Otterbein, Keith F., and Charlotte S. Otterbein (1965). An Eye for an Eye, a Tooth for a Tooth: A Cross-cultural Study of Feuding. *American Anthropologist* 67:1470–82.

Owsley, Douglas W., and Hugh E. Berryman (1975). Ethnographic and Archaeological Evidence of Scalping in the Southeastern United States. *Tennessee Anthropologist* 31:41–58.

Pauketat, Timothy R. (1994). *The Ascent of Chiefs: Cahokia and Mississippian Politics in Native North America.* University of Alabama Press, Tuscaloosa.

Pauketat, Timothy R. (1999). America's Ancient Warriors. *MHQ: The Quarterly Journal of Military History* 11:50–55.

Pauketat, Timothy R. (2002). A Fourth-Generation Synthesis of Cahokia and Mississippianization. *Midcontinental Journal of Archaeology* 27:149–70.

Pauketat, Timothy R. (2004). *Ancient Cahokia and the Mississippians.* Cambridge University Press, New York.

Pauketat, Timothy R. (2007). *Chiefdoms and Other Archaeological Delusions.* AltaMira, New York.

Pauketat, Timothy R., and Thomas E. Emerson (1991). The Ideology of Authority and the Power of the Pot. *American Anthropologist* 93:919–41.

Pauketat, Timothy R., and Thomas E. Emerson (1997). *Cahokia: Domination and Ideology in the Mississippian World.* University of Nebraska Press, Lincoln.

Pauketat, Timothy R., and Diana DiPaolo Loren, editors (2005). *North American Archaeology.* Blackwell, Malden (MA).

Peregrine, Peter N. (1993). An Archaeological Correlate of War. *North American Archaeologist* 14:139–51.

Perino, Gregory H. (1968). The Pete Klunk Mound Group. In *Hopewell and Woodland Site Archaeology in Illinois*, edited by James A. Brown, pp. 9–124. Bulletin 6. Illinois Archaeological Survey, Urbana.

Phillips, Philip, and James A. Brown (1978). *Pre-Columbian Shell Engravings from the Craig Mound at Spiro, Oklahoma*, Pt. 1. Peabody Museum of Archaeology and Ethnology, Harvard University, Cambridge (MA).

Piatek, Bruce J. (1994). The Tomoko Mound Complex in Northeast Florida. *Southeastern Archaeology* 12:109–18.

Pospisil, Leopold (1994). "I am Very Sorry I Cannot Kill You Any More": War and Peace Among the Kapauku. In *Studying War: Anthropological Perspectives*, edited by Stephen P. Reyna and R. E. Downs, pp. 113–26. Gordon and Breach, New York.

Potter, Stephen (1993). *Commoners, Tribute, and Chiefs: The Development of Algonquian Culture in the Potomac Valley.* University Press of Virginia, Charlottesville.

Powell, Mary L. (1988). *Status and Health in Prehistory: A Case Study of the Moundville Chiefdom.* Smithsonian Institution Press, Washington, DC.

Price, T. Douglas, and James A. Brown, editors (1985). *Prehistoric Hunter-Gatherers: The Emergence of Cultural Complexity.* Academic Press, New York.

Prosterman, Roy L. (1972). *Surviving to 3000: An Introduction to the Study of Lethal Conflict*. Duxbury-Wadsworth, Belmont (CA).

Raaflaub, Kurt, and Nathan Rosenstein, editors (1999). *War and Society in the Ancient and Medieval Worlds: Asia, The Mediterranean, Europe, and Mesoamerica*, Harvard University Press, Cambridge (MA).

Redmond, Elsa (1994). *Tribal and Chiefly Warfare in South America*. Memoir 28. Museum of Anthropology, University of Michigan, Ann Arbor.

Redmond, Elsa (1998). In War and Peace: Alternative Paths to Centralized Leadership. In *Chiefdoms and Chieftaincy in the Americas*, edited by Elsa Redmond, pp. 68–103. University Press of Florida, Gainesville.

Reid, Kenneth C. (1983). The Nebo Hill Phase: Late Archaic Prehistory in the Lower Missouri Valley. In *Archaic Hunters and Gatherers in the American Midwest*, edited by James L. Phillips and James A. Brown, pp. 11–39. Academic Press, New York.

Reyna, Stephen P. (1994). A Mode of Domination Approach to Organized Violence. In *Studying War: Anthropological Perspectives*, edited by Stephen P. Reyna and R. E. Downs, pp. 29–65. Gordon and Breach, New York.

Reyna, Stephen P., and R. E. Downs, editors (1994). *Studying War: Anthropological Perspectives*. Gordon and Breach, New York.

Rice, Glen E., and Steven A. LeBlanc, editors (2001). *Deadly Landscapes: Case Studies in Prehistoric Southwestern Warfare*. University of Utah Press, Salt Lake City.

Richter, Daniel K. (1983). War and Culture: The Iroquois Experience. *William and Mary Quarterly* 40:528–59.

Riley, Thomas J., and Glen Freimuth (1979). Field Systems and Frost Drainage in the Prehistoric Agriculture of the Upper Great Lakes. *American Antiquity* 44:271–85.

Rodbell, Donald T., Geoffrey O. Seltzer, David M. Anderson, Mark B. Abbott, David B. Enfield, and Jeremy H. Neuman (1999). An ~15,000-Year Record of El Niño-Driven Alluviation in Southwestern Ecuador. *Science* 283:516–20.

Ross-Stalling, Nancy (2007). Trophy Taking in the Central and Lower Mississippi Valley. In *The Taking and Displaying of Human Body Parts as Trophies by Amerindians*, edited by Richard J. Chacon and David H. Dye, pp. 339–70. Springer, New York.

Sahlins, Marshall D. (1961). The Segmentary Lineage: An Organization of Predatory Expansion. *American Anthropologist* 63:322–45.

Sahlins, Marshall D. (1968). *Tribesmen*. Prentice-Hall, Englewood Cliffs (NJ).

Sampson, Kelvin W., and Duane Esarey (1993). A Survey of Elaborate Mississippian Copper Artifacts from Illinois. In *Highways to the Past: Essays on Illinois Archaeology in Honor of Charles J. Bareis*, edited by Thomas E. Emerson, Andrew C. Fortier, and Dale L. McElrath. *Illinois Archaeology* 5:452–80.

Santure, Sharron K., Alan D. Harn, and Duane Esarey (1990). *Archaeological Investigations at the Morton Village and Norris Farms 36 Cemetery*. Report of Investigations No. 45. Illinois State Museum, Springfield.

Sassaman, Kenneth E. (1993). *Early Pottery in the Southeast: Tradition and Innovation in Cooking Technology*. University of Alabama Press, Tuscaloosa.

Sassaman, Kenneth E. (1995). The Cultural Diversity of Interactions Among Mid-Holocene Societies of the American Southeast. In *Native American Interactions: Multiscalar Analyses and Interpretation in the Eastern Woodlands*, edited by Michael Nassaney and Kenneth E. Sassaman, pp. 174–204. University of Tennessee Press, Knoxville.

Sassaman, Kenneth E. (1996). Technological Innovations in Economic and Social Contexts. In *Archaeology of the Mid-Holocene Southeast*, edited by Kenneth E. Sassaman and David G. Anderson, pp. 57–74. University Press of Florida, Gainesville.

Sassaman, Kenneth E. (2005). Structure and Practice in the Southeast. In *North American Archaeology*, edited by Timothy R. Pauketat and Diana Di Paolo Loren, pp. 79–107. Blackwell, Cambridge (MA).

Sassaman, Kenneth E., and Asa R. Randall (2007). The Cultural History of Banner-stones in the Savannah River Valley. *Southeastern Archaeology* 26:196–211.

Sasso, Robert F., Robert F. Boszhardt, James C. Knox, James L. Theler, Katherine P. Stevenson, James P. Gallagher, and Cynthia Stiles-Hanson (1985). *Prehistoric Ridge Field Agriculture in the Upper Mississippi Valley*. Reports of Investigations No. 38. Mississippi Valley Archaeology Center, University of Wisconsin, LaCrosse.

Saunders, Joe, Rolfe D. Mandel, Roger T. Saucier, E. Thurman Allen, C. T. Hall-mark, Jay K. Johnson, Edwin H. Jackson, Charles M. Allen, Gary L. Stringer, Douglas S. Frink, James K. Feathers, Stephen Williams, Kristen J. Gremillion, Malcom F. Vidrine, and Reca Jones (1997). A Mound Complex in Louisiana at 5,400–5,000 Years before the Present. *Science* 277:1796–99.

Scarry, John F. (1992). Political Office and Political Structures: Ethnhistoric and Archaeological Perspectives on the Native Lords of Apalachee. In *Lords of the Southeast: Social Inequality and the Native Elites of Southeastern North America*, edited by Alex W. Barker and Timothy R. Pauketat, pp. 163–83. Archaeological Papers of the American Anthropological Association No. 3. Washington, DC.

Schroeder, Sissel (2006). Walls As Symbols of Political, Economic, and Military Might. In *Leadership and Polity in Mississippian Society*, edited by Brian M. Butler and Paul D. Welch, pp. 115–41. Occasional Paper No. 33. Center for Archaeological Investigations, Southern Illinois University, Carbondale.

Schuldenrein, Joseph (1996). Geoarchaeology and Mid-Holocene Landscape History. In *Archaeology of the Mid-Holocene Southeast*, edited by Kenneth E. Sassaman and David G. Anderson, pp. 3–27. University Press of Florida, Gainesville.

Schurr, Mark R., and Margaret J. Schoeninger (1995). Associations between Agricultural Intensification and Social Complexity: An Example from the Prehistoric Ohio Valley. *Journal of Anthropological Archaeology* 14:315–39.

Seeman, Mark F. (1979). *The Hopewell Interaction Sphere: The Evidence for Interregional Trade and Structural Complexity*. Indiana Historical Society, Indianapolis.

Seeman, Mark F. (1988). Hopewell Trophy-Skull Artifacts as Evidence for Competition in Middle Woodland Societies Circa 50 B.C.–A.D. 350. *American Antiquity* 53:565–67.

Seeman, Mark F. (1992). The Bow and Arrow, the Intrusive Mound Complex, and a Late Woodland Jack's Reef Horizon in the Mid-Ohio Valley. In *Cultural Variability in Context: Woodland Settlement of the Mid-Ohio Valley*, edited by Mark F. Seeman. *Midcontinental Journal of Archaeology*, Special Paper 7:41–51.

Seeman, Mark F. (2007). Predatory War and Hopewell Trophy-Taking. In *The Taking and Displaying of Human Body Parts as Trophies by Amerindians*, edited by Richard J. Chacon and David H. Dye, pp. 167–89. Springer, New York.

Shetrone, Henry C. (1926). Exploration of the Hopewell Group of Prehistoric Earthworks. *Ohio Archaeological and Historical Quarterly* 35:1–227.

Shetrone, Henry C., and Emerson F. Greenman (1931). Explorations of the Seip Group of Prehistoric Earthworks. *Ohio Archaeological and Historical Quarterly* 40:341–509.

Shields, Ben M. (2003). An Analysis of the Archaic Human Burials at the Mulberry Creek (1CT27) Shell Mound, Colbert County, Alabama. Unpublished M.A. thesis, Department of Anthropology, University of Alabama, Tuscaloosa.

Simon, Mary L. (2000). Regional Variations in Plant Use Strategies in the Midwest During the Late Woodland. In *Late Woodland Societies: Tradition and Transformation across the Midcontinent*, edited by Thomas E. Emerson, Dale L. McElrath, and Andrew C. Fortier, pp. 37–75. University of Nebraska Press, Lincoln.

Smith, Bruce D. (1986). The Archaeology of the Southeastern United States: From Dalton to De Soto, 10,500–500 B.P. *Advances in World Archaeology* 5:1–92.

Smith, Bruce D. (1989). Origins of Agriculture in Eastern North America. *Science* 246:1566–71.

Smith, Bruce D. (1992). Prehistoric Plant Husbandry in Eastern North America. In *The Origins of Agriculture: An International Perspective*, edited by C. W. Cowan and Patty Jo Watson, pp. 101–19. Smithsonian Institution Press, Washington, DC.

Smith, Bruce D. (1996). Agricultural Chiefdoms of the Eastern Woodlands. In *The Cambridge History of the Native Peoples of the Americas*, Vol. 1, Pt. 1, edited by Bruce G. Trigger and Wilcomb E. Washburn, pp. 267–323. Cambridge University Press, New York.

Smith, Maria O. (1995). Scalping in the Archaic Period: Evidence from the Western Tennessee Valley. *Southeastern Archaeology* 14:60–68.

Smith, Maria O. (1997). Osteological Indications of Warfare in the Archaic Period of the Western Tennessee Valley. In *Troubled Times: Violence and Warfare in the Past*, edited by Debra L. Martin and David W. Frayer, pp. 241–65. Gordon and Breach, New York.

Smith, Maria O. (2003). Beyond Palisades: The Nature and Frequency of Late Prehistoric Deliberate Violent Trauma in the Chickamauga Reservoir of East Tennessee. *American Journal of Physical Anthropology* 121:303–18.

Snow, Dean R. (1994). *The Iroquois*. Blackwell, Oxford.

Snow, Dean R. (1995). Migration in Prehistory: The Northern Iroquoian Case. *American Antiquity* 60:59–79.

Snow, Dean R. (1996). More on Migration in Prehistory: Accommodating New Evidence in the Northern Iroquoian Case. *American Antiquity* 61:791–96.

Snow, Dean R. (2001). Evolution of the Mohawk Iroquois. In *Societies in Eclipse: Archaeology of the Eastern Woodlands Indians, A.D. 1400–1700*, edited by David S. Brose, C. Wesley Cowan, and Robert C. Mainfort, Jr., pp. 19–25. Smithsonian Institution Press, Washington, DC.

Snow, Dean R. (2007). Iroquois-Huron Warfare. In *North American Indigenous Warfare and Ritual*, edited by Richard J. Chacon and Ruben G. Mendoza, pp. 149–59. University of Arizona Press, Tucson.

Souza, Philip de, editor (2008). *The Ancient World at War*. Thames and Hudson, London.

Stahle, David W., Edward R. Cook, M. K. Cleaveland, M. D. Therrel, D. M. Meko, H. D. Grissino-Mayer, E. Watson, and B. H. Luckman (2000). Epic 16th Century Drought over North America. *Eos* 81:121–25.

Stahle, David W., Falko K. Frye, Edward R. Cook, and R. Daniel Griffin (2007). Tree-Ring Reconstructed Megadroughts over North America since A.D. 1300. *Climatic Change* 83:133–49.

Starna, William A., and Ralph Watkins (1991). Northern Iroquoian Slavery. *Ethnohistory* 38:34–57.

Steadman, Dawnie W. (2008). Warfare-Related Trauma at Orendorf, a Middle Mississippian Site in West-Central Illinois. *American Journal of Physical Anthropology* 135:51–64.

Steinen, Karl T. (1992). Ambushes, Raids, and Palisades: Mississippian Warfare in the Interior Southeast. *Southeastern Archaeology* 11:132–39.

Steinen, Karl T., and Russell Ritson (1996). Defense of the Frontier: Considerations of Apalache Warfare during the Period 1539–1540. *Florida Anthropologist* 49(3):111–20.

Stoltman, James B. (1986). The Archaic Tradition. In *Introduction to Wisconsin Archaeology*, edited by W. Green, James B. Stoltman, and Alice B. Kehoe. *Wisconsin Archaeologist* 67:207–38.

Strezewski, Michael (2006). Patterns of Interpersonal Violence at the Fisher Site. *Midcontinental Journal of Archaeology* 31:249–80.

Stuiver, M., P. M. Grootes, and T. F. Braziunas (1995). The GISP2 $\delta^{18}O$ Climate Record of the Past 16,500 Years and the Role of the Sun, Ocean and Volcanoes. *Quaternary Research* 44:341–54.

Swanton, John R. (1911). *Indian Tribes of the Lower Mississippi Valley and Adjacent Coast of the Gulf of Mexico*. Bulletin 43. Bureau of American Ethnology, Smithsonian Institution, Washington, DC.

Taylor, Colin F. (2001). *Native American Weapons*. University of Oklahoma Press, Norman.

Thwaites, Ruben G., editor (1896–1901). *The Jesuit Relations and Allied Documents*. Burrows Brothers, Cleveland.

Trigger, Bruce G. (1967). Settlement Archaeology: Its Goals and Promise. *American Antiquity* 32:149–60.

Trigger, Bruce G. (1990). *The Huron: Farmers of the North.* 2nd edition. Holt, Rinehart and Winston, New York.

Trubitt, Mary Beth D. (2003). Mississippian Period Warfare and Palisade Construction at Cahokia. In *Theory, Method, and Practice in Modern Archaeology,* edited by Robert J. Jeske and Douglas K. Charles, pp. 149–62. Praeger, Westport (CT).

Tschauner, H. (1994). Archaeological Systematics and Cultural Evolution: Retrieving the Honour of Culture History. *Man* 29:77–93.

Tuck, James A. (1978). Northern Iroquoian Prehistory. In *Handbook of North American Indians,* Vol. 15, Northeast, edited by Bruce G. Trigger, pp. 332–33. Smithsonian Institution Press, Washington, DC.

Turney-High, Harry H. (1991). *Primitive War: Its Practice and Concepts.* 2nd edition. University of South Carolina Press, Columbia.

Van Geel, B., J. van der Plicht, M. R. Kilian, E. R. Klaver, J. H. M. Kouwenberg, H. Renssen, I.

Van Geel, B., O. M. Raspopov, H. Renssen, J. van der Plicht, V. A. Dergachev, and H. A. J. Meijer (1999). The Role of Solar Forcing upon Climate Change. *Quaternary Science Reviews* 18:331–38.

Van Horne, Wayne W. (1993). The Warclub: Weapon and Symbol in Southeastern Indian Societies. Unpublished Ph.D. dissertation, Department of Anthropology, University of Georgia, Athens.

Vayda, Andrew P. (1961). Expansion and Warfare among Swidden Agriculturalists. *American Anthropologist* 63:346–58.

Vencl, S. (1999). Stone Age Warfare. In *Ancient Warfare: Archaeological Perspectives,* edited by John Carman and Anthony Harding, pp. 57–72. Sutton, Stroud (UK).

Walker, Phillip L. (1997). Wife Beating, Boxing, and Broken Noses: Skeletal Evidence for the Cultural Patterning of Violence. In *Troubled Times: Violence and Warfare in the Past,* edited by Debra L. Martin and David W. Frayer, pp. 145–79. Gordon and Breach, New York.

Walker, Phillip L. (2001). A Bioarchaeological Perspective on the History of Violence. *Annual Review of Anthropology* 30:573–96.

Wallace, Anthony F. C. (1972). *The Death and Rebirth of the Seneca.* Random House, New York.

Walthall, John A. (1980). *Prehistoric Indians of the Southeast: Archaeology of Alabama and the Middle South.* University of Alabama Press, Tuscaloosa.

Walthall, John A., and Brad Koldehoff (1998). Hunter-Gatherer Interaction and Alliance Formation: Dalton and the Cult of the Long Blade. *Plains Anthropologist* 43:257–73.

Waring, Antonio J., Jr. (1968). The Southern Cult and Muskogean Ceremonial. In *The Waring Papers: The Collected Works of Antonio J. Waring, Jr.,* edited by Stephen Williams, pp. 30–69. Papers of the Peabody Museum of Archaeology and Ethnology 58. Harvard University, Cambridge.

Watts, William A., Eric C. Grimm, and T. C. Hussey (1996). Mid-Holocene Forest History of Florida and the Coastal Plain of Georgia and South Carolina. In *Ar-*

chaeology of the Mid-Holocene Southeast, edited by Kenneth E. Sassaman and David G. Anderson, pp. 28–38. University Press of Florida, Gainesville.

Webb, Thompson, III, Patrick J. Bartlein, Sandy P. Harrison, and Katherine H. Anderson (1993). Vegetation, Lake Levels, and Climate in Eastern North America for the Past 18,000 Years. In Global Climate since the Last Glacial Maximum, edited by Herbert E. Wright, J. E. Kutzbach, T. Webb III, W. F. Ruddiman, F. A. Street-Perrott, and P. J. Bartlett, pp. 415–67. University of Minnesota Press, Minneapolis.

Webb, William S., and David L. DeJarnette (1942). An Archeological Survey of the Pickwick Basin in the Adjacent Portions of the States of Alabama, Mississippi, and Tennessee. Bulletin 129. Bureau of American Ethnology, Smithsonian Institution, Washington, DC.

Webster, David (1999). Ancient Maya Warfare. In War and Society in the Ancient and Medieval Worlds: Asia, The Mediterranean, Europe, and Mesoamerica, edited by Kurt Raaflaub and Nathan Rosenstein, pp. 333–60. Harvard University Press, Cambridge.

Webster, David (2000). The Not So Peaceful Civilization: A Review of Maya War. Journal of World Prehistory 14:65–119.

Whallon, Robert (1989). Elements of Cultural Change in the Later Paleolithic. In The Human Revolution: Behavioral and Biological Perspectives on the Origins of Modern Humans, edited by Paul Mellars and Chris Stringer, pp. 433–54. Princeton University Press, Princeton.

White, Richard (1991). The Middle Ground: Indians, Empires, and Republics in the Great Lakes Region, 1650–1815. Cambridge University Press, New York.

Widmer, Randolph J. (2004). Explaining Sociopolitical Complexity in the Foraging Adaptations of the Southeastern United States: The Roles of Demography, Kinship, and Ecology in Sociocultural Evolution. In Signs of Power: The Rise of Cultural Complexity in the Southeast, edited by Jon L. Gibson and Philip J. Carr, pp. 234–53. University of Alabama Press, Tuscaloosa.

Willey, Patrick S. (1990). Prehistoric Warfare on the Great Plains: Skeletal Analysis of the Crow Creek Massacre. Garland Press, New York.

Willey, Patrick S., and Thomas E. Emerson (1993). The Osteology and Archaeology of the Crow Creek Massacre. In Prehistory and Human Ecology of the Western Prairies and Northern Plains, edited by J. Tiffany. Plains Anthropologist 38:227–70.

Williamson, Ron (2007). "Otinontsiskiaj ondaon" ("The House of the Cut-off Heads"): The History and Archaeology of Northern Iroquoian Trophy Taking. In The Taking and Displaying of Human Body Parts as Trophies by Amerindians, edited by Richard J. Chacon and David H. Dye, pp. 190–221. Springer, New York.

Willoughby, Charles C., and Earnest A. Hooton (1922). The Turner Group of Earthworks, Hamilton County, Ohio. Papers of the Peabody Museum of Archaeology and Ethnology, Vol. 8(3). Harvard University, Cambridge (MA).

Wilson, Gregory D., Jon Marcoux, and Brad Koldehoff (2006). Square Pegs in Round Holes: Organizational Diversity between Early Moundville and Cahokia. In Leadership and Polity in Mississippian Society, edited by Brian M. Butler and Paul D.

Welch, pp. 43–72. Occasional Paper No. 33. Center for Archaeological Investigations, Southern Illinois University, Cardondale.

Wolf, Eric R. (1987). Cycles of Violence: The Anthropology of War and Peace. In *Waymarks: The Notre Dame Inaugural Lectures in Anthropology*, edited by Kenneth Moore, pp. 127–50. University of Notre Dame Press, Notre Dame (IN).

Yerkes, Richard W. (2006). Middle Woodland Settlements and Social Organization in the Central Ohio Valley: Were the Hopewell Really Farmers? In *Recreating Hopewell*, edited by Douglas K. Charles and Jane E. Buikstra, pp. 50–61. University Press of Florida, Gainesville.

Zhang, David D., Peter Brecke, Harry F. Lee, Yuan-Qing He, and Jane Zhang (2007). Global Climate Change, War, and Population Decline in Recent Human History. *PNAS* 104:19214–19.

Index

Note: Page numbers in *italics* indicate illustrations.

207

About the Author

David H. Dye is associate professor of archaeology at the University of Memphis. With over thirty-five years of archaeological experience in eastern North America, he is interested in the relationships of conflict, cooperation, politics, and religion. He specializes in archaeological photography and the archaeology of the Mississippian culture. His photographs have appeared in numerous books, including *The Southeastern Ceremonial Complex, Artifacts and Analysis* (1989) and *Hero, Hawk, and Open Hand* (2004). He has presented more than 80 conference papers and authored over 40 book chapters and journal articles. His edited books include *Towns and Temples Along the Mississippi* (with Cheryl A. Cox, 1990), *The Taking and Displaying of Human Body Parts as Trophies by Amerindians* (with Richard J. Chacon, 2007), and *Cave Archaeology of the Eastern Woodlands* (2008).